July 1987

Mum,
Happy Birthday
lotsalove

THE
GRAND
TOUR

THE GRAND TOUR

—

CHRISTOPHER HIBBERT

THAMES METHUEN

FOR FRANCIS AND THÉRÈSE

First published in Great Britain 1987
by Methuen London Ltd, 11 New Fetter Lane, London EC4P 4EE
in association with Thames Television International,
149 Tottenham Court Road, London W1P 9LL
© 1987 Christopher Hibbert

Filmset by Jolly & Barber Ltd, Rugby
Printed and bound in Spain by Cayfosa, Barcelona.
Dep. legal: B-13.288 - 1987

British Library Cataloguing in Publication Data
Hibbert, Christopher
The grand tour.
1. Grand tour
I. Title
914′.04253   D917

ISBN: 0-423-02040-4

CONTENTS

ACKNOWLEDGEMENTS

This book has been written to accompany the Thames Television series, 'The Grand Tour', with whose producer, Richard Mervyn, I have enjoyed long and profitable discussions while we were writing the scripts together. I am also most grateful to Suzanne O'Farrell, who has read numerous manuscript journals and letters for us in the British Library and elsewhere; to Lady Elton for permission to consult Ellen Hallam's diary at Clevedon Court; to Viscount Cobham for use of the Lyttelton Papers at Hagley Hall; and to John Bell for access to his family papers at Thirsk Hall.

I am much indebted, too, to Nicholas Jones, Ann Mansbridge and Alex Bennion of Thames Methuen; to Diana Potter of Thames Television International; to my agent, Bruce Hunter, and to John Rush of David Higham Associates; to Margaret Lewendon, Sheila Kidd and Alison Riley; to Julia Brown who has chosen the illustrations for the book; and to Peter Campbell who has designed it. Gerard Vaughan of Wolfson College, Oxford and Helen Valentine, Library Assistant of the Royal Academy of Arts, have given us much useful advice.

C.H.

Sir William Watkin Wynn

LIST OF ILLUSTRATIONS

The publishers are grateful to the following collectors, copyright owners and photographers for permission to reproduce the illustrations. All possible care has been taken to trace and acknowledge the owners of the illustrations. If any errors have accidentally occurred, however, we shall be happy upon notification to correct them in any future editions of this book.

Picture research by Julia Brown.

Within the painting:

SIR RICHARD WENMAN KNIGHT, MARRIED,
ISABELLA ELDEST DAUᵗʳ OF JOHN LORD
WILLIAMS OF THAME OBIIT MAR. 9ᵗʰ 1572.

1 An English gentleman, probably Sir Richard Wenman, in Venice in the late sixteenth century.

PROLOGUE

'A great desire to see forraine Countries'

Chaucer's 'worthy woman from bath', who accompanies her fellow pilgrims from the Tabard inn at Southwark to Canterbury, riding easily along on her ambling horse, has been far further afield than to Kent. She has been three times to Jerusalem; she has 'seen many strange rivers and passed over them'; she has 'been to Rome and also to Boulogne, St James of Compostella and Cologne'.

She was by no means unique. For generations English travellers had been sailing regularly from south coast ports on pilgrimages to France, Italy, Spain and the Holy Land, braving pirates and highway robbers and, as one of them recorded, enduring the unplesantness of seasickness in small boats crowded with a hundred passengers, of noisome smells aboard, of swearing sailors who roughly pushed the landlubbers about the deck under the pretext of working the ship – bawling out to anyone who appeared particularly ill, 'Cheer up, be merry! We shall soon be in a storm!' – and of captains as coarse as their men, shouting above the roar of the wind and the splash of the rain,

> Hale the bowelyne! Now vere the shete!
> Cooke, make redy anoon our mete,
> Our pylgryms have no lust to ete,
> I pray God give hem rest!

In the fourteenth and fifteenth centuries the number of pilgrims who sailed across the Channel and through the Bay of Biscay increased each year: in 1434 King Henry VI granted licences permitting 2,433 pilgrims to go to the shrine of St James of Compostella alone, and some years later one of the first books printed in English by Wynkyn de Worde was *Informacion for Pylgrymes unto the Holy Londe*. This ran to three editions and contained the kind of advice with which later travellers were to be assailed in treatise after treatise, book after book – advice on how to negotiate with ships' captains, how to obtain the best berth, the most comfortable quarters at inns, the first seating at the dinner provided, the strongest horses and asses. Travellers were also advised as to what they should take with them: no one should set out on a long journey across the Continent without a cage of half a dozen hens and chickens and seed with which to feed them, 'a lytell cawdron, a fryenge panne, dysshes, platers, cuppes of glasse . . . a fether bed, a matrasse, a pylawe, two payre sheets and a quylte'.

To many observers, indeed, it seemed that the care which most pilgrims by then took to ensure their comfort was quite incompatible with the religious zeal that ought to have inspired them. In one of his colloquies, Erasmus condemned the idea that pilgrimages were pious, arguing that they were frequently made by restless people seeking no more than change and adventure and an opportunity to shine at dinner tables upon their return, that the journeys were frequently accompanied by dissipation, and that the money and time spent upon them would be much better expended upon good works at home. Yet, while such charges did have an effect upon the numbers of people travelling abroad on pilgrimages, there were other purposes of travel which had been widely recognised as worthwhile and beneficial by the time Erasmus died in 1536.

Erasmus himself had studied and taught in Paris where one of his pupils, Lord Mountjoy, invited him to make his first visit to England; he subsequently lived in France for several years, and then, as he told a friend, felt it was 'very necessary' to go to Italy, to gain for his 'poor learning some authority from the celebrity of the place'. He went to Venice where he contentedly wrote in a printing-house, undisturbed by the clatter of printers and their type, so busy, as he put it, that he scarce had time to scratch his ears; he went to Rome where he was tempted to stay for ever, enjoying its lovely 'sky and fields, its libraries and pleasant walks, sweet conversations with learned men'; and, as tutor to the natural son of King James IV of Scotland, he went to Padua to whose university, as one of its students wrote, 'Gentlemen of all nations come . . . some coming to study the Civill Law, others the Mathematickes and Musick, others to ride, to practice the art of Fencing, and the exercises of dancing and activity, under most skilful professors of those Arts'.

Many of these students came from England. Reginald Pole, who was to be consecrated Archbishop of Canterbury in 1556, was one of them. Others were Thomas Winter, natural son of Cardinal Wolsey; Thomas Starkey, who was later to write *A Treatise Against the Papal Supremacy;* Richard Morison, one day to be ambassador to the Emperor Charles V; Edward Wotton, the naturalist, sent here by Richard Fox, Founder of Corpus Christi College, Oxford, 'to improve his learning and chiefly to learn Greek'; and Richard Pace, the future Dean of St Paul's, whose patron was Thomas Langton, Bishop of Winchester. Indeed there were few English scholars of the time who did not go to Italy for some part of their education. Thomas Lupset, the learned friend of Erasmus and of Thomas More; William Lily, who was to become the first Master of St Paul's School; John Colet, the school's founder; Thomas Linacre, the great physician; William Grocin, the humanist scholar; William Latimer, the Fellow of All Souls who was so esteemed for his knowledge of Greek that he was chosen to teach it to the Chancellor of Cambridge University; Cuthbert Tunstall, the learned Bishop of Durham; and Walter Grey, the Bishop of Ely, had all studied in Italy, mostly at Ferrara, Bologna or Padua, and all, on their return, made notable contributions to the dissemination of the new learning of the Renaissance in England, particularly in Oxford.

Nor was it only scholars who went abroad. Increasing numbers of young English gentlemen were sent on their travels to gather information which could be turned to the nation's advantage and to train them as representatives of England's prestige at foreign courts. Sir Richard Wingfield, English ambassador at the court of France from 1520, had travelled in Italy and studied at Ferrara; and Nicholas Wotton, one of King Henry VIII's ambassadors sent to the Duke of Cleves to negotiate the marriage of the Duke's sister, Anne, to the King, had also travelled in Italy, had lived for a time at Perugia and had witnessed the Sack of Rome in 1527. The King himself sometimes paid for a promising young man's education and travels, as, for example, those of John Mason, the son of a cowherd and one day to be ambassador in Brussels, whose good looks and presence had so impressed Henry on a visit to Oxford that he was sent to France at the royal expense.

The King's daughter, Queen Elizabeth I, followed her father's example in maintaining 'young men of promising hopes in foreign countries for the more complete polishing of their Parts and Studies'. She sent them to learn foreign languages, to broaden their minds, to help them to acquire self-reliance and self-possession as well as a highly developed taste and grace of manner. They were urged also to talk with learned men so that they might be imbued with their learning, as men in an apothecary's shop 'carrie away the smell of the sweet spices even in their garments', to study the fortifications of the towns and the fertility of the countryside through which they passed, and, as Lord Burghley told Edward Manners, to 'make a booke of paper wherein you may dayly or at least weekly insert all things occurent to you'. With such precepts in mind courtiers like Sir John Harington, the Earl of Essex, the Earl of Hertford, Sir Christopher Hatton and Sir Philip Sidney set off upon their travels, 'intending the end thereof', in Essex's words, 'to attain to true knowledge and to better [their] experiences', so that they might return 'acceptable servants' to sovereign and state. Many were away for long periods. Sir Philip Sidney, who was to be appointed ambassador to the German Emperor in 1577, travelled with a half-Italian tutor, three servants and four horses, not only through France, Germany, the Low Countries and Italy, but also through Poland and Hungary, and was away from home for over three years.

Others remained abroad even longer. Thomas Coryate, the eccentric, odd-looking son of a Somerset rector and the butt of many a practical joke at court, announced that he was going on his travels which would occupy him for ten years; and he might well have done so had he not died on the way. Travel for him was the 'sweetest and most delightful . . . of all the pleasures in the world'. 'The mere superscription of a letter from Zurich sets him up like a top,' so Ben Jonson said. 'Basil or Heidelberg makes him spin. And at seeing the word Frankford or Venice, though but in the title of a Booke, he is readie to breake doublet, cracke elbows, the overflee the roome with his murmure.' On a journey previous to his fatal one, he had covered 1,975 miles, most of them on foot, and in the space of five months had visited forty-five cities.

Fynes Moryson, a young gentleman from Lincolnshire and Fellow of Peterhouse, Cambridge, who confessed that he had from his 'tender youth a great desire to see forraine Countries', spent nearly six years abroad, landing on the Netherlands coast after spending ten days at sea – during which he narrowly evaded capture by pirates from Dunkirk – then travelling through Germany, the Low Countries, Poland, Italy and France, going as far south as Naples and as far east as Vienna. On his return he published an account of his travels, together with *Precepts for Travellers*, containing page after page of advice which Englishmen abroad were later to find indispensable. He demonstrated from his own experiences how dangers could be escaped and how forbidden places could be seen: he himself had visited the Jesuit College in Rome in the character of a Frenchman, and, disguised as a German, had been permitted to enter a Spanish fort. Set upon by marauding French soldiers who stole the money he had sewn up in his inner doublet, he managed to escape with the gold crowns he had concealed in a box of 'stinking ointment' which they threw away in disgust; and walking down the coastal roads of East Friesland, which were infested with Spanish freebooters, he had pretended to be 'a poore Bohemian':

I bought me an old Brunswicke thrummed hat [he recorded], and made mee a poore Dutch suite, rubbing it in the dust to make it seeme old, so as my Taylor said, he took more paines to spoyle it, than to make it. I bought me linnen stockings and discoloured my face and hands, and so without cloake, or sword, with my hands in my hose, tooke my place in a poore waggon. I practised as much as I could, Pythagoricall silence; but if any asked me who I was, I told him that I was a poore Bohemian, and had long served a Merchant at Leipzig, who left mee to dispatch some businesse at Stoke, and then commanded me to follow him to Emden. If you had seene my servile countenance, mine eyes cast on the ground, my hands in my hose, and my modest silence, you would have taken me for a harmlesse young man.

His general advice to travellers was highly practical: do not trust chance companions on the road who, when they question you, should be told that you are going only as far as the next city; keep your temper if men try to quarrel with you, for 'we are not all like Amadis or Rinalldo to incounter an hoste of men'; tell no one that you can swim for, in case of shipwreck, 'others trusting therein take hold of you and make you perish with them'; in all inns, 'especially in suspected places', take careful heed of those who share your chamber, always keep your sword by your side, and keep your purse under your pillow; if you also keep a book there, make sure that it is never one that might reveal your Protestant faith.

The Inquisition and its agents were said to be always on the watch for heretics; and the authorities at home took care to ensure both that Englishmen did not fall into their clutches and that the temptations of conversion to Roman Catholicism were so far as possible avoided. Licences to travel, which had to be obtained from the Privy Council, frequently stipulated the places that the traveller was not to visit. St Omer, Rheims and Douai were usually placed upon this list because of the number of English Roman Catholics at the Jesuit and Benedictine colleges there. Rome also was often forbidden the English traveller, since Cardinal Allen, whose zeal for the Catholic faith had driven him from Oxford into exile, was known to be plotting there the overthrow of the Queen's government with other English dissidents. After the defeat of the Spanish

Armada visits to Rome could be conducted more openly. No longer was it necessary to visit the city in disguise as Sir Henry Wotton had done, pretending to be a German Catholic with a 'mighty blue feather' in his hat, explaining the reason for the feather as follows: 'First, I was by it taken for no English. Secondly, I was reputed as light in my mind as in my apparel (they are not dangerous men that are so). And thirdly, no man could think that I desired to be unknown, who, by wearing of that feather, took a course to make myself famous through Rome in a few days.'

Yet while the Inquisition was no longer so feared towards the end of the sixteenth century, there were still exceptional examples of its continuing baleful influence. As late as 1638 John Mole, Lord Roos's eighty-year-old Protestant tutor, died in its prison in Rome after spending thirty years in confinement. And care had still to be taken to avoid the priests who went from house to house, particularly at Easter, to ensure that all the inmates received the Sacrament. Fynes Moryson, who was in Rome some time after the failure of the Armada and was able to visit the antiquities through the offices of Cardinal Allen, nevertheless thought it prudent to leave the city on the Tuesday before Easter for Siena and, upon Easter Eve, 'pretending great business', to rush over to Florence for the day, then go on to Pisa before going back to Siena. 'Thus by often changing places,' he explained, 'I avoyded the Priests enquiring after mee, which is most dangerous about Easter time, when all men receive the Sacrament.' Yet, provided the traveller did not provocatively proclaim his distaste for popery like William Lithgow, the Scottish traveller who, in the course of his 36,000 miles of tramping through foreign parts, indignantly tore the rich clothing off the images that offended him in the churches he entered, it was possible to live undisturbed as an avowed Protestant in any Italian city, including Rome. Sir Edward Herbert spent several weeks there quietly enjoying the antiquities in 1614, having introduced himself at the English College as a Protestant who was in the city for that sole purpose.

After the marriage of Charles I in 1625 to Henrietta Maria, the King of France's sister, who was allowed to bring priests with her to London where a chapel was specially built for her, the English traveller, with his country now at peace with both France and Spain, had less and less to fear from the attentions of the Inquisition. John Milton, who left on his continental travels in 1638, who met Galileo in Florence and Tasso's patron, Manso, in Naples, did not trouble to conceal his convinced Protestantism.

While the dangers to an English traveller threatened by the Inquisition gradually receded, the likelihood of becoming involved in a continental war remained. Indeed, there were travellers who went abroad specifically in search of war, either for adventure or for military experience. The principal intention of the diarist and virtuoso John Evelyn, when he sailed for the Continent, after leaving Balliol College, Oxford without taking a degree, was to 'hasten towards the Army'. He landed at Flushing, took a wagon to Rotterdam, went on to the Hague and hurried to Genepp, where Dutch forces had laid siege to the Spanish garrison, hoping to observe the operation and perhaps play some part in it. Arriving a fortnight after the surrender, he joined the Dutch army as a volunteer, trailed a pike around the horn-works, and 'went to view all the trenches, aproches, and Mines etc of the besiegers'. In particular he took 'notice of the Wheele-bridg, which Engine his Excellency [the Prince of Orange] had made to run over the moate, when they storm'd the Castle'. Soon 'pretty well satisfied with the Confusion of Armies', however, Evelyn took his leave of his 'Camerades; and on the 12 of Aug embarked upon the Wahal [actually the Maas] in the company of three grave divines who entertayned us a greate part of our passage with a long dispute concerning the lawfulnesse of Church Musick'.

Two years later, after the outbreak of the Civil War in England, Evelyn returned to the Continent for fear lest his Anglican and Royalist sympathies might endanger his brother's estate, then in Parliamentary territory. Joined by others anxious not to become entangled by political disputes at home, he took boat for Calais, travelled through France, sailed down the Loire, went to Lyons, Avignon, Marseilles and Cannes where he 'agree'd with a Sea-man to transport [him] to Genoa'. From here he sailed in a felucca, a coasting-vessel with oars and lateen sails, towards Leghorn; but, the seas being very high, he had to put in at Porto Venere 'between two such narrow & horrid rocks, as the waves dashing with extraordinary velocity against them, put us in no small peril'. Continuing his journey by land, he took a post-horse to Pisa (where he thought the cathedral 'superbe' and the problem of how the leaning tower is prevented 'from immediately falling would puzzle a good Geometrician'). He went on to Florence which was 'beautified by more than a thousand houses and country Palaces of note', to Siena, which 'presents the Traveller with an incomparable Prospect', and down to Rome where, under the guidance of a 'Sights-man, for so they name certaine Persons who get their living onely by leading strangers to see the Citty', he stayed over seven months, fulfilling his resolve 'to spend no moment idly' and setting down his impressions in page after page of his diary. Then, having visited Naples and climbed Vesuvius from whose 'gaping clefts & chasms issu'd such sulphurous blasts and Smoake that [he] durst not stand long neere them', he made for Venice, Padua and Vicenza by way of Bologna, and set off for Switzerland, through Verona, Milan and the Simplon Pass to Brieg at the foot of the Alps in the Valais. From here he went on to Geneva and then journeyed home through Orléans, Paris (where he married the British ambassador's only daughter), Rouen and Dieppe. He had been away for nearly four years, and had accomplished that continental journey which, with infinite variations, was later to be known as the Grand Tour.

The term first appeared in a printed work, Richard Lassels's *Voyage of Italy*, in 1760, thirteen years after Evelyn's return to London, although the word 'tourist' did not appear until 1800. But travel and study on the Continent, not only as a training for diplomats, public servants and soldiers but also as an ideal means of imparting taste, knowledge, self-assurance and polished manners to young gentlemen of fortune, had already become accepted as an invaluable alternative, or supplement, to a university education.

CHAPTER I

*

PREPARATIONS

AND

PRECAUTIONS

*

*''Tis the way to
be respected'*

SHORTLY BEFORE HIS FIFTEENTH BIRTHDAY in 1752, Edward Gibbon arrived at Magdalen College, Oxford and was flattered to be given the velvet cap and silk gown which distinguished a gentleman commoner from plebeian students and which enabled him 'to command, among the tradesmen of Oxford, an indefinite and dangerous credit'. His status also allowed him to join the Fellows at high table as the port went round, and the possession of a key to the 'numerous and learned library'. Yet, so Gibbon said, he was given no guidance as to the use of the library, his tutor virtually ignoring him and never summoning him to attend 'even the ceremony of a lecture'; while the conversations at high table, which he had hoped to be of Cicero and Chrysostom, were limited to gossip and scandal and occasional comment on a local election. His fourteen months at the university, until he professed himself a Roman Catholic and left his College, were 'the most idle and unprofitable' of his whole life.

His experiences were far from exceptional. A few years later, the Earl of Malmesbury came up to Oxford to spend his days in idleness: 'The discipline of the University happened at this particular moment to be so lax that a Gentleman Commoner was under no restraint and never called upon to attend either lectures, or chapel or hall.' 'They are perfectly their own masters,' the *Gentleman's Magazine* commented, 'and they take the lead in every disgraceful frolic of juvenile debauchery. They are curiously tricked out in cloth of gold, of silver and of purple, and feast most sumptuously throughout the year.'

Even had they wanted them, there were few facilities at either Oxford or Cambridge for the study of modern languages or, indeed, for most other subjects, apart from the classics, history and philosophy. Having been whipped through a public school and acquired the doubtful merits of its equally narrow curriculum, most of them left university scarcely better educated than when they had entered it. Examinations were oral and widely considered no more than a formality. They were even said to be conducted during drinking bouts or on horseback. John Scott, later Lord Chancellor Eldon, maintained that his examination in Hebrew and History for his Bachelor's degree consisted of just two questions:

Examiner: What is the Hebrew for the Place of a Skull?
    Scott: Golgotha.
Examiner: Who founded University College?
    Scott: King Alfred.

Examiner: Very well, sir, you are competent for your degree.

The discredit into which English universities had fallen in the eighteenth century was in fact, so Adam Smith, the Scottish economist and philosopher, declared in 1776, the principal reason why the Grand Tour had been brought into repute as an important, if not an essential, part of upper-class education.

The quality of this education depended largely upon the tutor – or, as he was more usually called, bear-leader – who was employed as a travelling instructor and companion. Ideally, in the words of Vicesimus Knox, a recognised authority on the subject whose *Liberal Education* was published in 1789, the tutor was a grave, respectable man of a mature age, with 'that natural authority and that personal dignity which command attention and obedience. In addition to his duties as teacher, mentor and guide, he would have to watch over the morals and religion of his pupil', both of which would be constantly in danger of being 'shaken from the basis and levelled with the dust before the end of the peregrination'. Knox considered it surprising, therefore, that more trouble was not taken over the selection of tutors by the parents of those to whose care they were to be entrusted.

There were undoubtedly conscientious tutors and there were several distinguished men who had been employed as such. Among them were Adam Smith, who was paid £300 a year (the equivalent of about £18,000 a year today) and a pension for life of the same amount, plus all his expenses, to accompany the third Duke of Buccleuch; and Dr John Moore, author of books on Italy and France, who was travelling tutor to the eighth Duke of Hamilton. Robert Wood, the politician and author of *The Ruins of Palmyra*, was bear-leader to the Duke of Bridgewater. William Whitehead, the future Poet Laureate, travelled with Lords Villiers and Nuneham; Thomas Hobbes, the philosopher, with both the second and third Earls of Devonshire; Paul Henri Mallet, the Swiss historian, with Lord Mountstuart; Joseph Addison, the essayist, with Edward Montagu, a young relative of the Earl of Sandwich; John Locke, the philosopher, with the son of Sir John Banks; the travel writer, Francis Misson, with the first Duke of Ormonde; and John Horne Tooke, the politician, with the son of John Elwes, the celebrated miser who died worth £250,000 though he lived in penury in a house with a leaking roof, wearing an old wig he had found in a ditch.

There were other bear-leaders who, while achieving no comparable fame, were men of worth and ability, like Joseph Spence, Professor of Poetry at Oxford, who paid three visits to Italy with various young Englishmen; Edward Holdsworth, the Virgilian scholar and Latin poet, who made five Grand Tours between 1719 and 1740; Dr James Hay who is depicted in a famous caricature by Pier Leone Ghezzi; and Thomas Hobart, a learned Fellow of Christ's College, Cambridge

2 (Left) A caricature by Pier Leone Ghezzi of Dr James Hay, an experienced bear-leader, with one of his young charges.

3 (Right) Robert Wood, author of The Ruins of Palmyra, *who was tutor to the Duke of Bridgewater on his Tour, portrayed by Allan Ramsay in 1755.*

who possessed 'sound judgement and admirable addresse', as well as the qualifications of a doctor of medicine, and was given leave of absence for three years to supervise the tour of the first Earl of Leicester. Yet most travelling tutors were fussy, incompetent clergymen, pedagogues or place-seekers, paid about £100 a year or less, quite incapable of controlling their high-spirited young charges and 'not infrequently', as one contemporary observer remarked, 'as new to the scenes they experience as the very pupils entrusted to their care'. In the extreme but not altogether unjustified opinion of Horace Walpole, who was himself twenty-one when he set out on the Grand Tour not with a tutor but with his fellow Old Etonian, Thomas Gray:

There is an animal still more absurd [than an English boy on his travels] and that is travelling governors, who are mischievous into the bargain, and whose pride is always hurt because they are sure of its never being indulged. They will not leave the world because they are sent to teach it, and as they come far more ignorant of it than their pupils, take care to return with more prejudices, and as much care to instill all theirs into their pupils.

Certainly the first Earl of Salisbury's son was entrusted to the care of a tutor chiefly remembered for his skill in composing 'bawdy songs', Sir Walter Ralegh's son to a bear-leader whose charge exhibited him in the streets dead drunk upon a cart, and the ninth Earl of Derby to a 'master of too mild a nature to manage his pupil' whose friends in Paris tossed the poor man in a blanket. In his *Voyage of Italy*, Richard Lassels, who had 'travelled through Italy five times as Tutor to several of the English Nobility and Gentry', warned against these ill-qualified tutors who might lead their pupils to Geneva where they would lose 'all their true English allegiance and respect for monarchy', who might keep them in dull provincial cities where they happened to have a wife or mistress, or who would take bribes 'from masters of fencing or dancing to bring their charges to them, maintaining that the worst academics were the best'. 'Others I have known,' he continued, 'would have married their pupils without their parents' knowledge.'

As well as by a tutor, incompetent or able, the richer tourists were accompanied by a governor. Paul Henri Mallet's pupil Lord Mountstuart, for example, whose father was the Prime Minister, Lord Bute, was supervised by Lieutenant-Colonel James Edmonstone, a Scot of ancient family whose difficulties with his wayward charge are vividly recorded in James Boswell's journal. The party was also accompanied by several servants. The choice of these was also important, since much was required of them. In larger retinues the servants had specified duties. When the immensely rich third Earl of Burlington set out from his Piccadilly mansion in 1714 he was accompanied not only by a tutor, an artist to make drawings of the buildings which appealed to his young master, an accountant to keep a record of all expenses incurred and at least three other gentlemen, but also by five or six servants, probably a postilion, a groom, a valet and three liveried footmen.

Such an imposing suite was, of course, highly exceptional, though the sixth Lord Baltimore arrived in Vienna with, amongst others, a doctor, two black eunuchs and eight women; and when asked by the police to indicate which was his wife replied that, being an Englishmen, it was not his practice to discuss his sexual arrangements with foreigners and that, unless permitted to continue his journey as he intended, he would settle the matter with his fists. Yet few tourists did not take at least one servant with them and most, like James Boswell, hired an additional *valet de louage*, or local servant, in each town in which they were expected to spend any length of time. Tourists were urged to be extremely cautious in hiring these servants. 'Trust nothing to them, I mean of your linen, wearing apparel etc,' Boswell was advised by his father's experienced friend, Dr McKinlay. 'Some honest fellows you may meet with, but in general they are rogues. You give all over Italy to your servant three *paolis* (eighteen pence sterling) a day without eating or anything else.' They were considered necessary, however, even if only as

4 (Opposite) The second Duke of Northumberland with his dog and his tutor, Lipyeatt, painted in Rome by Nathaniel Dance, who lived there from 1755 to 1764.

interpreters, since it was improbable that their employer's English servant would live up to the ideal recommended in one of those numerous guide-books which were published for the benefit of the tourist:

A servant selected to accompany a gentleman on his travels should be conversant with the French language; write a legible and quick hand, in order to be able to copy whatever is laid before him: know a little of surgery, and to bleed well in case his master should meet with an accident where no chirurgical assistance is to be expected. Gentlemen should endeavour to attach such useful servants to their persons, by showing the same care as a father has for a child, and promise him a settlement for life upon their return.

The tourist's servant was far less likely to resemble this paragon, or the companionable Matthew Todd – a young Yorkshire gentleman's valet who dealt as efficiently with grasping innkeepers as he did with his master's accounts, clothes and comfort – than Byron's tiresome servant, of whom his master wrote:

The perpetual lamentations after beef and beer, the stupid, bigoted contempt for everything foreign, an insurmountable incapacity for acquiring even a few words of any language, rendered him, like all other English servants, an incumbrance. I do assure you, the plague of speaking for him, the comforts he required (more than myself by far), the [dishes] which he could not eat, the wines which he could not drink, the beds where he could not sleep, and the long list of calamities, such as stumbling horses, want of *tea* !!! &c., which assailed him, would have made a lasting source of laughter to a spectator, and inconvenience to a master.

So long as servants were likely to be as useless as Byron's and tutors as incompetent as Walpole said they were, it behoved the tourist to pay due attention to the advice the guide-books and the accounts of experienced travellers had to give him. First of all he must make sure that he had everything requisite for this long journey. He would need the best historical accounts of the countries and cities he would be passing through, and the most up-to-date maps 'properly fitted up on linen in order to render them convenient to the pocket'. ''Tis proper also,' recommended one of the most useful of all guides, Sir Thomas Nugent's *The Grand Tour*, published in four volumes in 1749, 'to be provided with prospective glasses, a mariner's compass and quadrant'. Another widely read vade-mecum, F. M. Misson's *A New Voyage to Italy*, suggests that the traveller should carry with him a cane divided into several measures, or a piece of pack-thread well twined and waxed so that he can measure the height of towers and the dimensions of 'all buildings worth considering'.

Notebooks, dictionaries and grammars would also be required as a matter of course, as well as crayons; a pocket sun-dial or a watch; pens and a pocket inkstand; a penknife (as well as a pocket-knife to eat with); a passport holder stamped with name, rank and family crest; an inflatable bath with bellows; a tinder-box to light a fire in case of accidents on the road at night; a medicine chest (since foreign doctors were 'quacks to a man'), containing, in particular, remedies against sickness caused by the rolling both of the sea and of the swaying post-wagons in Germany; 'a bottle of vinegar, Ditto best French brandy, Ditto spirit of salmiac, against fits, Ditto Hoffman's Drops'. The eighteenth-century tourist was no longer in danger from the plague as he had been in the days of the third Lord North, who attributed his permanent ill health to the immoderate doses of hot treacle he drank to escape the plague in Venice, but other diseases and complaints were said to be rife. Outbreaks of typhoid were common, malaria was endemic in the Campagna, and it was well known that James Dawkins had had a twenty-four-yard tapeworm removed in Dresden, and that Lord Balgonie had narrowly escaped being bitten by a scorpion which had crawled into his bed in Padua.

As well as medicines, the traveller should also have boxes of spices and condiments, tea, salt, mustard, cayenne pepper, ginger, nutmegs, oatmeal, sago, sugar, and a bag stuffed with powdered bay salt to be applied to the stomach when this, inevitably, became upset. The anonymous author of *Letters from Italy, 1792 to 1798* further recommended a supply of 'essential oil of lavender' to drive bugs from the beds of inns and 'vitriolic acid to put into decanters of bad water to make the noxious particles deposit themselves at the bottom and render the water wholesome'. This author comforts the reader with the name of a shop in Florence, 'Molini's near the Royal Gallery', where a variety of trustworthy English goods could be purchased, including James's powders, Reeve's colours, tea, sago, wax candles for coach-lamps, painting-brushes, paper, pens, pencils, ink and English books, 'likewise excellent rum'.

Other authorities suggested that while it might not be so essential as it had been in the seventeenth century to have a linen overall to be worn over the clothes in bed at night, nor lice-proof taffeta-lined undergarments, plenty of shirts strong enough to resist the treatment of continental washerwomen were required, as were several pairs of shoes, silk stockings, waterproof buckskin breeches, a large supply of handkerchiefs 'which come in useful when you perspire', a pair of eye-preservers, a wide-brimmed hat as a protection against the sun, and, for the same purpose, an umbrella such as were used in Italy, though these, as Fynes Moryson was warned by a 'learned Physician', could be dangerous, 'because they gather the heate into a pyramidal point and then cast it down perpendicularly upon the head, except they know how to carry them for avoyding that danger'.

The sun, however, was the least of the dangers likely to be encountered. Touring, it was conceded, was not as hazardous as it had been in Fynes Moryson's day, and for several years after his death in 1630, when it was

A NEW MAP
OF
EUROPE
From the latest Observations

Inscrib'd to the Honble Samuel
Molyneux Esq. Secretary to his R.
H. the Prince

by Jn Senex

THE
NORTHERN
OCEAN

ICELAND

NORWAY

LAPLAND

SWEDISH LAPLAND

MOSCOV

SWEDEN

FINLAND

THE BALTICK SEA

G. OF FINLAND

FARRO I.

ORKNEY I.

NORTH
SEA or
GERMAN
OCEAN

THE WESTERN ISLES

POLAND

DENMARK

GERMANY

LITHUANIA

PRUSSIA

BRANDENBURG

SAXONY

BOHEMIA

MORAVIA

COURTLAND

LIVONIA

BAY
OF
BISCAY

S. GEORGE'S CH.

FRANCE

BAVARIA

AUSTRIA

HUNGARY

TURKEY
IN
EUROPE

TIROL

CARINTHIA

STIRIA

ITALY

GULF OF VENICE

DALMATIA

BOSNIA

SERVIA

POR TUGAL

SPAIN

GRANADA

MURCIA

MINORCA I.
MAJORCA I.

THE
MEDITER RANEAN
SEA

GULF OF LYONS

GENOA

TIRRHENIAN
SEA

SICILY

IONIAN SEA

ALBANIA

MACEDONIA

GREECE

ACHAIA

MOREA

CANDIA

PART OF AFRICA

Malta I.

AFRICA

6 *A passport issued in 1780 by a French cardinal and minister of state to Mr Neville, 'Gentilhomme Anglois, retournant en Angleterre avec un Domestique'.*

5 *'A new map of Europe from the latest observations', published in about 1720.*

considered inadvisable to travel from Rome and Naples without a guard of sixty musketeers as a protection against *banditti*, when the roads around Genoa were infested both by native brigands and Turkish pirates, when it was inadvisable in some inns to ask for wine and spend freely lest reports of a customer with money to spare reached the ears of freebooters, when in Germany during and immediately after the Thirty Years War peasants as well as bandits went about armed and cannibalism was said to be common in Brandenburg county, and when one traveller, riding to Hamburg in 1652, counted in a single day thirty-four piles of faggots each marking a spot where a previous wayfarer had been murdered. Yet, even so, the eighteenth-century traveller was constantly warned that when on the road in certain places he must always be on his guard, most especially when traversing dense forests. He should carry pistols as well as a sword, preferably, as one book of advice suggested, 'double-barrelled pistols, very well calculated for the defence of the traveller, particularly those which have both barrels above and do not require turning'. These he might well need in the Papal States in Italy and in other places where two states bordered, 'for there most robberies and murders are committed, as the offenders in half an hour may get out of the reach of justice from that territory where the act is committed'. The tourist should also have with him an iron fastener for securing the door of his inn room at night, whenever he was fortunate enough to have a room of his own, for there were numerous well-attested stories of travellers being attacked and robbed in their beds.

There were also often-repeated stories of travellers being murdered on the open road. Three Englishmen, who had been seen changing their money in Calais, were stopped and killed just outside Paris in 1723; in 1725 another young Englishman, William Yates, on his way to Italy was murdered near Ghent; and, some years later, James Walker narrowly escaped death when his carriage was stopped by highwaymen on the road to Frankfurt. But the chances of being killed on the road were not, in fact, high and it was often asserted, indeed, that the roads in France at least were safer than those in England where highwaymen, in the words of one experienced traveller, were 'as common as crows'. Accustomed to a strong force of *maréchaussée* to protect their main roads, visiting foreigners were astonished by the state of affairs in England, where a Swiss tourist described the number of robbers as 'amazing', and a Frenchman wrote that all the main roads within thirty or forty miles of London were '*garnis de voleurs à cheval*'.

Tourists on the Continent, then, had good cause to feel safer on the main roads than they did at home. Lady Mary Wortley Montagu averred that such good care was taken against robbers in France that 'you may cross the country with your purse in your hand'. 'It is a compliment to Italy,' wrote Adam Walker in the 1780s, 'that we neither were robbed, attempted to be robbed, or heard of a robbery, the time we travelled through it, and we travelled early and late.' Martin Sherlock, writing at about the same time, confirmed that the English traveller abroad was relatively safe.

The nation [Italy] is exceedingly poor, and that counsellor of evil, Hunger, makes them commit many rogueries. It is not, however, as is generally believed, a country of robbers and assassins. My countrymen travel there almost continually, and for thirty years past there has been but one accident which has happened to them, or to any of their people; and even that ought not to be mentioned as an exception. As the courier of an English duke was passing a river, he struck one of the boatmen with his whip, and the boatman shot him.

Indeed, when there was trouble it was as likely as not to be caused by an Englishman hitting postilions or guides, or getting drunk like Lord Charles Fitzroy who, inflamed by Rhenish wine in Vienna, knocked down 'every Austrian within reach'. Tobias Smollett, the irascible novelist who freely admitted to having wrangled with numerous innkeepers and to having questioned bills with sword in hand, was so provocative that Philip Thicknesse, author of *Observations on the Customs and Manners of the French Nation*, wondered that he ever got home alive to tell the tale of his altercations with guides whom he insultingly contradicted, with recalcitrant postmasters to whom he read out the rules in the post-book with 'great vociferation', with landlords whom he threatened with 'manual correction', and with importunate crowds whom his servant dispersed by a discharge from his blunderbuss.

If, however, despite the provocation offered, English travellers were very rarely killed and not all that often robbed, even in the unlighted streets of towns at night, pickpockets and petty pilferers were to be encountered everywhere. Tourists were therefore advised to be careful not to display their wealth in front of strangers, or pull valuables from their pockets in wayside inns. They must never allow more than one trunk at a time to be opened at the customs, 'as the owner's eyes and attention may be fixed on one revenue officer at the great hazard of his being pillaged by the other'; and they must always ensure that a servant kept a careful eye on their baggage when travelling. 'Travellers should not permit strangers to place themselves beside the vehicle, under any pretext whatsoever,' wrote Count Leopold Berchtold in a book of advice published in London in 1787. 'In suspicious places, the trunk should be placed before the coach; which place should generally be made use of as often as circumstances will permit.'

Such books also warned tourists against inadvertently breaking some local law and rendering themselves liable to arrest, as Fynes Moryson had done in Tuscany when he had broken off the bough of a mulberry tree to serve as a parasol. 'Those trees planted in the high waies belonged to the Duke, who preserved them for silkewormes,' he was afterwards told, 'and a great penalty was imposed upon any that should break a bough thereof.' In Dieppe and St Omer, for example, 'every person who is abroad without a lanthorn after ten at night is taken into custody by the police'. And here, as elsewhere, the gates were shut at nightfall, so care had to be taken to arrive at walled cities in daylight.

Care had also to be taken to learn in advance what troubles were likely to be encountered at customs posts where thievish officials were quite likely to throw small parcels under the coach to be gathered up later:

> Since it is impossible to know what goods are forbidden in different countries, information on that head should be had before foreigners enter into another territory, in order to avoid many inconveniences which might arrive from trifles: in some countries the whole luggage is confiscated if prohibited goods are found with them; and the owners condemned to imprisonment, or to pay a heavy fine.

At Pistoia, for instance, so John Northall said in 1766, they searched all baggage for tobacco and any quantity over a pound in weight was seized; they seized new clothes as well, 'at least they oblige strangers to pay for them, if only a pair of shoes'. At Rome they searched closely for prohibited books and for silk stockings bought in Naples; in Prussia in 1766 for no less than 490 commodities which were expressly forbidden even on the payment of heavy duties; on the Carinthian frontier, so one traveller reported in the 1790s, they seized 'gold and silver lace, snuff, and tobacco, and for unmade silks, gauzes, etc., they oblige you to deposit double the worth to be paid back, however, when you quit the imperial territories. They accept no fees, and are slower in their operations than it is possible to conceive'. Elsewhere, in addition to being slow, they were likely to be rough and clumsy, tumbling baggage about in 'a most disagreeable manner'. 'Everything was thrown into beautiful confusion,' runs one characteristic complaint of an inspection at Ostend, 'and besides half-a-crown for three yards of small cord, and two leaden seals about the size of a half-penny, I was sentenced to pay one shilling and sixpence for two pairs of unwashed stockings. My new shoes escaped taxation by my putting them on in presence of the inquisitors.'

At most places, so it was suggested, an adequate bribe usually settled all argument and immediately 'cooled the zeal of the inspectors'. This was certainly the experience of the great majority of tourists who, like James Edward Smith, found that the offer of a gratuity to the officials was 'generally the best way' to get baggage past the customs. 'We were stopt,' wrote James Essex in 1773 in a passage which may be taken as representative, 'as we were going out of the Gates of Calis by the Custom-house Officers who wanted to search our baggage, but seeing a 12 sou piece in our valet's hand, they turned their attention that way and suffered us to pass'. At the Milan custom-house, another tourist complained, tips were 'importunately' demanded.

Payment of bribes and of frequent tolls exacted on both carriages and river transport accounted for a large part of the allowance the young tourist was granted by his father or guardian. The amount of this allowance was the subject of anxious discussions in houses all over the country. As well as bribes and tolls, payments to lock-keepers and large fees paid to redeem confiscated weapons, there were all manner of incidental expenses apart from the ordinary costs of travel, clothes, board and lodging and the payment of servants, guides, barbers, laundry women, fencing and dancing masters. There were tips and gifts to the poor and to the galley slaves at Marseilles; there were presents to buy in addition to books, manuscripts and works of art – gloves in Turin; prints and scent in Rome; 'stockings, waistcoats, breeches, caps, and other works of silk . . . snuff and perfum'd soap' in Naples; leatherwork in Florence; 'all sorts of works in glass and crystal' in Venice; lace in Bruges; watches, tea cups, buckles, snuff-boxes, dressing-gowns, silk suits and shoes in Paris. The account books of Thomas Coke, first Earl of Leicester – who set forth on his six-year tour when he was only fifteen with a bear-leader and various servants including two grooms, a valet and a steward to keep the accounts – contain references to payments for musical instruments, tickets to the opera, repairs to the coach, for 'a dog fowling a silk carpet', a present 'given to too pretty women by my master's order', the salaries of 'mathematik and french masters', as well as to payments for drawing, dancing and fencing lessons, and such items as 'gave my master for his pocket 20–00', 'for letters and a poor woman by order, 01–12', 'a sute of silk cloaths for my master, 160–02', 'a masquerade, 05–00', '6 payor of gloves, 03–00', 'a black silk bag for my master's perriwig, 03–00', 'half a pound of chocolat, 02–00', 'ink, 00–03', 'washing, 10–00', 'cards, 01–12'.

Young men from families as rich as the Earl of Leicester's might receive as much as £2,000 a year – that is to say the equivalent of about £120,000 in present-day terms. The young man who was to become the seventh Earl of Salisbury was allowed £130 a month with an additional £400 to cover the expense of staying in Paris. Most tourists, however, managed on considerably less than this. Ashe Windham was allowed £600 a year when he was abroad in the 1690s, and Lord Boston spent £566 in twelve months in 1715–16. John Evelyn had managed on about half that sum, and in 1775 a tourist wrote from Paris, 'I think one might live very comfortably on £300 a year or with a little management for £250.' Arthur Young, who travelled extensively on the Continent before the Revolution, calculated that a man could live better on £100 a year in Italy than he could on £500 a year in England; and in 1785 it was estimated by William Blackett that many young travellers on the Continent were, indeed, making do with £100 a year, like Thomas Martyn who observed in his *Gentleman's Guide on his Tour through France*:

7 *An account kept by one of his servants of the Earl of Leicester's expenses in Rome in 1714.*

I must beg leave to observe, it is a general conceived notion in England that it is necessary to have considerable fortune to make the tour of France, so it is – if a man is determined to be a dupe to Frenchmen and enter into all the follies vices and fopperies of that vain superficial people. During eighteen months that I was abroad it did not cost me 150 livres sterling. In this time I learnt the language, made myself acquainted with their laws customs and manners, never omitted examining with care all the curiosities worthy of a stranger's inspection, always appeared in genteel company, kept my servant when in town, and in all respects supported with reputation the character I assume.

Early in the nineteenth century, when inflation had slightly increased the cost of living on the Continent, particularly in Paris, it was still considered possible to undertake a tour of Europe on seventeen shillings a day, provided one avoided those places where the reckless extravagance of rich Englishmen had increased prices too much.

For most tourists, however, economy was neither practicable nor even advisable. Spending in the grand manner was, so one guide-book put it, 'the way to be respected'. It was better, of course, to avoid losing such sums as those dissipated at the gaming tables and in tailors' shops by Charles James Fox, who once posted all the way from Paris to Lyons just to buy patterns for his waistcoat and who returned to London wearing extremely expensive red-heeled shoes and blue hair powder. It was also unwise to behave as profligately as 'the young nobility and gentry' whom one of their disapproving countrymen frequently saw 'collecting mobs in the streets, by throwing money from the windows, and in their daily actions confirming Frenchmen in their unalterable opinion that the English are all immensely rich and consequently can afford to pay double what a

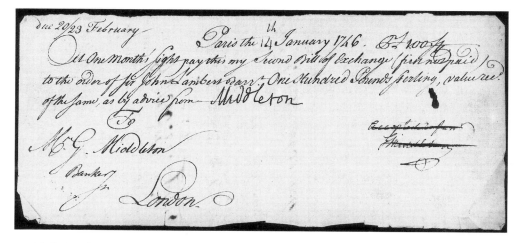

8 *A bill of exchange issued in January 1746.*

Frenchman will pay for the same article'. Few could contemplate giving a ball for 250 people at Lausanne as Lord Duncannon did at a cost believed to be in excess of £600. Yet the Grand Tour was made only once, and it was surely sensible to enjoy it as well as to profit by it and to take enough money to ensure that pleasures need not be stinted.

The manner in which money was taken, or arranged to be available on the Continent, required careful planning. A few tourists took a fairly large supply of English money with them, for this was accepted in most large towns in France and the Low Countries and in several in Switzerland and Germany. But to travel with substantial amounts was both tiresome and risky; and it was far more common either to ask a London banker to arrange with his foreign correspondents to have sums available for collection in foreign currency, or to take bills of exchange which would theoretically be cashed by any continental banker. Bills of exchange presented problems, though, as the commissions charged were often exorbitant and some bankers in a small way of business looked askance at them or even affected not to know what they were; while letters of credit were frequently delayed in the post, a communication from London to Florence commonly taking six weeks and sometimes much longer or not arriving at all. Tourists were, therefore, frequently obliged to borrow from other travellers or from a consul or resident minister.

Even when a reasonable and accommodating banker could be found, it was unwise for the tourist passing through a town to take much of the local currency as this might either not be accepted in a neighbouring state or exchanged only for a fraction of what it had cost him. Since he would constantly be having to change money, it was advisable for the tourist to know something about continental currency. The value of those relatively few coins in France was not too difficult to master, but in Italy he would have to contend with the *sequin* and the *scudo*, the *livre* and the *paul*, with *louis d'ors* and ducatoons, *soldi, pichioli, grosses* and *lire*, silver crowns and *genoins*, philips, testoons, *julios*, three sorts of *pistole* and four sorts of ducat. German money was equally confusing. 'In a country divided into so many petty sovereignties there must be a great variety of money,' Sir Thomas Nugent warned in *The Grand Tour*.

Almost every free town coins small pieces of its own, which are current over the whole empire. The German coin in general is neither true sterling nor true weight, being clipt, it is thought, more than any coin in Europe. The pieces that ought to be round are all shapes. The corruptors, particularly the Jews, do not trouble themselves to file it, but snip large bits off of the sides: This, with the variety of money that is current there, is no small disadvantage to trade. . . . As knowledge of the coins is extremely necessary for a traveller, we shall give here a short account of the general species that are current.

This 'short account' fills seven pages.

Nugent's and similar manuals left no aspect of the Grand Tour unremarked. Tips and warnings, words of guidance and moral injunctions followed each other and were repeated in publication after publication: never travel by night when it is possible to go by day, avoid the company of young women in the interests of virtue and of old women because they always want the best seats, when travelling by sea keep clear of the sailors who are sure to be covered with vermin and take off your spurs otherwise they will be stolen while you are being sick, always carry something to eat with you on a journey not only to satisfy your own hunger but also to keep off starving dogs, on reaching your inn at night look behind all the big pictures and looking-glasses in your room to ensure they do not hide secret doors, and never fail to make a bargain with the landlord before you touch anything. Failure to make a bargain could certainly lead to the grossest impositions. 'Let no one go to Cherbourg without making a bargain for everything he has, even to the straw and stable, pepper, salt and table-cloth,' warned Arthur Young.

I was here fleeced more infamously than at any other town in France. The two best inns were full; I was obliged to go to the *barque*, a vile hole, little better than a hog-sty where for a miserable dirty wretched chamber, two suppers composed chiefly of a plate of apples and some butter and cheese, with some trifle besides too bad to eat, and one miserable dinner, they brought me in a bill of 31 liv. (1 7s 1d). They not only charged the room 3 liv. a night, but even the very stable for my horse, after enormous items for oats, hay and straw.

It was the same in Italy. At Lerici, said James Edward Smith, 'we bargained beforehand as is necessary for our supper and lodging; but, having had coffee next morning, were surprised to find it charged about as much as all the rest put together. On complaining, we were told with the utmost effrontery, that coffee was not in the original bargain.' Tobias Smollett had similar experiences in both countries. In France the *auberges* were 'execrable' places in which one found 'nothing but dirt and imposition. One would imagine the French were still at war with the English, for they pillage them without mercy.' In Italy the houses were 'abominably nasty and generally destitute of provision: when eatables were found, we were almost poisoned by their cookery: their beds were without curtains or bedstead, and their windows without glass; and for this sort of entertainment [you are asked to pay] as much as if [you] had been genteely lodged, and sumptuously treated'.

From such accounts as these, the young tourist turned with relief to guide-books like *The Gentleman's Pocket Companion for Travelling into Foreign Parts* (1722) which, while not suggesting that continental inns were as clean as they might be, indicated that a night's stay might have its compensations. The section headed 'At the Inn' in *The Gentleman's Pocket Companion* contained a list of useful phrases in French, Italian and German in the form of a dialogue between the tourist, the innkeeper and Joan, the chambermaid:

> 'God keep you from misfortune, my host!'
> 'You are welcome, Gentlemen!'
> 'Shall we be well lodged with you for this night?'
> 'Yes, very well, Sir.'
> 'Have you good stable, good hay, good oats, good litter, good wine?'
> 'The best . . .'

[The tourist alights with his companions and enters the inn where he drinks too heavily with his meal.]

> 'By your leaves, Gentlemen, I find myself somewhat indispos'd.'
> 'Sir, if you are not well, go take your rest, your chamber is ready.'
> 'Joan, make a good fire in his chamber, and let him want for nothing.'
> 'Sweetheart, is my bed made? Is it good, clean, warm?'
> 'Yes, Sir, it is a good featherbed. The sheets are very clean.'

'Pull off my stockings, and warm my bed, for I am much out of order. I shake like a leaf in a tree. Warm a Napkin for my head and bind it well. Gently, you bind it too hard. Bring my pillow and cover me well: draw the curtains, and pin them together. Where is the chamber-pot? Where is the privy?'

'Follow me and I will show you the way. Go straight up and you will find it on your right hand; if you see it not you will soon smell it. Sir, do you want anything else?'

'Yes, my dear, put out the candle and come nearer to me.'

'I will put it out when I am out of the room; what is your will? Are you not well enough yet?'

'My head lies too low, raise up the bolster a little. I cannot lie so low. My dear, give me a kiss, I should sleep the better.'

'You are not sick since you talk of kissing. I would rather die than kiss a man in his bed, or any other place. Take your rest in God's name. God give you a good night and good rest.'

'I thank you, fair maid.'

James Boswell had more success than this tourist in his encounter with a young woman who came into his room at eight o'clock one morning in Berlin with a basket of chocolates to sell: 'I toyed with her and found she was with child. Oho! a safe piece. Into my closet. "Have you a husband?" "Yes, in the Guards at Potsdam." To bed directly. In a minute – over. I rose cool and astonished, half angry, half laughing. I sent her off.' Yet while it was considered inevitable that young gentlemen should enjoy themselves in this way on their travels, and, since they must sow their wild oats, it was better that they should do so abroad, it was hoped that they would not do so 'with such low women as may be injurious to their health'. In his celebrated letters to his natural son, Philip Stanhope, the fourth Earl of Chesterfield, who had himself set out on the Grand Tour in 1714, wrote that there was no need for a young man of any address to make love to his laundress, so long as ladies of his own class were ready to stoop to folly. And many undoubtedly were. Lord Carpenter in Paris in 1717 could not

omit setting down an adventure that happened to Mr Dixon at the Comte de Douglass assemblee: after he had played at cards some times with Madam de Polignac: a very handsome lady: she preferred to sett him at home in her coach: which he very willingly accepted of: this young gentleman (who was a man of pleasure) finding himself alone with a fine young lady: could not forbear putting his hand where some women would not let him: after he had pleased himself thus for some time and she had bore it with a great deal of patience: she told him (in a pleasant manner) that since he had been so very free with her: she could not forbear being familiar with him: upon which she handled his arms: and finding them not fitt for present service: she beat him very heartily: he said all he could for himself: telling her that he had been upon hard duty for some time in the wars of venus: and if she would give him but one day to recruit in: he would behave himself like a man: she minded not his excuses but turned him out of the coach: and gave him this advice – 'Never to attack a young handsome lady as she was when his ammunition was spent.'

Inevitable as sexual adventures might be, however, the young tourist was urged always to remember that he was being sent abroad to gain knowledge rather than to spend his days in dissipation and idleness. He was to travel, as the Earl of Cork and Orrery put it, 'not to see fashions but states, not to taste wines but different governments, not to compare laces and velvets but laws and politics'. He must not only learn the languages of the countries through which he passed, but study their history, geography, trade, climate, crops, minerals, food, clothes, customs, manners, fauna, flora, politics, laws and military fortifications. He must display a lively interest by asking questions and setting down the answers. One book lists 117 suggestions for the guidance of those without natural curiosity. No subject was considered too recondite for his consideration, be it grounds for divorce or corporal punishment at the university, the care of paupers or the pay of the clergy, water supply or fire precautions. Count Leopold Berchtold's *Essay to Direct and Extend the Inquiries of Patriotic Travellers*, after recommending inquiries as to 'Charitable Institutions for recovering Drowned and Strangled Persons' and the 'Extent of Liberty to Grown-up Young Ladies', goes on to give examples of the kind of questions that might be asked:

'Which are the favourite herbs of the sheep of this country?'
'Are there many examples of people having been bit by mad animals?'
'Which food has been experienced to be most portable and most nourishing for keeping a distressed ship's crew from starving?'
'How much is paid per day for ploughing with two oxen? With two horses?'
'What is the value of whales of different sizes?'

On entering a strange town the tourist should at once ascend the highest steeple to gain a good view of it and take note of any interesting buildings worthy of further inspection. He must then make drawings, take measurements, study the details of architecture and decoration, list valuable contents, sketch the layout of their courtyards and gardens, constantly bearing in mind his future as the inheritor of family possessions and as patron of artists who would one day enhance them. 'Take particular note of the French way of furnishing rooms,' Lord Annandale advised his nephew in 1725, 'especially with double doors and windows and door curtains and finishing them with looking-glass, marble, painting, and gilded stucco.'

As was to be expected, Lord Chesterfield's concern in his long and scrupulously regular correspondence with his son was not only to widen his knowledge and improve his taste but also to impose upon the shy, good-natured and rather clumsy boy the polished manners and graceful deportment which the Grand Tour was intended to provide. Philip was to spend five years on the Continent from the age of fourteen to acquire a better preparation for life than could be afforded by Oxford or Cambridge, whose education could not even prevent a young man from being flurried on being presented to his sovereign. He was to have a travelling tutor, of course, Walter Harte, a friend of Alexander Pope and son of a former Fellow of Pembroke College, Oxford, who was recommended to Chesterfield by Lord Lyttelton. But 'long accustomed to college life', Harte was 'too awkward both in his person and address to be able to familiarise the graces with his young pupil'. Chesterfield, therefore, urged his son to study the manners of those he would find in attendance at foreign courts and of the best company in the major towns of Switzerland, Germany and Italy to which numerous letters of introduction would be sent.

The first year would be spent in Lausanne (where Edward Gibbon was also to be sent) 'for the rudiments of languages'; this would be followed by a year in Leipzig for a thorough grounding in history and jurisprudence; a third year would be spent in visits to such cities as Berlin, Dresden and Vienna for a view of the various courts. Then it would be time to travel in Italy to shake off the manners of Germany: there must be no more 'scrambling at your meals as at a German ordinary: no awkward overturns of glasses, plates, and salt cellars'. Finally there was to be a long sojourn in France, mostly in Paris, where he would be given the ultimate polish, 'the supreme touch of gentlemanly complaisance, politeness and ease'. For the first six months in Paris, Philip was to live in an academy with young Frenchmen of fashion, then in lodgings of his own. The mornings were to be devoted to study and to serious conversation both with men of learning and of good family, the afternoons to exercise, the evenings to balls, to opera, or play, to establishing an intimacy with the best Parisian families, to becoming fashionable among the French so that he would be fashionable in London. At the end of those six months he would be eighteen and would be provided with a generous allowance, a coach, a footman, two valets, the very best French clothes and such items as a gold snuff-box and a handsome sword; but there would be no fancy cane-heads or extravagant fob-chains, no excessive gambling – no gambling at all, indeed, except in the presence of ladies – no supper in common taverns, no consorting with opera singers, and certainly no association with his fellow countrymen.

There were numerous tourists who had no need to be told to avoid the company of other Englishmen. William Hazlitt related the story of a journey he made in France with a man who took no notice of him, 'preserving an obstinate silence'. 'We pretended not to recognise each other, and yet our saying nothing proved every instant that we were not French. At length, about half way, my companion opened his lips, and asked in thick, broken French, "How far it was to Evereux?" I looked at him and said in English, "I did not know." Not another word passed.' Tobias Smollett encountered an Englishman of equal reserve on the beach at Antibes. This man, so his valet told Smollett's servant, had journeyed for three days in company with two other English tourists and in all that time had not addressed a single word to either of them.

More gregarious tourists, however, found it all too easy to spend their time in the company of their fellow countrymen. As early as 1592, and again in 1595, the Pope had been induced to complain about the number of English heretics in Paris, and in 1612 James I's ambassador in Venice told the Doge that there were then more than seventy Englishmen in the city whereas 'formerly' there had been only four or five. Throughout the seventeenth and eighteenth centuries the number of English travellers on the Continent increased year by year, most appreciably after the end of the Seven Years War in 1763 and the improvement of relations between England and the Roman Catholic courts of the Continent. 'Where one Englishman travelled in the reign of the first two Georges,' wrote one observer in 1772, 'ten now go on a grand tour. Indeed, to such a pitch is the spirit of travelling come in the kingdom, that there is scarce a citizen of large fortune but takes a flying view of France, Italy and Germany.' Adam Smith, also writing in the 1770s, said that it had become 'every day more and more the custom to send young people to travel in foreign countries'.

As early as 1713 Henry Lee Warner had written to his uncle from Paris, 'There are so many English that we must not stay long, and we hear that there are more at Montpellier.' In 1740 Horace Walpole described the English in Rome as 'numberless'. Edward Gibbon, while in Switzerland in the summer of 1785, was assured that 40,000 English were on the Continent. And in Paris the following year, according to the *Daily Universal Register*, 'to such an amazing pitch of folly is the rage for travelling come, that in less than six weeks, the list of Londoners arrived in Paris has amounted to three thousand seven hundred and sixty, as appears by the registers of that city'. In 1727 the numbers of English in Paris had been described as 'swarms'; the same word was used by the English Resident in Venice in 1733, and by more than one tourist in Rome in the 1780s. By then not a day passed, so it was said, when carriages could not be seen rattling out of the courtyard of the George at Southwark, and of other coaching inns, carrying rich young men to Dover.

9 A crowded coach rolling down to Dover from Canterbury by Rowlandson, who went to study in Paris at the age of sixteen and thereafter made regular trips to the Continent.

CHAPTER 2

*

ACROSS THE
CHANNEL

*

'A desperately rough passage'

'I NEED NOT TELL YOU THAT THIS IS THE worst road in England,' wrote Tobias Smollett with characteristic vituperation of the services offered to travellers between London and Dover. 'The chambers are in general cold and comfortless, the beds paltry, the cookery execrable, the wine poison, the attendance bad, the publicans insolent, and the bills extortion.' Dover itself, he continued, was a den of thieves, the inhabitants were said to live by piracy in time of war, and 'by smuggling and fleecing strangers in time of piece. . . . Without all doubt a man cannot be much worse lodged and worse treated in any part of Europe.'

There were, of course, alternatives to the Dover to Calais crossing. It was possible to go all the way by water from London to Dunkirk and Boulogne, to sail from Harwich to Helvoetsluys, from Yarmouth to Cuxhaven, London to Hamburg and Amsterdam, Brighton and Weymouth to Dieppe and Cherbourg, Dover to Ostend, to take boats, too, from Southampton to Le Havre and from Folkestone and Newhaven. It was possible also, at a cost of about three and a half guineas, to hire a sloop, or be rowed across the Channel 'in an open boat of six oars for thirty shillings'. But all these routes and methods had their disadvantages, and most entailed spending a long time at sea.

When Fynes Moryson had crossed from Leigh to the Netherlands in 1591 the voyage – made through fog and tempest and threatened by pirates from Dunkirk – took ten days. Thomas Coryate went by the shorter route from Dover to Calais but even so was ten hours at sea. Since Coryate's time crossings of this duration had been uncommon, although adverse winds frequently detained passengers for days on end: in September 1759 John Leake was kept waiting for five days at Harwich and in 1772 Dr Charles Burney, the musicologist, for nine. Delays of three days were not at all unusual. Nor were sudden storms which drove ships off course, forcing them to land at ports their passengers had not bargained for or to lie under storm-sails in imminent danger of shipwreck. Even when winds were favourable, a comfortable crossing was exceptional. Matthew Todd, Andrew Barlow's servant, described a voyage between Harwich and Helvoetsluys for which they paid £5 9s for two places in a boat carrying seventy-five passengers with berths for only twelve:

10 (Opposite) Guests entertained at a luncheon of oysters, by Jean François de Troy.

The weather was uncommonly cold and forced the passengers all below, when such a scene could never be imagined by any one excepting those who were of the party. The wind being pretty fresh there was a great motion in the vessel and those who had snugly stowed themselves in the side berths soon began to feel the effects and cascaded upon their friends and brother sufferers sleeping on the deck below them. The deck was too small for the party and actually many were laying in bread and butter fashion, and with the heat of the cabins the black of the boots had daubed the faces of some, and others in the pains of sickness overturning a *pot de chambre* with its contents, and no chance of getting out as the door of the cabin had about half a dozen people sleeping against it. Old Mr Ravie was very pressing for me and his son to take some tumblers of sea water, but could not succeed, tho' he offered to give his son a guinea to drink a glass, and by way of example drank one himself.

Even in less crowded and smelly boats nearly everyone was as seasick as the fellow-passengers of Thomas Brand who 'in almost the quickest passage ever known [between Dover and Calais], 2 hours and 40 minutes . . . had no other amusement than to watch the Seagulls, Willocks and Porpoises, unless [he] chose to pity the pale and wan faces of [his] fellow travellers or to listen to the splash of their evacuations which were most copious indeed'.

A crossing in two hours and forty minutes was certainly a quick one. Although the March wind was fresh, it took Walpole and Gray five hours to reach Calais from Dover in 1739, while the Earl of Cork and Orrery considered himself very lucky to get across in three hours and ten minutes in 1754, and in 1773 James Essex counted four and a half hours as a good passage. In one of his crossings Arthur Young spent fourteen hours between Dover and Calais.

11 Rowlandson shows passengers enduring a passage in choppy seas in a packet, 1791.

12 The first exasperating experience of douaniers at the custom-house in Boulogne.

When the French coast came into sight, the sufferings of the traveller were not over, since the packet could often not get into harbour because of the low tide or rough seas, and then rowing boats, rocking unnervingly, would appear and French sailors would demand a fee for carrying passengers and baggage ashore, sometimes as much as two guineas a boatload, though the fare of the packet crossing would probably not have been more than a guinea a head and in 1763 a packet-boat could be hired for five guineas.

Having crossed from Dover to Boulogne in a cramped and dirty cutter, sitting up all night 'in a most uncomfortable situation, tossed about by the sea, cold and weary and languishing for want of sleep', Smollett was told that, with the wind blowing offshore, the boat could not possibly get into the harbour and he would have to be rowed ashore. When Smollett objected to this, the captain replied that it was 'a privilege which the watermen of Boulogne had, to carry all passengers ashore, and that this privilege he durst not venture to infringe'. 'The French boat came alongside half filled with water,' Smollett continued, 'and we were handed from the one to the other. . . . We were afterwards rowed in a rough sea, against wind and tide before we reached the harbour, where we were landed, benumbed with cold, and the women excessively sick. From our landing place we were obliged to walk very near a mile to the inn, attended by six or seven men and women, bare-legged, carrying our baggage.' All the rooms at the inn were taken when they arrived, so that they were obliged to sit up for the rest of the night in a cold kitchen.

As other tourists discovered, being rowed ashore in an open boat was but the first of the annoyances that faced them in Calais. They had to look on helplessly as their bags were tossed about 'by men and boys, half naked and in wooden shoes' who carried them off to the custom-house where touts from the various inns bawled in their ears and where the officials, 'the most shocking sharks' imaginable, put hands into pockets and felt down sides and legs as far as the ankles for contraband goods.

They only allow one watch for each person [according to Nugent], and if they find any new cloathes, they will stop them. After your baggage has been searched, you had better have your trunk plumbed with a leaden stamp for Paris, for this will prevent the trouble of any further search of your baggage upon the road, or its being carried to the custom-house when you come to Paris; you must take care not to open the custom-house cordage and plumbing till you get to that metropolis; for on going out of Calais, and at several other garrison towns, both your Calais custom-house pass . . . and also the plumbing of your trunk are examined. . . . The fees at the custom-house for the pass, for your cloathes and necessaries, and for the plumbing of your trunks are very trifling; but if they are civil and do not tumble your cloathes, it is customary to give the officer half a crown. The porters who carry your goods from the ship to the custom-house, and from the custom-house to the inn, are, like our watermen, never satisfied.

Several of the inns which the touts in the custom-house so vociferously recommended were abominable. In one of these a weary traveller was shown into a comfortless room 'but a step raised above the courtyard, a tiled floor without carpet and two very high windows, with very thin muslin curtains half-way up, opening into the public entrance, so that it was exactly like sleeping in the street. To add to which the upper half of the windows was overlooked by the huge kitchen on the opposite side of the court.'

Most tourists, however, took care to avoid such places in Calais, where, unlike so many towns of comparable size in France, there were several reputable inns, among them the Silver Lion, the French Horn, the Table Royal, the Golden Arms, the Golden Head, the Prince of Orange and the Hôtel Angleterre which, in the Rev. William Jones's opinion, was 'well worth an Englishman's while to visit' and in James Essex's one of the best hotels in France, with forty or fifty carriages always ready for guests. It was kept during the second half of the eighteenth century by a M. Dessin who, by means of selling and hiring carriages and changing money as well as keeping an excellent and expensive table, famous for its succulent fish (especially crabs), was said to have made a fortune of over £50,000 between 1766 and 1776. Laurence Sterne stayed here and, as he recorded in *A Sentimental Journey*, 'incontestibly in France' dined upon 'fricasee'd chicken'. The Russian historian Nikolai Karamzin also stayed here on his way to England in 1789. He asked for Sterne's room and was told it was occupied by an English widow and her daughter. Indeed, as Karamzin discovered, Dessin's was always 'full of Englishmen'. Soon after his arrival he came across seven or eight of them

13 A French table d'hôte *at which the food was variously described as 'uneatable', 'preposterous' and 'delicious'.*

having supper and calling out, 'Wine! Wine! The very best! *Du meilleur! Du meilleur!*' They were equally noisy after supper, shouting and stamping their feet and banging their fists upon the table, but eventually they were persuaded to go to bed to allow the other guests to get to sleep and, after several 'God damns', they fell into silence.

In the morning arrangements had to be made for the onward journey, usually towards Paris. Before leaving England the tourist was advised that, if he had not brought his own carriage over with him, it would be advisable to hire one in Calais or even buy one and sell it there on his return. The convenience of having one's own carriage was naturally expensive and those who could not afford it had to rely upon public transport – upon the *carosse*, a vehicle rather like an English stage-coach carrying six passengers; the *coche*, a larger, heavier carriage with sixteen passengers; or the diligence, a public coach which could accommodate as many as thirty people and, by a change of horses every twelve miles or so, could cover up to a hundred miles a day at a gallop. Both *carosses* and *coches* carried great quantities of baggage, the immense wicker baskets of the *coche* sometimes accommodating additional passengers as well, and since they were usually drawn by extremely small horses they travelled at a very slow pace – on certain roads no more than three miles an hour.

14 Beggars pestering travellers upon their arrival at a French inn.

They were often, however, preferred to the faster diligence which Arthur Young described as 'detestable' after having travelled in one, 'overcrowded and badly sprung', whose French passengers so stunned him with their noisy singing of French airs that he 'would almost as soon have rode the journey blindfold on an ass'. 'A more uncouth clumsy machine can scarcely be imagined,' another traveller thought. 'All the carriages of this description have the appearance of being the result of the earliest efforts in the art of coach building.' The body of the carriage rested upon 'large thongs of leather, fastened to heavy blocks of wood' and was consequently exhaustingly bumpy until springs were introduced in the last quarter of the eighteenth century. Moreover, 'you are hurried out of bed at four, three, nay often at two in the morning. You are obliged to eat in the French way, which is very disagreeable to an English palate . . . and you are crowded into the carriage so as to sit very uneasy, and sometimes run the risk of being stifled among very indifferent company.'

There were those like Sacheverell Stevens who found the 'odd assemblage of passengers, such as monks, pilgrims, officers, courtezans etc.' most diverting, but most English travellers were more inclined to share the view of Samuel Ireland who, 'for the sake of novelty' took 'one stage on the diligence' which presented itself at the door of his hotel. This diligence was unusually small and slow, moving at the rate of 'about four miles an hour', and held twelve passengers:

Such a heterogeneous medley were scarce ever assembled. The lower orders of people in this country are not remarkable for their attentions to the decorum of cleanliness, and you may conceive that a mixed company of both sexes, crouded together in a clumsy trundling vehicle, in which the characteristic habits of each were freely indulged, could

15 (Left) A Frenchman greets a tourist: 'Que je suis enchanté de vous voir!'
16 (Right) Bunbury's caricature of a tourist arriving with his tutor and servant at a French inn, the tourist clutching a copy of Chesterfield's Letters, *the* 'grenouille traiteur' *standing beside the postilion in his huge boots 'as big as oyster barrels'.*

not be very pleasant to an Englishman. We were fairly smoked out of all patience and we left in disgust. . . . Before we reached one post we were overtaken by a storm of rain and thunder, so tremendous [that] the poor [horses] were so alarmed that they refused to proceed on their journey. . . . The driver was equally obstinate for their proceeding and, having vented all his hereditary stock of oathes, added many of his own invented on the emergency of the occasion, for which to give the French their due they have a happy talent. The enormous size of the postillions boots (huge appendages as big as oyster barrels and rimmed with iron to protect the legs in case of accidents) were at this actual juncture particularly unfortunate as they held such an immense quantity of water that they formed two reservoirs in which the poor fellows sat up to their knees full three hours.

The diligence was at least cheap, a journey of some 200 miles in 1775 costing 'only 3 *louis* for which you are provided with supper the first night and dinner and supper the next day besides your journey'. Also, later models were

capacious and lofty, lined with leather, padded and surrounded with little pockets in which the travellers deposit their bread, snuff, night caps and pocket handkerchiefs. . . . From the roof depends a large net work, which is generally crowded with hats, swords and band-boxes; the whole is convenient, and when all parties are seated and arranged, the accommodations are by no means unpleasant. Upon the roof, on the outside, is the imperial which is generally filled with six or seven persons more, and a heap of luggage, which latter also occupies the basket, and generally presents a pile, half as high again as the coach, which is secured by ropes and chains, tightened by a large iron windlass, which also constitutes another appendage of the moving mass.

Above all, by travelling in a diligence, it was possible to avoid 'the insolence of the Post-Masters and squabbling with Postilions', the plagues of the post-routes.

It was almost universally agreed that the French postilion in his dirty sheepskin coat, his greasy night-cap and gigantic boots was a rascal, 'a lazy, lounging, greedy and impertinent' rascal, so Smollett decided. 'If you chide them for lingering, they will continue to delay you the longer; if you chastise them with sword, cane, cudgel or horse-whip, they will either disappear entirely, and leave you without resources, or they will find means to take vengeance by overturning your carriage.' Lady Craven and the Earl of Leven agreed with him. You might 'just as effectively argue with a horse as with a French postilion', Lady Craven considered, while Leven lamented, 'Oh! its miserable posting in this country, 5 or at most 6 miles in one hour . . . and an old surly rascal as post boy, who will do nothing but what he pleases. One of them had the impudence this day to tell us, after we had given him sixpence to drink, that we payed like Frenchmen and not like Englishmen, and gave us names, upon which Sandie thrashed him.'

The only way to deal with the monsters, Smollett recommended, was to tip them generously, at least three *sols* (about threepence) a post, thus forcing up the price of travelling from Calais to Paris, a distance of thirty and a half posts or 183 miles, to almost £3. It was admittedly an extravagance, but long delays on the road were unthinkable, most of the inns on the way being, in Thomas Gray's words, 'terrible places indeed'.

There were a few tourists who could find favourable comments to make on their first experience of French inns, but most condemned them outright and, unless commenting upon the best places in the larger towns, continued to do so throughout their stay in France. John Eustace warned that:

An English traveller must, the very instant he embarks for the Continent, resign many of the comforts and conveniences he enjoys at home. . . . Great will be his disappointment if, on his arrival, he expects a warm room, a newspaper, and a well-stored larder. These advantages are common enough at home, but they are not to be found in any inn on the Continent. . . . The principal and most offensive defect abroad is the want of cleanliness, a defect in a greater or less degree common to all parts of the Continent.

Such comments can be found in book after book, journal after journal, letter after letter. Abraham Goelnitz wrote that 'in certain villages, in certain towns even in the centre of France, the inns lack everything. One can hardly find bread and a fire. Beds are wanting.' At Marquise, fifteen miles from Calais, in 1783, Horatio Nelson was taken to an inn, or what they called an inn: 'I should have called it a pigstye: we were shown into a room with two straw beds, and, with great difficulty, they mustered up clean sheets; and gave us two pigeons for supper, upon a dirty cloth, and wooden-handled knives – Oh what a transition from happy

England!' At Moulins, Arthur Young went to the Belle Image and found it so bad he left it for the Lion d'Or which was worse, and at Saint-Girons in a 'hideous' inn, presided over by a 'wretched hag, the demon of beastliness', he was almost poisoned by the smell of the stables that seeped up through the broken floor of his bedroom. At Montreuil, Walpole and Gray dined on 'stinking mutton cutlets, addled eggs, and ditch water'. 'Through the whole of the south of France, except in large cities,' recorded Smollett, 'the inns are cold, damp, dark, dismal and dirty; the landlords equally disobliging and rapacious; the servants aukward, sluttish and slothful.' 'I have one thing very extraordinary to observe of the French *auberges*,' he wrote elsewhere.

The landlords, hostesses and servants of the inns upon the road have not the least dash of complaisance in their behaviour to strangers. Instead of coming to the door to receive you as in England, they take no manner of notice of you; but leave you to find or enquire your way into the kitchen, and there you must ask several times for a chamber before they seem willing to conduct you upstairs. In general you are served with the appearance of the most mortifying indifference, at the very time they are laying schemes for fleecing you of your money.

'They have not heart to provide handsomely for their guests,' Horace Walpole confirmed, 'and are so saving and penurious that they count every bit one puts into one's mouth. They are well pleased to see their dishes not touched as a hearty English landlord is displeased when he thinks his guest does not like his victuals.'

Fault particularly was found with the beds, and if travellers did not bring their own bedding with them, as they were advised to do, they were strongly recommended to make use of what Count Berchtold called 'a preventive of infection', in other words 'a light coverlet of silk, two pairs of sheets and two dressed hart's skins' to place upon the mattress, because 'the lodgers who slept in the beds before them' may well have been 'affected with the itch, venereal or other disease'. 'If the matresses are suspected,' Berchtold added, 'it will be preferable to lie down on dry and clean straw.'

Yet whatever the traveller did it was almost impossible in many places to escape the bugs, those 'ubiquitous parasites' which pestered Lady Knight, even at a place in Paris where the food was 'admirable'. In some of the most splendidly furnished bedrooms they were as numerous as they were in the poorest. The Rev. William Jones, who slept in a room 'with very large gilt glasses, tapestry, paintings and sattin beds', had to contend with 'a swarm of bugs and a dirty brick floor'.

Not only were beds flea-ridden, they were also likely to be damp and so high that a chair was sometimes needed to climb into them. 'After you have passed Boulogne,' so Sir Thomas Nugent informed his readers, 'you will not find the beds like ours in England; for they raise them very high with several thick mattresses: their linen is ill-washed and worse dried, so that you must take par-ticular care to see the sheets aired.' And even if you were shown into a clean room with a bed that did not threaten to break every bone in your body should you fall out of it onto the brick floor, you must expect to have to share the room with some other traveller, perhaps with a person of the opposite sex, as Sterne's 'Mr Yorick' has to do when, 'without much nicety', a lady is led into his bed-chamber and told 'there was nobody in it but an English gentleman and that there were two good beds in it', the beds being 'so very close to each other as only to allow space for a small wicker chair between them'.

Walter Stanhope, who was in France in 1769, the year after *A Sentimental Journey* was published, could

hardly remember one place where some of us did not sleep in the same room in which we supped. For it was generally furnished with beds, and those beds were almost as generally occupied with troops of bugs, and whole armies of fleas. The nightly excursions, and attacks of those hopping and creeping gentry were a great annoyance to all ye company except myself, who happily have not ye honour of being to their taste.

'You have no parlour to eat in, only a room with two, three or four beds,' Arthur Young confirmed in 1787, 'having crossed the kingdom and been in many French inns.'

Apartments are badly fitted up; the walls white washed, or with paper of different sorts in the same room . . . and the furniture such that an English innkeeper would light his fire with. For a table you have everywhere a board laid on cross bars which are so conveniently contrived, as to leave room for your legs only at the end. Oak chairs with rush bottoms, and the back universally a direct perpendicular that defies all idea of rest after fatigue. Doors give music as well as entrance; the wind whistles through their chinks; and hinges grate discord. Windows admit rain as well as light; when shut they are not so easy to open; and when open not easy to shut. Mops, brooms, and scrubbing brushes are not in the catalogue of the necessaries of a French inn. . . . The kitchen is black with smoke; the master commonly the cook, and the less you see of the cooking, the more likely you are to have a stomach to your dinner. . . . Copper utensils always in great plenty, but not always well tinned. The mistress rarely classes civility or attention to her guests among the requisites of her trade.

The tourist was at first as critical of the food and drink provided at French inns as he was of their accommodation, their scanty furniture, their dirty kitchens and floors, their tawdry decorations and creaking doors, their tapestries full of spiders, windows that would not open and drawers that would not shut, their soap – on those rare occasions when it was provided at all – such as ought to be taken away so that 'men of science might analyse it', and their lack of bells that made it necessary to bawl for the services of a chambermaid who, when she eventually appeared, was 'neither neat, well dressed or handsome'.

'I hate the French cookery and abominate the garlick with which all their ragouts are highly seasoned,' was one typical complaint of an Englishman longing for the plain roast beef or boiled mutton of his own country. 'At dinner they give you three courses,' another complained, 'but a third of the dishes is patched up with sallads, butter, puff-paste, or some such miscarriage of a dish.' ''Tis a great inconvenience to travel in France upon a fish-day,' wrote a third; 'for 'tis a hard matter to get anything to eat but stinking fish or rotten eggs.' One evening at some 'miserable inn' outside the walls of St Omer, where Charles Burney had arrived after the gates were shut, he was served with 'stale mackerel, a salad with rancid oil and an omelette made with raddled eggs.' As for the wine, it was as often as not condemned as being as sour and sharp as vinegar; the water served was equally undrinkable, while the coffee, in Lord Macaulay's opinion, was worse than any cook 'could make for a wager'. Even when the provisions were unexceptionable, the way in which some innkeepers presented them, carving and serving at their own *tables d'hôte*, was considered insupportable,

The master is such a Goth too [wrote William Hazlitt], a true Frenchman! When carving he flourishes his knife about in such a manner as to endanger those who sit near him, and stops in the middle with the wing of a duck suspended on the point of his fork, to spout a speech out of some play. Dinner is no sooner over than he watches his opportunity, collects all the bottles and glasses on the table, beer, wine, porter, empties them into his own, heaps his plate with the remnants of fricassees, gravy, vegetables, mustard, melted butter, and sops them all up with a large piece of bread, wipes his plate clean as if a dog had licked it, dips his bread in some other dish that in his hurry had escaped him, and finishes off by picking his teeth with a sharp-pointed knife.

Yet even the most disgruntled tourist had eventually to concede that such behaviour was out of the ordinary, that innkeepers were far from universally grasping and ill-mannered, that good small inns were, in fact, to be found, and that some of the larger ones were first-class. The inn at Châlons, for example, was 'furnished throughout with silk and damask, the very linings of the rooms and bed covers not excepted'. The Hôtel de Henri IV at Nantes was, in Arthur Young's opinion, 'the finest inn in Europe . . . and very cheap', while the principal hotel at Montélimar was 'a great and excellent inn'. And as they became accustomed to it, the food served in the better inns was allowed to be excellent, even though, on occasions, very strange. Robert Wharton wrote of a meal at Dijon in 1755,

I was helped to an excellent Fricasee, but was much puzzled to find out what it was, there being an uncommon quantity of bones and especially of small merry-thoughts . . . I found that I had been eating no small quantity of fricasseed frogs. I shall bring the receipt home with me. It will be at least a curiosity. They tasted exceeding like white veal which you know is so much approved of.

'The common cookery of the French gives great advantage,' Arthur Young considered. 'It is true they roast everything to a chip, if they are not cautioned, but they give such a number and variety of dishes, that, if you do not like some, there are others to please your palate. The dessert at a French inn has no rival as an English one.' Thomas Nugent agreed that they boiled and roasted their meat much longer than suited English palates, yet their diet was not 'near so gross as ours'. He went on:

Their bread is exceedingly good, and so is their beef and mutton. They are fond of soups, ragoos and made dishes, which they dress the best of any people in Europe. Their vegetable food consists of kidney-beans, white lentils, turnips, red onions, leeks, lettuce, white-beets and asparagus. They have scarcely any potatoes, but great quantities of sorrel and mushroom, especially the latter, of which they are very fond.

And, provided a bargain had been struck beforehand, a good meal was surprisingly cheap. At his inn at Dunkirk in 1773, James Essex shared a supper with four other guests at no more than 1s 3d a head. 'It consisted of two fowls boild, a Duck roasted, a very fine codling, a dish of artichoke and a fine sallad. These were replaced by a dish of Tarts, a plate of Apricots, a plate of maccaroons with other confectionarys.' Here, as elsewhere in recommended inns, the wines were 'not to be despised' and, in general, 'far better than English inns give'.

As it was with French food, so it was with the French people whom the English met in them and on the road. First impressions were not favourable. Needless to say, Smollett found little in the French character to please him:

If a Frenchman is capable of real friendship, it must certainly be the most disagreeable present he can possibly make to a man of a true English character. Your French friend intrudes upon you at all hours; he stuns you with his loquacity; he teases you with impertinent questions about your domestic and private affairs; he attempts to meddle in all your concerns. . . . If there are five hundred dishes at table, a Frenchman will eat all of them, and then complain he has no appetite. . . . Vanity predominates among all ranks, to such a degree, that they are the greatest egotists in the world. A Frenchman takes it for granted that his addresses cannot but be acceptable. . . . Of all the coxcombs on the face of the earth, a French *petit maître* is the most impertinent; and they are all *petit maîtres*, from the marquis who glitters in lace and embroidery to the *garçon barbier* covered with meal who struts with his hair in a long queue, and his hat under his arm.

Extreme as Smollett's views were, they were shared by others who had been warned before they left home in more than one guide-book that the French were 'fiery, impatient, inconstant and of a restless disposition', that the young were 'debauched and irreligious', and that they were all excessively garrulous, 'especially those of the female sex'. 'A Frenchman not only means nothing beyond common civility by the plentiful shower of compliments which he pours on every stranger,'

17 Barbers, hairdressers, postilions and maidservants attend upon travellers at breakfast-time in Breteuil.

wrote Dr Moore, 'but also he takes it for granted that the stranger knows that nothing more is meant.' This infuriated an acquaintance of Moore who insisted that there was 'nothing real in all the fuss these people make about us'. 'Curse their courtesies!' he continued. 'They are the greatest bores in nature. I hate the French. They are the enemies of England and a false, deceitful, perfidious . . .' He would have gone on had not Moore interrupted him: 'But as we did not come over to fight them at present, we shall suspend hostilities till a more convenient season.'

'The French only regard strangers according to the money they spend and the figure they make with their equipages,' thought Edward Mellish, echoing the words of Dr Moore's disgruntled acquaintance, while Lord Chesterfield wrote home to the Duchess of Marlborough:

I see nothing here that we have not better and finer in England. I shall not give you my opinion of the French, because I am very often taken for one; and many a Frenchman has paid me the highest compliment they think they can pay anyone which is – 'Sir, you are just like one of us.' I shall only tell you that I am insolent; I talk a great deal; I am very loud and peremptory; I sing and dance as I go along, and lastly I spend a monstrous deal of money in powder.

Despite their 'superficial airs and graces', the French, both men and women, were also widely condemned for their indelicacy. Elizabeth Wynne related the story of a French 'Lady in the Old Fashion which during her dinner at a Gentleman's was very uneasy; at last she cries to her footman, "*Jacques, cherchez ma puce,*" and Jacques put his hand in the lady's back and after having looked for a long while he says "*La voilà, Madame*", and she drowned it in her wine-glass.'

18 A French lady's knee was evidently quite 'as modest as the elbow of an English lady'.

Chesterfield's persistent critic, Samuel Johnson, who in 1775 went to France with Henry and Hester Thrale, their daughter, 'Queeney', and 'Queeney's' Italian tutor, Giuseppe Baretti, spoke for most Englishmen when he pronounced,

The French are an indelicate people; they will spit upon any place. At Madame's [du Boccage], a literary lady of rank, the footman took the sugar in his fingers, and threw it into my coffee. . . . The Spout of the tea-pot did not pour freely; she bade the footman blow into it. France is worse than Scotland in everything but climate. . . . What I gained by being in France was learning to be better satisfied with my own country. . . . The French are a gross, ill-bred, untaught people; a lady will spit on the floor and rub it in with her foot.

This habit of 'spitting up and down their houses and churches' was as strongly condemned as 'detestable' by Arthur Young who once saw a gentleman 'spit so near the cloaths of a dutchess' that he stared at the man's unconcern.

Several of Johnson's and Young's contemporaries complained, not only of the spitting in carriages and inns but also of the embarrassing conversations carried on openly in them. One particularly prim young man was much distressed to find himself in a coach with 'an elderly woman of genteel appearance', 'a beautiful girl of sixteen' and a French lawyer who chatted to each other with the most disturbing freedom. 'Shall I record that in this company,' he wrote disapprovingly, 'the most undisguised and shocking descriptions were given of the debaucheries of the capital, and particulars which would scarcely be whispered in English discussed with the utmost exactness.' Another shocked tourist wrote of 'a middle-aged widow' who was 'as dirty in her conversation as in her dress, and very fit company for the rest of the men'.

Few young men knew enough French at this stage of their journey to be shocked by such conversations, but the sights were often disconcerting enough. A young lady, on stepping out of a carriage, 'discovered a lapse of stocking, and continuing her chat with the gentleman who had handed her out, she deliberately adjusted it and tied her garter'. A French lady's knee was evidently 'as modest as the elbow of an English lady'. Indeed, French ladies were deemed to have little modesty at all and were 'so free with their favours' that their lovers 'could scarcely be distinguished from their husbands'. 'It is observable that the French allow their women all imaginable freedoms, and are seldom troubled with jealousy; nay, a Frenchman will almost suffer you to court his wife, and is even angry if you do not admire her person.'

Even the grandest ladies appeared to be not at all put out by the presence of men in circumstances which would have been inconceivable in England. William Jones once saw a countess sitting at the window of her dressing-room

under the hands of her waiting women and by her side one of her footmen [actually, so he discovered later, her hairdresser] was standing with his arms folded perfectly free and easy, as if he had access when he pleased to his lady's dressing room, there to spend as much of his time as he thought proper . . . I could not but conclude that the French ladies were very easy of access and not at all delicate in the choice of their company.

According to Smollett, in fact, a French lady 'who shifts her frowsy smock in presence of a male visitant, and talks to him of her *lavement*, her *médicine* and her *bidet*', had no compunction about being 'handed to the house of office by her admirer, who stood at the door, and entertained her with *bons mots* all the time she was within'. Smollett complained of another habit which disgusted him:

A true bred Frenchman dips his fingers imbrowned with snuff into his plate filled with ragout. Between every three mouthfuls, he produces his snuffbox, and takes a fresh pinch. . . . Then he displays his handkerchief and in the use of both scatters his favours among those who have the happiness to sit near him. . . . But I know of no custom more beastly than that of using water-glasses in which polite company spit, and squirt and spue the filthy scourings of their gums under the eyes of each other.

Nor had a Frenchman any sense of discretion: 'He pries into all your secrets with the most impudent and importunate curiosity, and then discloses them without remorse. If you are indisposed he questions you about the symptoms of your disorder with more freedom than your physician would presume to use, and very often in the grossest terms.'

The French, however, were often as puzzled by the English and had as good cause to be censorious of their conduct as the English were disapproving of the French. English gentlemen, in the first place, were frequently seen to be drunk, whereas, as William Jones observed, 'the vice of drunkenness [was] but little known' among the French. Also, the Englishman's rowdiness at meals was most tiresome and, if French people were given to spitting at table, the English lolled about in their chairs, their elbows on the table in a manner that Lady Charlotte Campbell's fourteen-year-old daughter described as 'most vulgar' after seeing a group of her fellow-countrymen behaving like this at Meurice's Hotel in Calais. Then, when they were not rowdy, they were often rudely taciturn. Dr Moore recalled a genial French marquis who addressed 'much of his conversation to' a peculiarly withdrawn English lord. He 'tried him upon every subject, wine, women, horses, politics and religion'. He admired his clothes, praised his dog, and 'said a thousand obliging things of the English nation. To no purpose; his Lordship kept up his silence and reserve to the last, and then drove away to the opera. "*Ma foi!*" said the Marquis as soon as he went out of the room, "That milord has a great talent for silence!"'

Perhaps he spoke no French. Certainly there were many English tourists who did not, and many more who spoke so little and so badly that they were reluctant to speak at all. Samuel Johnson spoke only Latin when in France on the grounds that 'there is no good in letting the French have a superiority over you every word you speak'. Yet it was admitted that the English who attempted to speak French were listened to 'with the most serious attention and never laughed at', even when they uttered the most absurd solecisms in the most atrocious accent. Indeed, after they had spent some time in France, most tourists were inclined to the view that the French were, after all, not the blackguards they had been led to believe they were and had sometimes initially taken them to be. 'During the time we were in France,' said William Wordsworth after a visit in 1790, 'we had not once to complain of the smallest deficiency of courtesy in any person, much less of any positive rudeness. We had also perpetual occasion to observe that cheerfulness and sprightliness for which the French have always been remarkable.' These were common sentiments with those who had spent some time in the country. The French were 'gay and volatile', full of 'vivacity and good humour', 'a people of quick understanding and nice taste', the men 'masters of good breeding', the women 'of a graceful and winning deportment', their lowest servants taking 'your hat and gloves as if you were doing them a favour'. 'Nothing struck us English more in the manners of the French than the sweetness of address in all classes.' Even the beggars were gracious and cheerful. On being refused they were quite likely to bow, saying, '*Pardon, Monsieur, une autre occasion.*' Or, if thrown a few coins from a carriage window, they might well dance about, waving their arms and joining in the common cry of '*Bon voyage! Vives les voyageurs!*'

'At the public ordinary of the Hôtel de Bourbon,' so Dr Moore said, 'a marked attention was paid us from the moment we entered; everybody seemed inclined to accommodate us with the best places. They helped us first and all the company seemed ready to sacrifice every little convenience and distinction to the strangers. For, next to that of a lady, the most respected character at Paris is that of a stranger.' Moore went on to describe an evening at the theatre where an Englishman was represented in a ridiculous light upon the stage: 'An old French officer, who was in the next box to us, seemed uneasy and hurt at the peals of laughter which burst from the audience at some particular passages. He touched my shoulder and assured me that no nation was more respected than the English.'

Anxious to reach Paris as soon as possible, most tourists rushed along the post-route through Boulogne, Montreuil, Abbeville, Amiens, Clermont, Chantilly and St Denis or along the *carosse-route* which, after Abbeville, diverged from it by taking the road through Poix, Beauvais and Beaumont. There was little deemed worthy of mention between these places, although the numbers of beggars by the roadside and outside the inns, and the impoverished appearance of many country people with what Lady Mary Wortley Montagu described as 'miserable starved faces and thin tattered clothes', seemed remarkable in view of the vast, fertile cornfields and rich pastures of Normandy and the Ile de France. A few travellers also commented upon the pervasive atmosphere of Roman Catholicism, the numbers of monks and priests, the people praying at shrines, the gaudily painted and clothed images of the Blessed Virgin and of saints, the constant ringing of bells, the processions following the Host through the streets. Some, already homesick, compared the strange landscape with that of England, much preferring what they had left behind; one, on approaching the 'boasted river of Seine', 'with some degree of exultation' reflected on the 'great superiourity' of the Thames Valley.

Nor were the towns themselves considered to have much to recommend them. The houses in Calais, a small place with a population of no more than four thousand, looked 'bleak and poor', though the bourgeoisie seemed 'to live at their ease, probably in consequence of their trade with the English'. Certainly they were affable and polite to the English on whom their prosperity largely depended. Some of them even looked English, being very fair, a circumstance attributed to the fact that when Edward III had captured Calais he had turned out the old inhabitants and replaced them with English citizens. When Fanny Burney was in the port a band played 'God Save the King' outside her bedroom window.

Halfway between Calais and Paris, Amiens was described in Thomas Martyn's *Gentleman's Guide on His Tour through France* (1787) as a 'clean though ancient town set on the banks of the River Somme in the midst of a most beautiful plain. . . . You should visit the Cathedral for it was built by the English in the gothic taste.' It was also, so this and several other guide-books claimed, an excellent place for a tourist to 'get hold of the French language before he goes to Paris', since 'it is little frequented by the English' and the language was taught there by monks who charged no more than half a guinea a month. A brief stay at Chantilly, famed for its fine lace and porcelain, was also recommended if only to see the Prince of Condé's magnificent palace, one of 'the most charming places upon earth', its stables for 240 horses 'beyond any Palace' Richard Pococke had ever seen, its gardens 'laid out in a most elegant taste' with canals, fountains and cascades and ornamental birds swooping through the spray and darting over the neat walks.

Just south of Chantilly was St Denis, whose white marble abbey was filled with treasures, including, so one young Englishman breathlessly recorded, Charlemagne's golden crown, his diamond-encrusted sword, spurs and ivory chess men, Roland's hunting horn, 'precious stones and cups made of them, busts of saints, silver gilt crowns of many Kings, that of the present set very richly with jewels there is likewise all the habit of the King when he is crowned which was always deposited here. Nextly we saw the picture of the maid of Orleans and the very sword she made use of and I don't doubt that this treasury is worth millions.' Here were buried numerous kings who had ruled in France from the time of the seventh-century Dagobert I, their tombs constituting a remarkable collection of funerary sculpture which afforded Smollett 'some amusement'. And here, too, were numerous relics which John Evelyn listed with characteristic thoroughness:

a pretended naile of the real Crucifix . . . a Crucifix of the true Wood of the Crosse carved by Pope Clement the 3d . . . A Box wherein is preserv'd some of the B: Virgin's haire . . . some of the linnen our B. Saviour was envelop'd in at his Nativity . . . Something staind red which the Father would have us believe was the natural blood of our Saviour, as also some of his haire, Cloaths, Linnen with which he wip'd the Apostles feet: Something of the Crowne of Thornes, a piece of the Sponge . . . some of the B: Virgins milke . . . an arme of St Simon . . . the right hand of St Thomas the Apostle . . . the chin of their St Lewes, the shoulder bone of St Jo: Baptist, the finger of St Bartholomew . . . Some of the Prophet Isaias bones . . . a cup in which Solomon was used to drink . . . a morcel of one of the Water-potts our Saviour did his first Miracle in . . . the brasse Lanterne sayd to have conducted Judas to apprehend our B.S. . . . and a world of other rarities I was forc'd to pass over: But thus having rewarded our Courteous Fryer, we tooke horse for Paris.

CHAPTER 3

*

PARIS

*

'When an Englishman comes to Paris he cannot appear until he has undergone a total metamorphosis'

AFTER EXPERIENCING THE HORRORS OF SOME French inns in the remoter countryside, English travellers were in general well satisfied with the accommodation provided for them in Paris, particularly at the hotels in the faubourg St Germain, the rue Mazarin and the rue St Denis, at the Hôtel d'Espagne in the rue de Seine and the Grand Hôtel de Luine on the quai des Augustines. 'We drove to the Hôtel de l'Impératrice in the Rue Jacob,' wrote one tourist in 1773.

Here we have an elegant dining-room, with two bed chambers on the first floor, and a bed chamber in the *entre-sol*, with an apartment for the servant, for three guineas a week. I confess the lodgings are dear, but the situation is good, and the furniture magnificent. . . . We generally dine at a *Table d'Hôte* where we find genteel people and good dinners. The price is different at different houses; but for forty *sous* a head, which is twenty-pence English, we dine most sumptuously on two courses of seven and five, with a dessert and a pint of Burgundy. . . . We always sup at home. We buy our wine of the merchant, and our supper is sent from the neighbouring *traiteurs*.

There were, of course, bad hotels in Paris: the Hôtel de la Ville de Rome was evidently 'a very dirty inn indeed' where the staircase shook, the maids were 'bold and impertinent, the treatment sparing and the charge exorbitant'. But such places were rare, and the food in most others excellent, not expensive and, as Robert Wharton discovered to his surprise and pleasure, 'not stuffed with garlic'. In private houses the food was even better; and many tourists chose to take private lodgings either because the family speaking only French at table would help them to learn the language more quickly or because they were cheap, being readily available at £2 12s 6d a month, including dinner and supper and a pint of wine at each meal. Having stayed at the Hôtel de Luxembourg for half a guinea a week, Robert Wharton moved to lodgings which cost him nine *louis* a month; this was comparatively expensive but he could have had other lodgings 'further from the spectacles' for only two *louis* a month. Other tourists chose to rent furnished rooms and eat out at a public *ordinaire*, as Edward Gibbon did in 1763, paying six guineas a month for 'an Antichamber, a dining room, a bedchamber and servant's room' in the rue du Colombier, now the rue de l'Université. Lady Sarah Lennox could not have been more pleased with her rooms when she went to stay in 1765 with Lord Hertford, then British ambassador. 'The rooms are large,' she excitedly wrote to a friend, 'the windows immense & all down to the ground, the furniture very fine . . . for there are commodes even

19 In Paris a 'variety of dress [was] absolutely essential for all those [of] any rank above the mere bourgeois'.

in our lodgings, & looking glasses in every part of the room & very large ones.'

Once he had settled in at his hotel or lodgings, and delivered his letters of introduction at the British Embassy, and at those private houses to which he had hopes of being invited, the tourist's first destination after his arrival in Paris was a tailor's shop where, so he was warned in *The Gentleman's Guide* of 1770, he would be asked to pay as much as sixteen guineas for a black suit with 'gold waistcoat and two pairs of breeches'.

Smollett observed that:

When an Englishman comes to Paris he cannot appear until he has undergone a total metamorphosis. At his first arrival he finds it necessary to send for the taylor, peruquier, hatter, shoemaker, and every other tradesman concerned in the equipment of the human body. He must even change his buckles and the form of his ruffles; and, though at the risk of his life, suit his cloaths to the mode of the season. For example, though the weather should be never so cold, he must wear his *habit d'été* or *demi-saison*, without presuming to put on a warm dress before the day which fashion has fixed for that purpose; and neither old age nor infirmity will excuse a man for wearing his hat upon his head! A variety of dress is absolutely indispensable for all those who pretend to any rank above the mere bourgeois. On his return to his own country all this frippery is useless.

Even Samuel Johnson, who was quite content to be seen in London shambling along in an ill-fitting wig, creased black stockings, and a shabby brown coat, its pockets bulging with books, decided that in Paris he must provide himself with

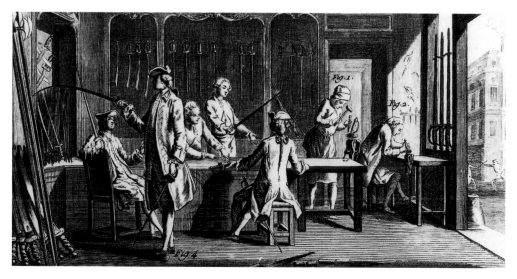

20 *Elegant, well-made swords were also purchased in Paris.*

new white stockings, a new hat and a 'French-made wig of handsome construction'; while the young Scottish architect, Robert Adam, who arrived in Paris with the Hon. Charles Hope in 1754, confessed that he often 'burst out a-laughing' when he wondered what his mother would say if her 'once plain friend' were to show himself in her drawing-room with his now 'most Frenchified head of hair, loaded with powder', his velvet suit of two colours with a white satin lining, his white silk stockings with embroidered silk gussets, his 'Mariguin pumps' with red heels and diamond buckles, his gold-handled sword, his Brussels lace and solitaire ribbon.

Tourists soon grew accustomed to wearing such 'Frenchified' clothes, but they could not get used to Parisian ladies looking so 'fantastically absurd in their dress,' as Lady Mary Wortley Montagu described them, 'so monstrously unnatural in their paint'. They seemed to have no resemblance to human beings, she continued, with their hair cut short, curled round their faces, and 'loaded with powder that makes it look like white wool, and on their cheeks to their Chins, unmercifully laid on, a shineing red Japan that glistens in a most flameing manner'. William Jones agreed with her: women of rank in Paris made themselves 'hideous by great blotches of paint upon their cheeks which in some ladies [were] as well defined as the circumference of a circle and as red as the Saracen's Head upon a sign post'. Smollett thought that the rouge they wore rendered them 'really frightful', though he supposed the white with which their necks and shoulders were plastered was 'in some measure excusable', since their skins were 'naturally brown or sallow'.

'When I see one of those fine creatures sailing along in her taudry robes of silk and gauze, frilled and flounced and furbelowed, with her false locks, her false jewels, her paint, her patches, and perfumes,' he protested, 'I cannot help looking upon her as the vilest piece of sophistication that art ever produced.'

Several English visitors were as uncomplimentary about the city, the 'ugly and slovenly city', as they were about its ladies. As soon as you entered Paris, you were stopped 'in your chaise and your pass and plumbings and every corner of your chaise' would be examined, 'while menservants out of place, who could speak a little English, urged you to employ them and your postilions pressed upon you the advantages of hotels which paid them to bring custom to their doors'. In winter the dining-rooms of these places were likely to be bitterly cold since the Parisians, so Walpole said, had 'not the least idea of *comfortable*, but sup in stone halls, with all the doors open'. Even the houses of the nobility were cold, one of Walpole's contemporaries complained, and while they far exceeded in handsomeness those of London, they were 'so shut up from the streets that they [added] little of ornament to the city'.

The streets were admittedly supplied with a very large number of candles 'in damaged lanterns', but these 'went out every now and then with a gust and left all in darkness'. The streets were also for the most part narrow, almost universally dirty and noisy, and extremely dangerous because of the hundreds of one-horse cabriolets and the thousands of carts, coaches, chaises and hackney-carriages which were driven so recklessly about the city that pedestrians were forced to jump out of their way, frequently knocked over, or, at least, splashed by the mud that oozed down the gutters. Passers-by were also liable to be drenched by the contents of chamber pots emptied from windows by maidservants with the perfunctory cry of '*Gare l'eau*!' Many houses still had no latrines or even pits for nightsoil; and in royal palaces heaps of ordure were piled up in the courtyards and gentlemen could be found defecating behind doors, creating what was described in an official report as '*milles puanteurs insupportables*'. One tourist described a scene in a provincial town which might well have been witnessed in Paris:

The side of the stone steps which lead from near Cathedral . . . is a perfect lavatory; and as I descended that hill by the carriage way, a full-dressed *avocat*, his tie-wig nicely powdered, his hat under his arm, was squatting with his bare backside completely exposed to view. Two women, not of the first rank indeed, but full dressed, walked by while he very composedly pulled up his breeches.

Ordinances were frequently issued in an attempt to make Paris a cleaner city, but they were largely ignored. After a magistrate had fallen to his death while emptying a chamber pot from a high window, a minister strongly complained of the Parisians' indifference to hygiene and of their city's 'excessively dirty' streets.

21 Despite his purchases, so Bunbury suggested in 1767, the Englishman in Paris remained an unmistakable figure.

Even the famous equestrian bronze statue of Louis XIV was surrounded by filth so that there was no approaching it 'even in winter; and in summer no doubt the smell will caution all persons to admire this costly work of art at a very respectable distance'.

'It is the ugliest beastliest town in the universe,' Horace Walpole decided. 'A dirty town with a dirtier ditch calling itself the Seine . . . a filthy stream, in which everything is washed without being cleaned, and dirty houses, ugly streets . . . and churches loaded with bad pictures.' It was 'a beast of a city to be in', Addison concurred. 'Rousseau said well that all the time he was in it, he was only thinking how he should leave it.' Everywhere there was excrement, 'filth and even blood streaming from the butchers' stalls'. 'You must call Paris,' Nikolai Karamzin concluded, 'the most vile . . . the most foetid city.' But it was also, he added, 'magnificent'. He was fascinated by the constant bustle:

Go from one end of the city to the other. Everywhere there are crowds of people on foot or in carriages; everywhere noise and hubbub, in large and small streets, and there are a thousand streets in Paris! At ten, at eleven o'clock at night there is still life, movement, noise everywhere. At one and two o'clock many people are still about. At three and four you hear the occasional rattle of a carriage. . . . Everyone is hurrying . . . they guess at what you want so as to be rid of you as quickly as possible. . . . Before you have finished your question, the Parisian has answered you, bowed and taken his leave.

Everywhere, too, there were magnificent sights to be seen in a city which, even Walpole admitted, 'beat us vastly in buildings, both in number and magnificence. The tombs of Richlieu and Mazarine at the Sorbonne and the Collège de Quatre Nations are wonderfully fine.' Although he for his part considered Paris 'much inferior to London in size and beauty', Philip Thicknesse, writing twenty-five years later in the 1770s, thought that Paris's 'every street furnishes either a church, a convent, or something worthy of attention'. Nugent advised beginning with the Palais Royal, where three whole days might be spent 'examining the finest collections of paintings in Europe'.

There were further fine art collections at the Louvre and the Tuileries; there were several splendid libraries including the King's library, the nucleus of the Bibliothèque Nationale, which already contained by the middle of the century 'ninety thousand printed volumes and near forty thousand Mss'; there were visits to be made to the cathedral of Notre Dame on the Ile de la Cité, 'fine and crowded with ornament', in William Jones's opinion, if 'not so grand as either Westminster Abbey or the great church of Canterbury'; to the Champs Elysées, planned by André Le Nôtre to open up a fine view from the Tuileries Palace to the Etoile where the Arc de Triomphe now stands; to the lovely gardens of the Luxembourg, the Palais Royal and the Tuileries to which 'persons decently clad' were admitted free of charge, 'domestics in livery or women of servile appearance' being turned away; to the five bridges over the Seine; to the Louvre with its splendid array of domes and cupolas, spires and turrets; to Perrault's grandiose Observatory and Jules Hardouin-Mansart's church of the Invalides; to the Invalides hospital itself, one of the most splendid monuments of the seventeenth century, built in 1671–76 to the designs of Bruant; to the Place des Victoires and the lovely octagonal Place Vendôme with its statue of Louis XIV; to the immense complex of the hospital buildings of the Saltpêtrière; to the hotels of the nobility and of rich merchants and financiers which were approached across oval or rectangular courtyards from the *porte-cochère* besides which liveried servants stood ready to receive the guests of their master whose name, proudly emblazoned on a marble plaque, was usually to be seen above the doorway.

On his visit to Paris in 1775 Samuel Johnson also went to the Ecole Militaire, to many churches, to the courts of justice, to the King's cabinet and the King's library as well as to the libraries of the Sorbonne and St Germain. He looked into the dried-up moat of the Bastille; he went to the porcelain works at Sèvres, so lavishly patronised by Mme de Pompadour, and to the Gobelins tapestry factory which took its name from the family who had established a scarlet dyeing

22 *Boats on the Seine beneath the houses on the Pont Notre Dame.*

workshop on the outskirts of Paris in the fifteenth century and which, so Philip Thicknesse learned with 'great delight', was managed by an Englishman. Johnson went on to watch the rope-and-egg dancing on the boulevards; he went round the brewery of M. Antoine Santerre, who was soon to achieve fame in the Revolution as commander of the National Guard; and he went to court where he saw the King and Queen at dinner.

While most young tourists went to court, if only to catch a glimpse of the royal family, very few were as conscientious in their sight-seeing as Johnson or Robert Adam, who reported that 'we breakfast by eight, go out by nine in our machine and travel from one church to another with our books in our hands, making such remarks as we think proper of buildings, pictures and statues until half an hour past two when we come home for dinner, you may be sure well-disposed and wholesome'. Indeed, according to Lord Chesterfield,

the life of *Milords Anglais* in Paris is regularly or, if you will, irregularly thus: As soon as they rise, which is very late, they breakfast together, to the utter loss of two good morning hours. Then they go by coachfuls to the Palais, the Invalides, and Notre-Dame; from thence to the English coffee houses, where they make up their tavern party for dinner. From dinner, where they drink, they adjourn in clusters to the play, where they crowd up the stage, drest up in very fine clothes, very ill made. . . . From the play to the tavern again, where they get very drunk, and where they either quarrel among themselves, or sally forth, commit some riot in the streets, and are taken up by the watch.

Certainly, as Thomas Gray remarked, it was not the fashion to display much curiosity in Paris. His friend Conway, who had been there some time, 'had not seen anything at all' until Walpole and Gray arrived; and their sight-seeing days were soon over. They subsequently spent much of their time lounging about in their rooms.

About two days ago, about four o'clock in the afternoon [Walpole wrote], as we were picking our teeth round a littered table and in a crumby room, Gray in an undress, Mr Conway in a morning-grey coat and I in a trim white night-gown and slippers, very much out of order . . . a message discomposed us all of a sudden, with a service to Mr Walpole from Mr More, and that, if he pleased, he would wait on Mr Walpole. We scuttle upstairs in great confusion, but with no other damage than the flinging down two or three glasses and the dropping a slipper by the way. Having ordered the room to be cleaned out, and sent a very civil response to Mr More, we began to consider who Mr More might be.

Many young English gentlemen seem to have been content to wander about in their new clothes and, with powdered and scented hair, to look into the shops, to read the English newspapers at the Cabinet Littéraire in the rue Neuve des Petits Champs, to stroll along the walks of the Boulevard, sip a cup of coffee or a

23 Rowlandson's 'La Belle Liminaudiere au Caffee de Mille Collone' an amply proportioned and much admired attendant in a well-known refreshment room.

glass of wine or lemonade at the Café des Milles Colonnes, or a cup of *bavaroise* at the Café de Valois or the Café du Caveau, to throw a handful of coins to the singing-girls and musicians who went from table to table, and, after the theatre, perhaps to visit a brothel. This James Boswell did almost immediately after his arrival in Paris, having been given advice by 'a young fellow' at the custom-house and been driven in a fiacre to the recommended establishment, one of two run by Mme Charlotte Genevieve Hecquet, where he enjoyed himself much more than he later did at the more celebrated brothel, the Hôtel Montigny. It was indeed certain, Philip Thicknesse thought, 'that men of large fortunes' could 'in no city in the world indulge their passions in every respect more amply than in Paris and occasion such immense sums to be lavished away in debauchery of every kind'. Thicknesse verily believed 'Paris to be the theatre of more vice than any city in the world, drunkenness excepted'.

As well as in brothels and in the streets, prostitutes were also to be found at one or other of Paris's numerous theatres where the tourist spent much of his time, not always pleasurably. Walpole declared the music at the opera resembled a gooseberry tart as much as it did harmony; David Garrick considered the singing in Paris very bad when he was there in 1751; and Robert Wharton 'could not help asking the gentleman who sat next to [him] whether they were singing an air or a Recitative. It mattered not which for both [were] equally detestable. . . . The eye is the only organ to be pleased at the french opera.' Henry Ellison thought so too. So did William Bennett and Lord Rolle who went 'to the opera of the Danaides' and praised both the scenery and a marvellous

representation of Hell in which the fifty Danaides were hauled and pulled about as if the Devils had been going to ravish them . . . being literally thrown upon their backs and at last buried in such a shower of fire that [it was a wonder] the Playhouse was not burned to the ground. We paid somewhat more than six shillings each for our places and were on the whole well entertained . . . [but] the music was loud and noisy in the French taste, and the singers screamed past all powers of simile to represent.

These, however, were minority verdicts. Thomas Nugent considered the 'operas at Paris extreamly fine, the music and singing excellent. The most sprightly and fashionable people of both sexes flock to these entertainments and listen with unrelaxed gravity and attention.' 'There was no mobbing,' Wharton conceded. 'They dare not be noisy for there are soldiers ready to arrest the troublesome person. This may appear a mark of despotism, but it is yet comfortable to the peaceable spectators.' The silence and attention of one particular audience were 'astonishing'. Wharton 'thought of the English audience and felt for [his] countrymen'. 'Not a whisper was to be heard' when the young Irishwoman, Catherine Wilmot, who accompanied Lord and Lady Mount Cashell on their European tour, attended a performance at the Paris Opera. 'Every eye was turned upon the stage, with most devotional attention.' 'The ballets are enchanting,' she went on enthusiastically. The performances exhibited 'more grace, dexterity of pointed toes, variety and elegance of attitude, and sparkling shows of dress etc., than any spectacle I ever saw in my life'.

Parisian audiences were not, however, prepared to sit through bad performances without protest, as Charles Burney discovered at the Théâtre Italien where a comic opera was hissed and booed by an audience who 'thoroughly damned it . . . in all the English forms, except breaking the benches and the actors' heads'. Nor were French audiences any more tolerant than English ones of foreign visitors who disregarded the customs of the house. When Mrs Crewe went to see a burlesque play in Paris, the people in the pit shouted at her for having hung her cloak over the front of the box, making her think that 'the Etiquettes' of the Parisians were 'cruel in the case of strangers' who had no means of knowing what might be offensive.

After the theatre many richer tourists went on to gamble. Indeed, there were those who contended that the only way to succeed in French society was to be prepared to gamble and to lose money. 'Without gaming,' wrote Andrew Mitchell, 'one can't enter into that sort of company that usurps the name of *Beau*

24 *(Above) Smart French society taking 'English tea' at the Prince de Conti's house.*

25 *(Below) The Grand Gallery in the Louvre in 1796, three years after it had been opened to the public by the revolutionary government.*

26 (*Left*) *Street vendors of all kinds were to be found on the Pont Neuf.*
27 (*Right*) *The Café du Caveau du Palais Royal, a favourite meeting place for tourists.*

Monde, and no other qualification but that and money are requisite to recommend one to the first company in France.' 'The French only regard strangers according to the money they spend,' agreed Edward Mellish. 'And provided you game and play you will be well received in the best company at Paris where one risques losing five, ten or fifteen pounds sterling in two hours time. Besides at games of hazard the French of the very best fashion make no scruple of cheating you, for they will do it to one another.' Nor was it only in Paris that, as the Duchess of Marlborough put it, 'when they find people won't play they grow very cool'. In Tours, so Mellish was told, 'if one expected to be well received by persons of the best fashion one must be obliged to play deep. . . . Every stranger that runs into this fashionable way of life ought to have about two or three thousand pound a year.' Dr John Moore, who did not himself gamble yet was nevertheless introduced into 'some of the most fashionable circles in Paris', considered that nothing could give greater proof of the influence and standing in society of the marquis who condescended to take such an unrewarding stranger under his wing.

Several tourists who could not afford to play for high stakes comforted themselves with the belief that Parisian society was not worth entering anyway. The upper-class Parisians' boasted knowledge of society, one disgruntled Englishman complained, was 'reduced to talking of their suppers and every malady they have about them, or know of'. Besides, they had no interest in anything which was not French: 'If something foreign arrives at Paris, they either think they invented it, or that it has always been there. . . . If we did not remember there was such a place as England, we should know nothing about it. The French never mention it, unless it happens to be in one of their proverbs.' So absorbed were the French nobility in the 'pleasures which this capital affords', wrote another English commentator, 'Nobody can persuade them that there is anything worth travelling to see. They spend their whole lives in Paris and its immediate neighbourhood and they believe that only Paris exists.'

As well as for being arrogant, Parisians, unlike the French in general, were condemned for being rudely insensitive to the feelings of foreign visitors. The London mob, it was acknowledged, could be rude enough to foreigners. 'When the people see a well-dressed person in the streets of London, especially if he is wearing a braided coat, a plume in his hat, or his hair tied in a bow, he will, without doubt, be called "French dog" twenty times before he reaches his destination,' wrote César de Saussure in 1726. 'This name is the most common and, evidently, according to popular idea the greatest and most forcible insult that can be given to any man, and it is applied indifferently to all foreigners, French or otherwise.' Yet Thomas Holcroft thought the Parisians even more derisive of an unusual appearance than Londoners were.

Being short-sighted I began to wear spectacles nearly thirty years ago when the custom of walking the streets in them was scarcely introduced [he wrote in a book published in 1804]. The English populace, when I passed, would often call me Mr Four Eyes, but I never met a greater instance of rudeness from them than this; whereas in Paris, the first time I went there, *voilà les quatre yeux* was much more frequently repeated, and with an air of great rudeness and contempt. One day a youth, who was nearly a man, tolerably dressed therefore not of the lowest order, suddenly darted his two fingers almost to my face, uttering the same exclamation.

Yet, for all the alleged rudeness of the populace, the supposed arrogance of the rich and the 'itch for gaming' that was 'deemed one of the plagues of the nation', the interesting and well-mannered young Englishman was likely to have as little cause for complaint as had Edward Gibbon, who arrived in Paris in 1763 and within three weeks had heard more memorable conversation and had met 'more men of letters among the people of fashion' than he had in as many months in London. He had been sadly neglected by the British ambassador, the Duke of Bedford, to whom he had been given a letter of introduction from the Duke of Richmond and from whom he had received 'not one invitation', but this was a 'general complaint'. He himself had few others. Paris was 'unavoidably a very dear place': there was such 'a concourse of strangers' in the city that the hirers of coaches hardly knew what to ask, and he had not been able to get one for less than sixteen guineas a month. His English clothes, looking 'so foreign here', had had to be discarded and replaced by a velvet suit 'of three colours, the ground blue' which seemed to him 'excessively long waisted'. And he had to admit that the reputation of his *Essai sur l'Étude de la Littérature* resulted in his being regarded 'solely as a man of letters', eclipsing 'the gentleman entirely'. 'I should have liked to add to [my literary reputation],' he confessed in his journal, 'that of a man of rank for which I have such indisputable claims.'

These reservations apart, however, Gibbon found Paris delightful. He was introduced to the Marquis de Mirabeau who 'acted a very friendly part'; he was welcomed by Mme du Boccage, and by Mme Geoffrin at whose salon he met Diderot and d'Alembert, d'Holbach (who gave excellent dinners) and Helvétius (who had a very pretty and witty wife). He also met the archaeologist, the Comte de Caylus, and J. J. Barthélemy, author of *Voyage du jeune Anarcharsis en Grèce*, who took him to see the King's collection of medals. He went often to the theatre, principally to the Théâtre Français, he visited all the usual sights, was conducted around the Carmelite church by a shy and sensitive young officer of the Guards, and judged Saint-Sulpice to be one of the finest structures in France. He seems to have had an affair with Mme Bontemps, a handsome woman of about forty-five and formerly Mirabeau's mistress, who took him to church in the rue St Honoré and on pleasant excursions to St Denis, St Germain and Versailles.

28 Promenading beneath the trees in the Tuileries gardens.

29 *An interior with card players by Pierre Louis Dumesnil the Younger. 'Without gaming one can't enter into that sort of company that usurps the name of* Beau Monde.'

CHAPTER 4

∗

TOURING

IN FRANCE

∗

*'The concourse of English who
come hither, like simple birds of
passage, allow themselves to be
plucked by the people of the country'*

NEARLY ALL TOURISTS WENT TO VERSAILLES and few liked what they saw. It was 'a huge heap of littleness', decided Lord Macaulay who, while doubting that there was any other single architectural composition of equal extent in the world, could think of a dozen country houses of private individuals in England which had 'a greater air of majesty and splendour than this huge quarry'. In the middle of the courtyard there was an equestrian statue of Louis XIV who 'showed his good sense, at least, in putting himself where he could not see his own architectural performances'. Smollett thought Versailles 'a dismal habitation'. Its apartments were 'dark, ill-furnished, dirty and unprincely'. Lady Mary Wortley Montagu considered it 'vast rather than beautiful' and its irregularity 'shocking', though the Petit Trianon 'in its littleness' pleased her 'better than Versailles, Marli better than either of them and St Cloud best of all, having the advantage of the Seine running at the bottom of the gardens'.

To Horace Walpole, also, the palace was a profound disappointment: 'Stand by, clear the way, make room for the pompous appearance of Versailles Le Grand. But no; it fell so short of my idea of it.' It was, after all, a mere 'lumber of littleness, composed of black brick, stuck full of bad old busts, and fringed with gold rails'. The rooms were 'all small, except the great gallery which is noble, but totally wainscotted with looking-glass' and, to make it all far worse, 'in the colonnades, upon the staircases, nay in the antechambers of the royal family, there are people selling all sorts of wares', while in the Dauphin's bedchamber two fellows, 'dancing about in sabots', were sweeping the floor. Later visitors were equally astonished by the dirty apartments through which all the world was evidently permitted to rove at pleasure. In 1787 Arthur Young was 'amused to see the black-guard figures that were walking uncontrolled even in the [King's] bedchamber; men whose rags betrayed them to be in the last stages of poverty'.

Official regulations required visitors to be reasonably well dressed, to wear a sword (which could be hired for the day from a palace official), and not to carry walking-sticks. Men were requested not to offer their arms to ladies; ladies were forbidden to have servants carrying their trains; all were warned not to push too close to the royal family and courtiers. Yet none of these rules was strictly enforced. Crowds gathered round Louis XVI when he was being dressed, and in

30 (Opposite above) The courtyard of the Royal Palace at Blois showing the famous spiral staircase.
31 (Below) Joseph Vernet depicts road-menders at work beside a river in France.

the chapel they pressed around him at Mass as he 'laughed and spied at the ladies', so Arthur Young reported. 'Every eye was fixed on the personages of the court . . . while the priest, who in the meantime went on in the exercise of his office, was unheeded by all present. Even when the Host is lifted up, none observed it; and if the people knelt, it was because they were admonished by the ringing of the bell; and, even in that attitude, all were endeavouring to catch a glimpse of the King.'

There were certain rooms containing art treasures which were not opened to the public, but these could be inspected by connoisseurs on the understanding that they would tip the guides. Elsewhere in the palace thefts were commonplace: silk tassels and bits of gold braid had constantly to be replaced; lead piping, nozzles and brass taps regularly disappeared from the fountains in the gardens.

Immense sums of money had been spent on these gardens in which no fewer than 1,400 fountains had been installed by direction of Louis XIV, who was repeatedly exasperated by the sprays dwindling to dribbles when the inadequate water supply failed to meet the heavy demands made upon it. Yet, despite the interest that the King took in them, and the talents which Le Nôtre expended upon them, the gardens at Versailles – 'littered with statues and fountains . . . the gardens of a great child', as Walpole described them – proved as disappointing to the eighteenth-century visitor as the palace itself. Arthur Young's comment, made two years before the Revolution, was characteristic:

Ramble through the gardens and by the grand canal, with absolute astonishment at the exaggeration of writers and travellers. There is magnificence in the quarter of the orangerie, but no beauty anywhere. . . . The extent and breadth of the canal are nothing to the eye: and it is not in such good repair as a farmer's horsepond. The menagerie is well enough, but nothing great.

Nevertheless, there were visitors enough who had been sufficiently impressed by Versailles to return home determined to use it as a model for a country house in England where, in the late seventeenth and early eighteenth centuries, several houses were built by men who had fallen under the spell of the palace. Montagu House in Bloomsbury, designed by Robert Hooke as what John Evelyn called 'a stately and ample palace' for Ralph Montagu, later first Duke of Montagu, was one example. Boughton House in Northamptonshire and Petworth House in Sussex were others; while the great marble entrance hall at Castle Howard, the Yorkshire mansion of the third Earl of Carlisle, was clearly inspired by the work of Louis XIV's architect Louis Le Vau. The interiors of these and many other houses were decorated throughout by French craftsmen and artists, several of whom, like the great master of wrought-ironwork, Jean Tijou, were Huguenots exiled by Louis XIV's ill-advised revocation of the Edict of Nantes. At Montagu

32 *Fountains playing in the gardens of the Orangery at Versailles.*

House the interior decoration was entirely entrusted to Jacques Rousseau, Charles de Lafosse and Jean-Baptiste Monnoyer, and when it was burned down within ten years of its completion a French architect and French craftsmen were employed in its reconstruction.

As well as to Versailles, trips were regularly made to Sèvres, to Saint-Cloud and to Fontainebleau. Most of these trips were made in a *coche d'eau*, a more pleasant method of travelling, it was generally agreed, than making the journey to Versailles in the crowded *coche d'osier* which left twice every day from the rue Saint-Niçaise and, although designed for sixteen passengers, commonly carried twice that number, several of them on the roof. Before proceeding on their journey south, many tourists also went along the well-paved road to Orléans to take a boat down the Loire to the coast at Nantes. In the seventeenth and first half of the eighteenth century particularly, the towns of the Loire were much favoured by the English, who were advised to stay in one or other of them for several months because of the purity of the French spoken there and of the possibility not only of learning to speak the language with a satisfactory accent, but also of acquiring skills in dancing, fencing and riding at a safe distance from the temptations of Paris. There were highly recommended academies where English students were welcomed at Tours and Angers as well as at Blois. Thomas Coke spent five months at the Academy at Angers in 1712–13. Blois was 'one of the pleasantest cities in France' and the food there was excellent. Edward Mellish, who often regaled himself here with 'much pleasure' on 'soupe, a joint of mutton, a fowl . . . and a good Bottle of wine', met Dr King, the Master of Charterhouse, in the town in 1731. King had come to Blois because of his asthma. 'However he has found so much benefit by this air that [at the age of seventy] he is become younger than any of us; and has a much better appetite for eating and drinking.' It was for reasons of health also that Lord Berkeley came to the Loire Valley four years later and stayed with Lord Bolingbroke, who had a house near Amboise.

In the seventeenth century Robert Montagu, later third Earl of Manchester, spent over a year at Saumur learning French and Latin, fencing and singing and how to play the guitar; and John Evelyn spent a happy time at Tours. He recorded in his journal that:

The streets very large and strait. The houses well built, & all exceeding Cleane: The Suburbs ample and pleasant. . . . The Mal is certainly the noblest for length, & the ranges of goodly tall Elms planted in Walks about it, superior to any in *France*. . . . Here in hot Weather walk the Ladys and persons of quality. The Citty is walled with square stone. . . . Indeed there is no Citty in the whole Kingdom that exceeds it for beauty, & agreeableness, so cleane, & aiery, without noise; the People of the best quality, & all in general extremely Civil to strangers.

Tours remained popular in the eighteenth century; while one English traveller at least, Arthur Young, considered that Nantes, in the admirable Hôtel de Henri IV, possessed the 'finest inn in Europe'. But towards the end of the century, most tourists, in their eagerness to reach Italy, avoided the Loire Valley, making south for Lyons. There were several alternative routes. The post-route took the traveller through Briare, Pouilly, Nevers, Moulins and Roanne. The diligence, which left every other day from the Hôtel de Sens in Paris, passed through Melun, Joigny, Vermenton and Arnay le Duc. But many tourists preferred to go at least part of the way by river, and so took the longer road through Dijon and then down the Saône past Châlon, Mâcon and Villefranche.

In good weather travelling by river was a pleasure. John Jervis St Vincent, later 1st Earl St Vincent, who took the boat to Lyons in November 1772, thought that it would be 'a very agreeable way of travelling in a more favourable season, being attended with no fatigue and affording a delightful prospect of the country on the borders of the river'. The 'very convenient passage boat' stopped 'to dine and lye, at different places in its course'. There were admittedly disadvantages: the boatmen and porters were paid before arrival at Lyons so that the passengers were 'entirely neglected and left a prey to a crowd of *canaille* . . . many of them sharpers and all imposters'. Moreover, 'this mode of travelling, so apparently commodious [had] one great inconvenience, the want of a necessary, which indeed may be supplied by a portable close stool'.

Other travellers, while agreeing that 'the charming prospects along the banks of the river' were 'very entertaining', complained of the disagreeable company with whom one was obliged to travel. To avoid such company it was advisable, where possible, to hire a *bateau de poste* which would take a carriage as well as passengers. One traveller, who hired such a boat for the equivalent of about £5 to take him down the Rhône from Lyons to Avignon in 1777, described his experiences:

Thursday 25th November, I embarked myself, servant and cabriolet in a *bateau de poste* navigated by two men . . . down the Rhone to Avignon, stopping when and where I pleased or proceeding all night if I chose it. These boats are flat bottomed and of very rude construction, the materials being always sold for plank and firewood on their arrival at Avignon. My cabriolet served me for a cabin: The wheels being taken off were laid flat at the bottom of the boat, and the body of the carriage, being set upon them was thus kept above the bilge water, which came in so plentifully as to require frequent bailing.

Those of a nervous disposition found the 'great velocity' with which the boats sometimes sped down the river most alarming, particularly those whose only previous experience of river travel in France was on the Seine, whose barges, drawn by three or four horses, took about twelve hours to cover forty-eight miles and about thirty-six hours to get from Paris to Rouen. On the Rhône the boats sped along between the villages and towns where they stopped so that the passengers could eat the *ordinaires*, and sometimes failed to stop as the boatmen with their clumsy oars fought vainly against the current. At the Pont Saint-Esprit, where most passengers got out to walk round the bridge, they had been know to capsize in the rushing waters, having struck the piers after attempting to shoot under the arches.

On disembarking at Lyons the travellers found themselves in what one of them described as 'the pleasantest city in France'. There were several good inns, among them the Three Kings, the Dauphin and the Auberge au Parc, while the *ordinaires* were often as good as those in Paris and considerably less expensive. One tourist described a meal, for which he paid 'half what it would have cost' in Paris, as 'exquisite'; Robert Wharton thought the peaches at Lyons the best fruit he had ever tasted; while Richard Pococke wrote, 'We had crayfish often at Lyons and were regal'd with fricassees of frogs which are very good like fish'. Robert Adam was much taken, too, with the shops of Lyons which sold the 'prettiest things for ladies'. Yet, although the inhabitants were 'civil to strangers', so Nugent said, and the women 'could be very handsome were it not for their losing their hair and teeth so soon', and although there were 'a great many remains of antiquity' to be seen in the town, Lyons was considered essentially as a terminus. Even Lady Mary Wortley Montagu considered it so, though she did take the trouble to see the sights, the Roman gate, the remains of the aqueduct, 'and behind the monastery of St Mary's, the ruins of the imperial palace where the Emperor Claudius was born and where Severus liv'd'. She remarked that,

The great Cathedral of St Jon is a good Gothic building, and its Clock much admir'd by the Germans. In one of the most conspicuous parts of the town is the late King's statue set up, trampling upon Mankind. I can't forbear saying one word here of the French Statues (for I never intend to mention any more of them) with their gilded full bottom'd wigs. If their King had intended to express, in one Image, Ignorance, Ill taste, and Vanity, his Sculpturers could have made no other figure to represent the odd mixture of an old Beau who had a mind to be a Hero, with a Bushel of curl'd hair on his head and a gilt Truncheon in his hand. The Houses are tolerably well built, and the Belle Cour well planted, from whence is seen the celebrated joyning of the Soane and Rhone.

Many tourists followed the Rhône from here to Geneva. Others stayed but a day or two before continuing their journey south to Avignon, and then on to Marseilles and Toulon or to Nîmes and Montpellier. A few went as far as Toulouse and from there went down the 150-mile long Languedoc Canal, the greatest work of its kind in Europe, to the shores of the Mediterranean.

The first stop on the route south was Vienne where, although the streets were

33 Louis XV enjoying a stag hunt by Jean Baptiste Oudry, the King's Court Painter, whose 'Hunts of Louis XV' were designed for the Gobelins tapestry works.

34 *Lyons drawn from the Rhône on his Grand Tour in 1754 by George Keate.*

'even narrower, crookeder and darker than most in France', the wine was deemed 'splendid'; then came Pont St Esprit, where Philip Thicknesse had a meal that he estimated would have cost him over eight times as much in England; and, just south of Pont St Esprit, was Avignon. 'Nothing worth our seeing,' was Robert Adam's comment here. A less dismissive traveller attempted a brief description which may be taken as a typically prosaic example of the kind of entry with which a conscientious young gentleman filled his diary of his Tour:

The walls and towers of Avignon, the ancient, are too perfect, and too regular to possess much of the picturesk: but the rock of the castle overhanging the road, which is a tangle against the river, and more particularly the ruined bridge, afford very picturesk parts as we draw near the landing place. The bridge is a fine object in many points of view both by itself and in composition, and Villeneuve directly opposite to Avignon, on the Languedoc side of the river, affords some rich assemblages of rock, river, trees, and buildings, which in some points of view are embellished with a fine distance of craggy hills. The prospect from the castle hill of Avignon is very amusing in the birds eye stile.

East of Avignon lies Nîmes and many tourists came here to see the Roman remains, above all the amphitheatre, the Pont du Gard – 'an Aqueduct to carry

35 The Pont du Gard, 'an Aqueduct to carry water to Nîmes built by the Romans', by William Marlow who was travelling in Italy in the 1760s.

water to Nîmes built by the Romans', as Richard Pococke economically described it – and the Maison Carrée. Even the grumpy and censorious Tobias Smollett was overwhelmed by both the aqueduct – 'a piece of architecture so unaffectedly elegant, so simple and majestic that I will defy the most phlegmatic and stupid spectator to behold it without admiration' – and the Maison Carrée, which was

an edifice . . . of the most exquisite beauty . . . built by the inhabitants of Nîmes, in honour of Caius and Julius Caesar, the grandchildren of Augustus . . . the proportions of the building are so happily united, as to give it an air of majesty and grandeur, which the most indifferent spectator cannot behold without emotion. A man needs not to be a connoisseur of architecture to enjoy these beauties. They are indeed so exquisite that you may return to them every day with a fresh appetite for seven years together. . . . It is ravishingly beautiful. The whole world cannot parallel it; and I am astonished to see it standing entire, like the effects of inchantment, after such a succession of ages, every one more barbarous than another.

The only trouble was that Nîmes was infested with 'shaby antiquarians' who offered to act as guides, offering for sale medals which they insisted had been dug out of the temple and baths. 'All these fellows are cheats; and they have often laid under contribution raw English travellers who have more money than discretion.'

South-west of Nîmes is Arles and here, too, there were Roman antiquities that attracted many tourists who chose to go by way of Arles, 'generally called a second Rome', on their way to the university town and health resort of Montpellier, 'whither vast numbers of consumptive people flock from all parts of Europe, especially from England' to breathe the clear and refreshing air.

Unfortunately, 'the concourse of English people' who flocked to Montpellier and 'like simple birds of passage' allowed themselves to be 'plucked by the people of the country' had made it an extremely expensive place. At the Cheval Blanc, for example, reputed to be the 'best *auberge* in the place' in the 1760s, prices were exorbitantly high even though, so more than one guest objected, it was none too clean, very dark and staffed by servants both lazy and impertinent. Further west at Toulouse, where far fewer travellers ventured, prices were a fraction of those demanded of the English at Montpellier. The impoverished Lady Knight, who considered that her countrymen paid 'double for everything in every country', settled at Toulouse in the 1770s because living there was so cheap. One day she provided a dinner for herself and two guests of soup, stewed beef, 'a very fine large eel, mutton chops, a brace of red partridges, an omelet with peaches in it, grapes, peaches, and savoy biscuits; a bottle of Bordeaux – sixteen pence – a bottle of our own wine, value three half-pennys. The whole expense amounted to ten shillings, wine included and a very fine cauliflower.'

Good meals were also reported from Aix-en-Provence, which with its spacious squares and sparkling fountains, so *The Gentleman's Guide* suggested in 1770, 'will perhaps please you better than any town you have yet seen in France'. A few *bon vivants* also spoke well of the two large coastal towns to the south of Aix, Marseilles and Toulon, though neither of these was then particularly distinguished for its gastronomy, Toulon being considered more remarkable for its naval arsenal, its busy foundry and vast rope yard, and Marseilles, 'a noble city', in Smollett's opinion, 'large, populous and flourishing', for the wonderful variety of its export trade and for the galleys in the harbour. John Evelyn had been welcomed aboard the Galley Royal by the captain and had been both fascinated and horrified by the spectacle below the ship's decks:

The captain of the Gally gave us most courteous entertainment in his Cabine, the Slaves in the interim playing both on loud & soft musique very rarely: Then he shew'd us how he commanded their motions with a nod, & his Wistle, making them row out; which was to me the newest spectacle I could imagine, beholding so many hundreds of miseraby naked Persons, having their heads shaven clooose, & onely red high bonnets, a payre of Course canvas drawers, their whole backs, & leggs starke naked, doubly chayned about their middle, & leggs, in Cupples, & made fast to their seates: and all

36 (Opposite) A picnic during a hunt, by Carle van Loo.

Commanded in a trise, by an Imperious & cruell seaman: One Turke amongst them he much favour, who waited on him in his Cabine, but naked as he was, & in a Chayne lock'd about his leg; but not coupled. . . . Their rising forwards, & falling back at their Oare is a miserable spactacle, and the noyse of their Chaines with the roaring on the beaten Waters has something of strange & fearfull in it, to one unaccustom'd. They are ruld, & chastiz'd with a bulls-pizle dry'd upon their backs, & soles of their feete upon the least dissorder, & without the least humanity.

Despite their ill treatment the slaves seemed 'Cheerful & full of vile knavery', while most had 'some occupation or other by which as leisure in Calmes, & other times, permitts, they get some little monye: in so much as some have after many Yeares of cruel Servitude been able to purchase their liberty'.

Later visitors reported that they were even permitted to have their own shops along the quay where they dealt in toys and cutlery, in combs, salted eels, anchovies, gum arabic and in many other of those commodities which were shipped all over the world from the port. Naturally, the insatiably curious James Boswell came to see the galley slaves when he was in Marseilles in December 1765.

It was [he recorded] curious to see a little row of booths, with signs, all occupied by slaves, many of whom looked as plump and contented as any decent tradesmen whatever. I went into one of the galleys where the slaves were mostly working in different ways in order to gain some little thing. I was told that many of them make rich, as they are allowed a great deal of time for themselves when lying in the harbours [which they nearly always were]. I talked with one who had been in the galleys twenty years. I insisted with him that after so long a time custom must have made even the galleys easy. They came about me, several of 'em, and disputed my proposition. I maintained that custom made all things easy, and that people who had been long in prison did not choose to come out. 'Ah,' said the slaves, 'it is otherwise here. It is two prisons. If we could escape, we should certainly do it. A bird shut up in a cage desires freedom, and so much the more should a man desire it. At first we shed tears, we groaned, but all our tears and groans availed us nothing.' I was touched with the misery of these wretches, but appeared firm, which made them not show much grief. . . . I was much satisfied with having seen a galley. I gave the slaves something to drink.

East of Marseilles and Toulon there were no other places along the Mediterranean coast which were recommended, even for a brief visit, apart from Nice. Fréjus, according to Nugent, had little more than 'some old fortifications, indifferently built . . . the old harbour is now a flat shore'; Antibes was dismissed by Boswell as 'a small and poor-looking place'; Cannes, which could be approached only 'on the sides of great stony mountains thick covered with pines and firs', by Smollett as merely 'a little fishing town'; Monaco by Dupaty in the 1780s as 'two

37 The Maison Carrée at Nîmes, a monument described by the novelist Tobias Smollett as of 'the most exquisite beauty'.

or three steps upon precipitous rocks; eight hundred wretches dying of hunger; a tumble-down castle, and a battalion of French troops'. The whole countryside around Menton was condemned out of hand by Henry Swinburne as a

calcined, scalped, tasped, scraped, flayed, boiled, powdered, leprous, blotched, mangy, grimy, parboiled country *without* trees, water, grass, fields – *with* blank, beastly, senseless olives and orange-trees like a mad cabbage gone indigestible; it is infinitely liker hell than earth, and one looks for tails among the people. And such females with hunched bodies and crooked necks carrying tons on their heads and looking like Death taken seasick.

Nice, however, was already quite fashionable. Advised, as Smollett was, that its climate was 'favourable to disorders of the breast', many foreigners came to live here in the eighteenth century. Smollett himself stayed several months and, for once, had little cause to grouse, plunging into the sea with pleasure, much to the astonishment of the local people:

The people here were much surprised when I began to bathe . . . they thought it very strange . . . and some of the doctors prognosticated immediate death. But, when it was perceived that I grew better in consequence of the bath . . . [the] example was followed by several inhabitants of Nice. There is, however, no convenience for this operation,

38 Dressmakers working in a shop at Arles.

*39 (Opposite) Lyons, although used mainly as a terminus, was considered
by at least one traveller 'the pleasantest city in France'.*

from the benefit of which the fair sex must be intirely excluded, unless they lay aside all regard to decorum; for the shore is always lined with fishing-boats, and crowded with people. If a lady should be at the expense of having a tent pitched on the beach where she might put on an off her bathing-dress, she could not pretend to go into the sea without proper attendants. . . . All that she can do is have the sea-water brought into her house, and make use of a bathing-tub, which may be made according to her own, or physician's direction.

Above the beach, the streets of the town were narrow and the windows of most of the stone houses were fitted with paper instead of glass; but, since storms and rain were rare, these paper windows answered tolerably well. When he stood upon the ramparts and looked about him, Smollett could 'scarce help thinking [himself] inchanted'. The countryside below appeared like one large cultivated garden 'full of green trees, loaded with oranges, lemons, citrons and bergamots', plantations of green peas ready to gather,

all sorts of sallading, and pot-herbs, in perfection . . . and roses, carnations, ranunculas, anemones, and daffodils, blowing in full glory, with such beauty, vigour, and perfume as no flower in England ever exhibited. . . . Amidst the plantations in the neighbourhood of Nice, appear a vast number of white *bastides*, or country-houses, which make a dazzling shew. . . . The hills are shaded to the tops with olive-trees, which are always green, and those hills are overtopped by more distant mountains, covered with snow.

The sight of those mountains filled many another traveller with apprehension, for the next stage in their journey involved a tiresome and possibly dangerous climb over them, unless they were to undergo, as Smollett was, an equally tedious, and perhaps hazardous, passage by sea.

40 Marseilles, 'a large, prosperous and flourishing port', from which some tourists sailed to Italy.

CHAPTER 5

*

THE WAYS TO

ITALY

*

'Dangerous waters' and 'frightful Alps'

TOBIAS SMOLLETT, HAVING CHOSEN TO MAKE the journey to Italy by sea, immediately regretted his decision. After providing himself with 'a proper pass, signed and sealed' by the British consul at Nice, as well as with letters of recommendation from him to the consuls at Genoa and Leghorn, he hired a boat in Nice harbour to take him to Genoa. It was a boat, rowed by four men and steered by the owner, with room for five passengers. In it Smollett left Nice on a fair September morning in 1774. After calling at Monaco, where the owner paid toll in the harbour, the boat was rowed on passed Menton and Ventimiglia and would have been taken another twenty miles had the water not begun to grow rough and the two female passengers seasick. The owner put in at San Remo and, leading the way to what he recommended as the best *auberge* to be found along the whole riviera of Genoa, he conducted the passengers up a 'dark, narrow, steep stair, into a kind of public room, with a long table and benches, so dirty and miserable, that it would disgrace the worst hedge alehouse in England'.

Not a soul appeared to receive us [Smollett recalled]. This is a ceremony one must not expect to meet with in France; far less in Italy. Our *patron*, going into the kitchen, asked a servant if the company could have lodging in the house; and was answered, 'he could not tell: the *patron* was not at home'. When he desired to know where the *patron* was, the other answered, 'he was gone to take the air'. E andato a passaggiare. In the meantime, we were obliged to sit in the common room among watermen and muleteers. At length the landlord arrived, and gave us to understand, that he could accommodate us with chambers. In that where I lay, there was just room for two beds, without curtains or bedstead, an old rotten table covered with dried figs, and a couple of crazy chairs. The walls had been once white-washed: but were now hung with cobwebs, and speckled with dirt of all sorts; and I believe the brick-floor had not been swept for half a century. We supped in an outward room and fared villainously. The provision was very ill-dressed, and served up in the most slovenly manner. You must not expect cleanliness or conveniency of any kind in this country. For this accommodation I payed as much as if I had been elegantly entertained in the best auberge of France.

The next morning the wind was so high that the boat could not put to sea, and Smollett and his companions were obliged to spend another twenty-four hours in their dreadful hovel. On the third day they re-embarked and were rowed along close to the shore, the weather still being unfavourable, though the wind had abated; in the evening they reached the waters of the Capo di Noli which were 'counted very dangerous in blowing weather' and even in a moderate breeze, when the waves were dashed against the echoing rocks and caverns, made such 'an awful noise and at the same time occasioned such a rough sea' that one could not but feel 'a secret horror'. Having passed the cape and followed the winding of the coast, the boat put in at Noli where the inn was so unspeakable that the passengers even regretted the one they had left at San Remo. Smollett had not been in bed more than five minutes when 'about a dozen large bugs' began to crawl over his body. So, still suffering from the effects of seasickness, he spent the rest of the night lying on a chest in an outer room. The next day, he was further distressed to find he could not procure a drop of milk for his tea. There were flocks of goats feeding among the rocks, yet 'the people here have no idea of using milk, and when you ask them for it, they stand gaping with a foolish face of surprise, which is exceedingly provoking'. So, having had to drink their tea without milk, the passengers re-embarked once more and were rowed past Pietra, Savona, Voltri and Sestri Ponente, and at last, at about five in the afternoon, they reached Genoa where at La Croce di Malta in the neighbourhood of the harbour they met with 'such good entertainment' that the tribulations of their journey seemed almost worthwhile.

Were he to make that journey again, Smollett said, he would hire a larger boat, a felucca, which had sails as well as oars and was large enough to take aboard a post-chaise. These craft, of which there were scores to be seen every day in the harbours of Nice, Marseilles, Toulon and other Mediterranean ports waiting to take passengers and goods to Genoa or Leghorn, had an awning over the stern sheets where the passengers sat to protect them from the sun or rain; and between the seats there were mattresses upon which they could lie down if they preferred. Yet even these boats kept close to the shore to escape the attention of Barbary pirates, and passengers who sailed to Italy in them did not speak highly of their comfort. Indeed, throughout the eighteenth century and well into the next, the sea voyage to Italy remained a trial for many of those who chose to go that way. The experience of Matthew Todd, who sailed to Leghorn with his master in the early nineteenth century was not exceptional.

First delayed by unfavourable winds, then by a striking crew, then by the need to take on ballast, the boat at length weighed anchor but made little way for several hours, the wind being so light. At four o'clock in the morning Todd was roused by the captain who pressed him to have a cup of coffee. Todd unwillingly accepted it and then, unable to get to sleep again, got up and dressed, whereupon the captain immediately took possession of his bed. As he slept the winds became unfavourable once more, and the boat was obliged to put in at Porto Fino. 'We had no table, nor chairs, 2 mouth glasses, one of which was broken, and nothing but bad wine and water to drink,' Todd mournfully recorded. 'Knives and forks such as they were, never cleaned, nor plates washed and little bits of beef . . . as tough as the Devil, no vegetables except raw onions which by the bye was by far the best thing we had.'

Todd went ashore in 'sad rainy weather' but could find 'nothing in the town (if it may be called one) worth looking at'. The next morning when he awoke he found the boat 'still sticking in the mud' and the captain in a foul temper because his passengers refused to sleep ashore, denying him and his cousin, the mate, the use of their beds. He threatened to seize their baggage until Todd showed him 'a brace of pistols which he did not much like the appearance of'. However, Todd and his master, considering it 'dangerous to sleep on board another night', eventually agreed to find rooms in the village, taking their pistols with them 'in case of surprise which was very probable in such an outlandish place as this'.

The next day continued 'rainy and unfavourable'; and on the day after that, the wind still being adverse, the captain showed no disposition to move, 'but a very great one' to cut his passengers' throats. So, Todd continued,

We accepted the offer of 2 of his sailors (who were dissatisfied with the Captain) to take the small boat, whilst he was out on shore with the mate, and leave the harbour, the ship and the Captain to their fate. And after a pull of about 4 hours along the coast we arrived at Ceste, a small village, and obliged to stop at a most miserable house, and shocking bad wine. Discharged our men and boat and gave them a couple of napoleons, with which they were well pleased.

At this village, Todd's master engaged another small boat to take them on to Leghorn; but they were woken early in the morning 'by the man belonging to the boat coming to say that he could not take [them] unless paid something more'. So they booked another boat, but the seas were by then so heavy again that it could not get off and they were obliged to continue their journey to La Spezia by land, hiring three ponies and a driver, travelling over hills, rocks and execrable roads from eight in the morning until late at night, and narrowly escaping being robbed and murdered in a house where they slept by a man 'with a countenance so fierce you might have taken him for some wild beast of the forest'.

It was possible to avoid the sea route by taking the winding road which ran along the coast at the foot of the Ligurian Alps. But this road was not only appallingly rough and slow – 'you take a mule and clamber along at two miles an hour at the risque of breaking your neck every minute' – it was also infested with bandits. Having quarrelled with his Swiss servant, and distrusting the master of the felucca that had brought them as far as Noli, James Boswell determined to go the rest of the way alone by land, and so set off crossly with Jachone, his dog, 'pulling him along with a good cord, and, whenever he was rebellious, beating him sorely'.

At last I arrived at Razzi at one in the morning [he recorded in his diary] and knocked up the landlord and landlady of a little inn. I found I had let my purse with two *louis* drop by the way, so I dispatched the landlord's two sons with a lantern to seek it for me, their father having charged them to pray to the Virgin that it might be found. I did not much like this Genoese inn. My room had two doors, one of which opened on a room where I saw one or two stout fellows. That door I bolted very well; the other, which opened on my landlord's room, I attempted to shut. He called to me that I had locked it, while I heard the sound of a lock, but I knew I had not turned the key, and discovered that he had bolted it on his side and would make me believe that I had locked it. This looked ugly. The sequel, however, proved that he had no other intention but merely to humour my resolution to have my door locked, for I was obliged to content my self with matters as they were. It was three o'clock before I got to bed. I did not throw off my clothes, but laid Jachone on the foot of my bed, and took my *couteau de chasse* and laid it at my side.

Alarmed by such accounts of the dangers and discomforts of the coastal route into Italy, tourists were often equally apprehensive when they caught their first sight of the mountain passes that offered an alternative path, 'those uncouth, huge, monstrous excrescences of Nature, bearing nothing but craggy stones'. One traveller in the late eighteenth century recorded his horror at coming into view of that 'awful and tremendous amphitheatre' which barred his road to the south. 'When first I turned my glass upon the mountains,' he confessed, 'and brought their terrors closer to my eye, I started with affright! My friend the curate perceiving my amazement said to me, "*Ah! Monsier l' Anglais, vous voyez là des belles horreurs!*" And in fact they were so . . . I could not behold them without terror, and even was pleased that I was distant from them.'

For long such sentiments had been common. In May 1646, on his return from Italy, John Evelyn approached the Alps with foreboding. Having exchanged their asses for mules at Domodossola, he and his companions rode through 'very steepe, craggy, & dangerous passages to . . . a very infamous wretched lodging' at the village of Dovedro. Next morning they mounted 'againe through strange, horrid & firefull Craggs & tracts abounding in Pine trees, & onely in-habited with Beares, Wolves and *Wild Goates*'. Above them rose the vast 'mountaines' whose tops were covered with snow and 'seem'd to touch the Skies, [and] 'twixt whose clefts now & then precipitated great Cataracts of Mealted Snow, and other Waters which made a tirrible roaring'. Soaked to the skin and concealed from each other by a thick mist, the party rode on, across narrow bridges made from felled fir trees and over 'Cataracts of stupendious depth' until stopped by 'a huge young fellow' claiming that a dog belonging to one of the travellers had killed his goat.

They spurred on their mules and tried to ride away from him but were soon surrounded by a crowd of villagers who knocked them from their saddles and

41 St Jean de Maurienne in the Savoyard Alps sketched on his Grand Tour in 1755 by George Keate before crossing Mount Cenis.

took away their carbines. Forced to pay compensation before proceeding, they continued their journey through the mountains, colder than ever, nearly losing all their baggage when the horse carrying it plunged through a bank of loose snow and 'Slid downe a firefull precipice, more than thrice the height of St Paule's'. 'Affritted with this disaster', they dismounted and 'trudg'd on foote', sometimes slipping and sometimes falling over, for 'seven long miles, plainely hearing the firfull roaring' of cascades of melted snow 'that had made Channels of formidable depth in the Crevices of the Mountains'. Late at night they came down to a 'Towne call'd Briga [Brieg] where, upon nearly every door, were nailed the heads of bears, wolves and foxes'. Here they 'tooke fresh Mules' and were soon passing through as pleasant a Country as that which before [they] had traveld was melancholy and troublesome'.

In the eighteenth century the most usual route into Italy was over Mont Cenis by

way of Susa and Lanslebourg, where the travellers' coaches were either dismantled and packed in separate pieces on the backs of mules or stored in one of the large sheds in the town until the day of their return. This was the way Boswell went in January 1765, carried by porters in 'the Alps machine which consisted of two trees between which were twisted some cords on which [he] sat. There was also a kind of back and arms, and a board before on which [he] put [his] feet.' The prospect was 'horribly grand', he thought, and in places alarming, but the road had been well hardened by other passengers and he crossed 'the immense mountain' without incident, swallowing some snow on the way so that he might say with Virgil, 'I have climbed the rudest heights and drunk the Alpine snow.'

Horace Walpole and his friend, Thomas Gray, who took that route some years before, were not so fortunate. The journey took them six days and it was, so Gray wrote, like 'eight days' journey through Greenland'. Mont Cenis, he added, carried the permission mountains had of 'being frightful rather too far'. 'Swathed in beaver bonnets, beaver gloves, beaver stockings, muffs and bear-skins', the two friends were carried in their chairs over the snow. And one day, adding horror to horror, Walpole's King Charles spaniel, Tory, while running along beside his master in the cold air, was seized by the throat by a wolf and, before anything could be done to prevent it, was carried away up the side of a rock and eaten.

The porters, Walpole had to admit, were extremely dexterous as they leaped from rock to rock with the poles of the chair on their shoulders. Inconceivably nimble, they ran 'down steeps and frozen precipices' where no other men, 'as men are now, could possibly walk'. 'Their quick short little Steps are superior in these places to those of a mule,' agreed Edward Gibbon, whose four porters, taking it in turn to carry him, 'made the five leagues across the mountain without stopping at all', moving slowly enough on the steep and painful ascent but then trotting down as though quite unimpeded by their burden. The one disadvantage about which some travellers complained was that the chairs had no floors and if the porters put them down to take a rest, the occupants were left sitting in the snow, as Mariana Starke was, clutching for warmth her little lap dog and a heated bag of semolina.

Although it took 'only two men to carry you', Dr Sharp explained, 'six, and sometimes eight, attend in order to relieve one another. The whole way you ride in this manner being fourteen or fifteen miles. When the person carried is corpulent, it it necessary to employ ten porters.' To determine how many porters would be required for each party, the travellers comprising it were examined

42 (Opposite above) Travellers climbing the summit of Mont Blanc in August 1785.
43 (Below) On Mont Cenis the Pass of Les Echelles was impassable for vehicles between Lanslebourg and Moualaise, and travellers had to cross on foot or by mule.

44 All travellers agreed that the porters who carried them across the Alps were extremely sure-footed.

before departure. 'Lord Middlesex,' wrote his tutor, Joseph Spence, who accompanied him across Mont Cenis in October 1731, 'had four assigned to him, ye Duke of Kingston six: and his Governor, who is a portly plump gentleman, no less than eight.' Spence, who was much slighter, 'was under terrible apprehension that they would allow [him] only two, but was overjoyed when the Manager said that my little lord (for [the] English are all lorded abroad) must have four too'. With the assistance of such skilled men, Sharp thought, crossing Mont Cenis was not nearly such an ordeal as timorous travellers made it out to be. 'A propos of Mont Cenis,' Giuseppe Baretti confirmed, 'let no one be frightened by the dismal accounts, so frequent in the books of travel writers, of the bad road over dangerous precipices.'

We passed Mt Cenis after bad weather and it was covered with snow six or eight inches deep [wrote Thomas Brand in 1783, expressing the view of those for whom the mountains held no terrors]. But even in that state we could not help shrugging our shoulders and shaking our heads at the extravagant exaggerations of danger which most travellers indulge themselves in describing that famous passage. It was indeed a little cold in going up but once on the plain the air was temperate enough and at the descent it was mild beyond expectation. We rode up upon mules and were carried down by porters . . . [who] whisk you with incredible strength and celerity down a steep stony road with sharp angles at each turn. Perhaps for the first five or six minutes I was under some fright but the firmness of their steps soon set me at ease.

Thomas Pelham concurred – crossing Mont Cenis was 'certainly a great undertaking in point of conveying the carriages' but, as to the travellers' own persons, there was 'neither danger nor inconvenience'. There was so hard a frost when Pelham himself came to the top of the mountain that the chairs had to be abandoned and the passengers transferred to sledges, 'which though very trying to the *nerves* was not unpleasant. It was the clearest day imaginable and our view beyond all description.' Others however, found these sledges 'quite the most frightful way of travelling in the world', while the kind of char-à-banc that was sometimes used, 'a species of jolting wheel-barrow', was 'the most infernal vehicle ever invented'.

Yet, if there was less danger of being killed or injured than some travellers suggested, there was always a strong likelihood of catching cold, as Lady Mary Wortley Montagu discovered on crossing Mont Cenis in 1718.

The prodigious Prospect of Mountains cover'd with Eternal Snow, Clouds hanging far below our feet, and the cascades tumbling down the Rocks with a confus'd roaring, would have been solemnly entertaining to me if I had suffer'd less from the extreme cold that reigns here [Lady Mary told Alexander Pope], but the misty rain, which falls perpetually, penetrated even the thick fur I was wrap'd in, and I was halfe dead with cold before we got to the foot of the Mountain, which was not till 2 hours after twas dark. . . . The Descent is so steep and slippery 'tis surprizing to see these chairmen go so steadily as they do, yet I was not halfe so much afraid of breaking my Kneck as I was of falling sick and the event has show'd that I plac'd my fears in the right place.

There is no mistaking, however, the real fear that gripped many travellers when they crossed the Alps in the worst weather, down the most slippery precipices, and through the thickest mists. The passage by the Col di Tenda could be particularly alarming, as Tobias Smollett discovered when he was going home after his Italian travels. The route was completely covered with snow, at the top nearly twenty feet thick. He and his party hired six men to assist them in the ascent, 'each provided with a kind of hough to break the ice, and make a sort of steps for the mules'. When they were near the top, however, they were obliged to alight and clamber up as best they could, supported by guides known as *coulants*. Even the mules, 'though very sure-footed animals and frost-shod for the occasion . . . stumbled and fell very often, the ice being so hard that the sharp-headed nails in their shoes could not penetrate it'.

The St Gotthard Pass could be equally frightening. 'The mountain is two miles high and very dangerous in winter, because of the great heaps of snow and stones which the violence of the wind rolls down the precipices,' warned Thomas Nugent. 'But the most hazardous part is the bridge on the Russ, called the bridge of hell from the horrid noise the water makes as it tumbles from the rocks, and from the slipperiness of the bridge which renders it difficult even to foot passengers who are obliged to creep on all fours, lest the fury of the wind should drive them down to the rocks.' On the Simplon route avalanches were common, and when Beaujolois Campbell went that way as late as 1817 fir trees uprooted by them lay on either side of the road, and melted snow ran in torrents 'furiously down the mountain in various directions'. As for the route that led from Grenoble through Briançon and Cesana, this lay among 'horrid mountains worse than the Alps', according to John Clenche, 'hewn out of the side of rocks in steps with continued precipices, a roaring torrent in the bottom, and through the melancholy shade of pine and fir-trees'.

'But the road, West, the road!' exclaimed Walpole in a letter to a friend he had made at Eton.

Winding round a prodigious mountain, and surrounded with others, all shagged with hanging woods, obscured with pines or lost in clouds! Below, a torrent breaking through cliffs, and tumbling through fragments of rocks! Sheets of cascades forcing their silver speed down channelled precipices, and hasting into the roughened river at the bottom! Now and then an old foot-bridge, with a broken rail, a leaning cross, a cottage or the ruin of a hermitage!

'Rocks and torrents beneath,' wrote Thomas Gray of that same countryside through which he had ridden on a mule. 'Pine trees and snows above; horrours and terrours on all sides. . . . Scenes which would awe an atheist into belief, without the help of other argument.'

The people encountered in these mountains seemed only too appropriate in that awesome landscape, 'meagre, ragged, barefooted, with their children in extreme misery and nastiness'. Many of them were disfigured by such grotesque goitres that it was sometimes hardly possible to discover where the face ended and the throat began. John Evelyn said that he had seen some inhabitants of these regions with

monstrous Gullets or Wenns of Flesse growing to their throats as big as an hundred pound bag of silver hanking under their Chinns; among the women especially, & that so ponderous, as that to ease them, they many of them wore linnen cloth bound about their head & coming under the chin to support it. . . . Their drinking so much snow water is thought to be the cause of it. . . . It runs as we say in the bloud, & is a vice in the race, & renders them so ougly, shrivel'd & deform'd, by its drawing the skin of the face downe, that nothing can be more fritefull; to which add a strange puffing habit, furrs & barbarous Language, being a mixture of corrupt high German, French, & Italian: The people are of gigantic Stature, extreamly fierce & rude.

The inns kept by these mountain people were execrable. There were only two at Lanslebourg, both of which were 'scarcely habitable'. The inn on the Col di Tenda was still in 1792 'a crazy hovel, containing scarcely one whole window, and no sitting-room, except that which serves in common, for postilions, porters, gentlemen, poultry, and hogs'. At Simplon, the 'inhospitable' place where Evelyn stayed was 'halfe cover'd with Snow' and, although the ceilings were 'strangely low for those tall people', it was very cold. He was given 'cheeze & Milke & wretched wine' for supper, then shown a bed in a cupboard so high from the floor that it had to be approached by a ladder. Two centuries later a guide-book warned that the post-house at Simplon was still 'dear and dirty', offering little but 'damp sheets, hard bread, hard water, hard old hens and of course hard eggs'.

After their discomfort and travails in these desolate mountains and this 'mis-shapen scenery', as Addison called it, the tourist who came down from them into the 'sweet and temperate air' of the Plain of Lombardy was all the more ready to appreciate the pleasures of Italy.

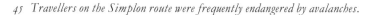

45 Travellers on the Simplon route were frequently endangered by avalanches.

46 The performance of an opera at the Teatro Regio in Turin.

CHAPTER 6

*

PIEDMONT

AND

LOMBARDY

*

'A true spring in the air in the midst of winter'

IT WAS ONE OF THE MOST BEAUTIFUL LAND-scapes imaginable, Gray decided when he saw the Plain of Lombardy for the first time, 'vast plantations of trees, chiefly mulberries and olives, and not a tree without a vine training about it'. William Beckford was equally impressed. Even the rocks were 'mantled with vines. Here and there a cottage, shaded with mulberries, made its appearance; and we often discovered on the banks of the river, ranges of white buildings, with courts and awnings' giving shade to peasants making silk. At Bolzano there were terraces of melons and Indian corn, 'gardens of fig trees and pomegranates hanging over walls'. Compared with the grotesque appearance of the mountain people of Savoy, the Piedmontese seemed as attractive as their countryside. The women combed their hair back from their foreheads and wound it in a large knot at the back, decorating the knot with pins almost a foot long with gold or white beads at the ends. They wore huge earrings and necklaces, Catherine Wilmot noticed, and jackets 'worked in gold threads, and as much ornamentation as the wearer can afford; white shift sleeves are tied over all, with bunches of the gayest coloured Ribbands. The only thing they have as a Hat, is a vast number of folds of white linen laid flat and square upon their heads about the size of a stiff pocket handkerchief with a tassle at one corner.'

Passing through Avigliana and Rivoli on his way from Susa, the tourist came to Turin where he was likely to spend some time, as Thomas Coke did, studying at the Academy. 'The principal advantage I shall reap here,' wrote Sholto Douglas, one day to become Bishop of Salisbury, 'is, I fancy, an *easier air* in company, as I am to be introduced to the king and the principal nobility at the return of the court.'

Edward Gibbon, who arrived in Turin in the spring of 1764, could have warned Douglas that he was not likely to find much either to entertain him or to improve his manners at the Piedmontese court. 'The court is old and dull,' he warned a friend, and the King a little old man whose uneasy manners and commonplace questions to visitors indicated 'a bourgeois' of limited intelligence and no sophistication, though his daughters were sociable enough. Gibbon chatted with them and 'grew so very free and easy' that he 'drew his snuff-box, rapped it, took snuff twice (a crime never known before in the presence chamber) and continued [his] discourse in [his] usual attitude of body bent forwards and forefinger stretched out'.

A court is for me simultaneously an object of interest and disgust [he decided]. The servility of the courtiers revolts me and I view with horror the magnificence of the palaces which have been cemented with the blood of the people. In a small and poor kingdom like this they must grind the people in order to be equal with other crowned heads and to keep up the air of grandeur and the long series of apartments filled with guards and officers whom one sees in the palaces of Turin.

The city itself was a disappointment. The pretty women, who were, in any case, not a common sight, were taken up with their *cicisbei*, their recognised male attendants who were, infrequently, their lovers; while the entertainments offered in the drawing-rooms where they were to be encountered were uniformly dull. 'If there is any pleasure in watching play [usually faro] which one does not understand, in listening to a Piedmontese jargon of which one does not take in a word, and in finding oneself in the midst of a proud nobility who will not speak a word to you, we had a most amusing time in this assembly.'

This was the drawing-room of Caterina Maria Theresa di San Gillio, who was married to an illegitimate son of the late King Victor Amadeus II and who, according to Casanova, superintended all the intrigues in Turin. She was said to have had a great predilection for young Englishmen, and when she was almost fifty inspired a violent passion in both the young Lord Charles Spencer and Sir Brooke Boothby.

James Boswell sought her out as a matter of course when he arrived in Turin the next year and, provided with a letter of recommendation, was received by her one afternoon at four o'clock: 'She was past fifty . . . but, being strong, was still well enough. She talked of Duke Hamilton [James, the sixth Duke] who had been a great gallant of hers. She had animal spirits and talked incessantly. She carried me in her coach to take the air. I was already then quite in the Italian mode. We returned to her house, where was a stupid *conversazione*, all men.' The next day Boswell returned to her house where he was 'tired to death'. 'The room was full of young rakes, mighty stupid, and old worn-out miscreants in whom impotence and stupidity were united. I attended her to the opera, as one of her [*cicisbei*]. She had two of us. One held her gloves or her muff, and another her fan. After being heartily wearied in her box, I went down to the parterre.'

Tedious as he and other tourists found life in Turin, Boswell was intrigued by the women in society whom, he was assured, he could have for the asking. Whenever he expressed admiration for one of them at a ball at the Théâtre de Carignan, he was told by the 'counts and other pretty gentlemen', 'Sir, you can have her. It would not be difficult.' At first he thought they were joking, but he soon discovered they were 'in earnest' and that the manners here were 'so openly debauched that adultery was carried on without the least disguise'. Encouraged

47 (Left) *Turin, drawn by an English tourist, Thomas Sutherland.*
48 (Right) *A travel pass issued at Leghorn to James Boswell for his voyage to Corsica and thence to Genoa.*

by this, the whim seized him of having an intrigue with an Italian countess, and as he 'had resolved to spend very little time' in Turin he thought 'an oldish lady most proper' as he would have an 'easy attack'. He therefore began throwing out hints at the opera to the Contessa di San Gillio. 'I sat *vis-à-vis* to her and pressed her legs with mine, which she took very graciously,' he recorded. 'I began to lose command of myself. I became quite imprudent.' But then he was taken away to the box of Contessa Burgaretta, a 'most beautiful woman' whom he was assured he could also have.

His mind was 'quite in fermentation' as he made overtures to both women; but then one morning, after having been dismissed by the Contessa di San Gillio who had, of course, heard of his passion for her rival, he went to 'Mme Burgaretta's where [he] found two more swains. She grumbled and complained of a headache, and she dressed before [them all], changing even her shirt.' 'We indeed saw no harm,' Boswell commented, 'but this scene entirely cured my passion for her.' He now set his sights upon another lady, reputed to be very debauched, Contessa di Scarnafigi, for whom he protested 'the strongest of passions' in a long letter, both abject and impertinent, in which he assured her that, although he had 'heard many tales' of her, he was 'determined to believe none'. 'No, Madame, I adore you,' he continued, 'and nothing can weaken that admiration. . . . If you accord me the supreme happiness, you will be showing yourself generous to an excellent man who would be attached to you for the rest of your life. . . . Ah! when we abandon ourselves to pleasures under the veil of darkness, what transports, what ecstasy will be ours! Pardon me, Madame, I am greatly agitated . . . have a care, Madame, there is here something important at stake. I tremble but have hopes. . . .'

Mme di Scarnafigi burned the letter, and Boswell had to be content with girls of the town provided for him by one Captain Billon, who took it upon himself to act as pimp. The willing and beautiful Italian countess whom nearly every young tourist hoped to possess on his Italian travels did not prove so easy to find.

Yet, while court life was undoubtedly dull, and amours with its more attractive denizens not so easy to arrange as he was led to suppose, the tourist had to concede that Turin – despite the often dirty oiled paper rather than glass in the windows of even larger houses – was a handsome city, if as the second Earl Stanhope thought a 'mournfull' one. It was notable, so Nugent said, 'for the magnificence of its buildings, the beauty of its streets and squares and for all the conveniences of life'. All in all, one tourist concluded in 1730, Turin was 'one of the prettiest towns' he had ever seen: ''Tis built very regular and almost all the streets cut each other at right angles so you see from one end of the town to the other. . . . Were it built of stone instead of brick, it would be the . . . finest town in Europe of its size.'

The Piazza San Carlo, rebuilt after it had almost been destroyed in a siege by the French in 1706, was particularly admired. So were the various handsome churches, the Jesuits' College and the Chapel of the Holy Handkerchief named after the cloth which Saint Veronica gave to the sweating Christ when he was carrying the cross to Calgary. So were the Villa Reale at Stupingi built by Filippo Juvarra in 1729–31 and the Villa Madama with its famous double staircase. So, too, were several of the city's well-run inns, notably the Bonne Femme and the Auberge d'Angleterre, the Spit and the Duke of Florence, where the macaroni soup with cheese and the veal cutlets with marsala sauce and asparagus tips were a revelation to most English palates, and where the prices were most reasonable: Boswell paid about £3 for six days' food and lodging at the Bonne Femme, and £3 6s for nine days at the Auberge d'Angleterre.

After supper in one of these inns tourists would take out their maps and guide-books to plan the next stage in their journey. Italian roads, they had been warned, were mostly very primitive. There were, indeed, a few good thoroughfares in Lombardy, Piedmont and Tuscany, but even here they could not all be relied upon. 'We are arrived at Turin,' wrote Dr Sharp in May 1766. 'The journey from Alessandria has been unpleasant. One night's rain has made the road almost impassable, so muddy and clayey is the soil.' Secondary roads frequently degenerated into cart-tracks; and in many hilly districts, particularly in Liguria, travellers were 'exposed to a variety of disagreeable adventures', including the necessity of abandoning carriages altogether for mules. 'The coach had been in the most imminent hazard of being lost with all our baggage,' wrote one disgruntled passenger, 'and at two different places it was necessary to hire a dozen of oxen and as many men to disengage it from the holes into which it had run.' In the south buffaloes, 'ugly, stubborn, and sometimes mischievous Animals', often took the place of mules; and in swampy areas both animals and carriages had to be abandoned for boats in which passengers were 'rowed through lines of willows' until dry land was reached again. In all areas there were either ferries to be paid for or fords to be negotiated. Crossing one deep ford in Piedmont, the guides had to 'wade naked up to their waists on each side of the carriage, feeling their way with poles. If any person be lost the guides are hanged without mercy. Yet their pay, as fixed by Government, is very low, three pence for each passage. All travellers, who have the least spark of Generosity, give them much more.'

In the Apennines the roads were as bad as they were anywhere, even on main routes. The way between Bologna and Florence, running 'over several ranges of mountains', so Addison discovered, was the worst road of any in that region. It was, in fact, 'So Incommodious for wheel-carriages,' Nugent advised, 'that those who travel [on it] choose either litters or mules, because of being obliged so often to alight and walk a-foot, rather than the calashes, in which they travel in the plain country.'

The calashes themselves were uncomfortable enough. The best of them, like the English carriages with which Mariana Starke suggested that every traveller in Italy who could afford one ought to provide himself, were 'strong, low-hung, double-perched with well-seasoned corded springs, iron axle-trees and two drag chains with iron shoes'. Drawn by two horses, they accommodated two people inside and two trunks behind. But in the worst and oldest carriages, as Goethe found, you 'were tossed about as you would have been centuries ago'.

The most satisfactory method of travelling was, as many tourists learned by experience, under the direction and with the help of a *vetturino* who drove the carriage, looked after the horses and acted generally as guide and courier. He and his client settled upon a fixed sum to include meals and accommodation, and usually tips, on the way.

Some travellers considered *vetturini* 'perfect pests'. Hazlitt complained that

they bargain to provide you for a certain sum, then billet you for as little as they can upon the innkeepers . . . who consider you as common prey, receive you with incivility, keep out of the way, will not deign you an answer, stint you in the quantity of your provisions, poison you by the quality, order you into their worst apartments, force other people into the same room or even bed with you, keep you in a state of continual irritation and annoyance all the time you are in the house.

But this was a rare verdict.

'Travelling with a *vetturino* is unquestionably the pleasantest way of seeing

Italy,' wrote Bayard Taylor, expressing a more common opinion. 'The easy rate of the journey allows time for becoming well acquainted with the country, and the tourist is freed from the annoyance of quarelling with cheating landlords.' James Edward Smith was equally satisfied with the arrangements he made with a *vetturino* to conduct him and a friend from Pisa to Florence, 'forty-nine miles, for fifty *pauls* (not twenty-five shillings), to be fed by the way into the bargain'. 'We were excellently accommodated,' Smith added, 'and we made use of this same honest fellow to carry us over most parts of Italy. We never had a word of dispute all the way.'

Travelling in the care of a *vetturino* was, however, slow – Smith covered no more than four miles an hour on his way to Florence, while others, Shelley among them, sometimes progressed no more than three. Also, the arrangement did not allow for diversions from the route, or for a day or two's sojourn in places which caught the tourist's fancy. It was for this reason that Goethe condemned the method as 'sorry travelling', believing that it was 'always best to travel at one's ease on foot', as he himself did when he walked from Ferrara to Pisa.

Those in a hurry – as so many always were – were recommended either to ride post-horses, to hire or buy their own carriage, or to travel by *cambiatura* where there was such a system. In Nugent's day the *cambiatura* operated 'in the ecclesiastical state, in Tuscany and the dutchies of Parma and Modena'. The price was 'generally at the rate of two *julios* a horse each post'. 'The greatest conveniency of this way of travelling,' in Nugent's experience, 'is that you may stop where you please, and change your horses or calash at every *cambiatura*, without being obliged to pay for their return; and, besides, you may take what time you please to satisfy your curiosity.'

As in France, a journey by water was sometimes preferred to one by land. Feluccas constantly plied between Rome or Ostia and Naples, taking about twenty-four hours, provided the wind was fair. Inland, it was possible to go from Ferrara to Bologna by canal, and thence to Venice, 'a voyage of eighty miles up the Po, and Adige, the Brenta and the Lagoons'.

The *burcello* in which the traveller made the last stage of this journey was 'sufficiently luxurious, with its mirrors, carpets and glass doors' and its pretty central room 'adorn'd with carving, gilding and painting'. It was 'drawn down the Brenta with one horse to Fusino, the entrance into the Lagune; and from thence to Venice, hawl'd along by another boat [called] a *Remulcio*, with four or six rowers'. But other boats, apart from those available for expensive private hire, were far from comfortable. James Edward Smith, 'after a confused kind of supper', was laid, 'or rather piled', with other passengers on an arrangement of mattresses spread haphazardly over 'chests, bales, and everything that could be thought of'. Arthur Young on his way to Bologna found the food and conditions aboard even more unappealing that Smith had done: 'The skipper takes snuff, wipes his nose with his fingers, cleans his knife with his handkerchief at the same time as he is preparing the food he offers you.'

109

The food the tourist was likely to be offered at many of the inns on his route was often just as unappetising. Indeed, the appalling discomfort and inedible meals provided at inns all over Italy called constantly for bitter complaint year after year, generation after generation. Italian inns of the eighteenth century did have their defenders. 'The little country inns are dirty,' John Chetwode Eustace conceded, but he went on to say, 'The greater inns, particularly in Rome, Naples, Florence and Venice are good, and in general the linen is clean, and the beds are excellent. As for diet, in country towns the traveller will find plenty of provisions, though seldom prepared according to his taste.'

The meat might not be as good as it was at home, other tourists thought, yet while dishes were cooked in a way that took some getting used to, Italian food had much to be said for it. On the Brenta, Adam Walker had fish cooked in oil for the first time and found it 'much better than [he] had expected', and at Milan he enjoyed

an excellent dinner of plump fowls, tolerable boiled beef, and the delicious small birds called *Bechia Fecchi*; and for the first time since we entered Italy, had a boat of melted butter to our greens. This was a great treat. . . . At the better inns we seldom sit down to less than a dozen dishes (half of which we cannot eat) and a dessert of peaches, pears, and delicious grapes. . . . The fish from the Mediterranean are very good — fine lobsters, plaice, sardines, mullets, etc. . . . I never saw such large and beautiful apples, melons, pompions, nor such quantities and variety of fine grapes.

It was just not true that the inns of Italy were 'detestable', wrote Charles de Brosses. 'One is very well entertained in the better towns. In the villages, to be sure, one is badly off; but that is no marvel, it is the same in France.' And James Edward Smith, in defending the 'poor traduced inns of Italy', mentioned the damp sheets he encountered in a little village twenty-two miles from Viterbo as his only experience of them in the entire country, where he had not discovered dirty sheets anywhere. In the north of Italy generally, Smith added, he found the innkeepers 'honest enough to be trusted, at least so much as only to ask the price of accommodation on entering', and, even if that precaution were neglected, he was 'seldom imposed upon'. Some inns left their charges to the discretion of their guests, and in such places it was as well to be travelling with an Italian. Smith himself travelled to Genoa with an Italian count and recalled, 'When we came to pay our bill in the morning, I was surprised to find no demand made but the whole left to the discretion of my companion, who paid in all, for himself and for me, much less perhaps than I should have paid alone; as was the case all the way

49 A posthouse in the hills above Florence, by William Marlow.

to Genoa. Such is the advantage of travelling under the protection of an inhabitant of the country.'

Dr Moore was another traveller who considered Italian inns to be less unpleasant than they were supposed to be. He attributed the average Englishman's 'fretting at Italian beds, fuming against Italian cooks, and execrating every poor little Italian flea' that he met with on the road, to his extreme ill humour at having been 'so ill advised as to come so far from home'. Nor were good inns necessarily expensive. Thomas Martyn said that even in Venice, 'not the cheapest place in Italy to live in', it was perfectly possible to find a good room for less than 10d a day, while a 'genteel apartment and dinner' might be had for less than 5s a day. At 'Kennets a very good English publick house, but more like a lodging', Richard Pococke paid no more than 1s 6d a night.

But these were lonely voices drowned in a torrent of disapproval. Needless to say, Smollett found fault everywhere, venturing to say that convicts in London prisons were 'more cleanly and commodiously lodged' than he and his companions were on certain roads in Tuscany where the inns were 'abominably nasty and generally destitute of provision'. 'When eatables were found, we were almost poisoned by their cookery; their beds were without curtains on bedstead, and their windows without glass.' Yet the bills were 'outrageous'. 'I repeat it again; of all the people I ever knew, the Italians are the most villainously rapacious.' Cantankerous as Smollett was, numerous other travellers vied with him in vituperation. In the words of Dr Sharp:

Give what scope you please to your fancy, you will never imagine half the disagreeableness that Italian beds, Italian cooks, Italian post-houses, Italian postilions, and Italian nastiness offer to an Englishman in an Italian journey. At Turin, Milan, Venice, Rome, and, perhaps, two or three other towns, you meet with good accommodation; but no words can express the wretchedness of the other inns. No other bed but one of straw, and next to that a dirty sheet, sprinkled with water, and, consequently, damp; for covering you have another sheet, as coarse as the first, and as coarse as one of your kitchen jack-towels, with a dirty coverlet. The bedsted consists of four wooden forms, or benches. An English Peer and Peeress must lye in this manner, unless they carry an upholsterer's shop with them. There are, by the bye, no such things as curtains, and hardly, from Venice to Rome, that cleanly and most useful invention, a privy; so that what should be collected and buried in oblivion, is forever under your nose and eyes.

The crockery and cloths set on the table, Sharp continued in mounting indignation, were filthy; the food was vile, the butter 'so rancid it cannot be touched'; the numbers of bugs, fleas, gnats and lice were infinite. Others complained of beds that were broken as well as damp and dirty, of mattresses filled with wet leaves, potatoes or even peach stones, of ceilings covered with spiders, of meals cooked in such a manner 'that a Hottentot could not have beheld them without loathing'.

At Capua the inn was 'so miserable' that the best room and bed in it would have provoked an English footman to 'grievous outcry'; the wine was 'intolerable, the bread ill-baked, the oil rotten', the victuals non-existent except for pigeons. At an inn of comparable atrociousness between Spoleto and Florence the rooms were 'dismal and dirty beyond all description'. In the main room in the inn at Parma – a house so uncommonly bad that 'all one could do was laugh at it' – there was an altar with a picture of a man being flayed alive. The Hotel di San Marco, supposedly the best in Piacenza, provided dinners which were 'scarcely eatable [having] a great profusion of oil but a general taste of dirt'; at Carrara the few inns were still 'only fit for labourers' a century after Fynes Moryson had pronounced them so; near Turin a traveller was still likely to pay an enormous price, as Peter Mundy had done, for 'an egg, a frog and bad wine'; at Tenda the only inn was 'frightful, black, filthy and stinking' without a single window pane; at Bologna, the Tre Maureti was nothing but 'an appalling hovel'; in Venice, where prices were unusually high, a guest at the Scudo di Francia, 'a celebrated hotel', was likely to be asked twenty sequins a month 'for only two miserable little rooms' which were unavailable for shorter periods.

The verdicts of Frenchmen were quite as harsh: Father Labat, who chose to sleep on a table in Siena rather than venture into the bug-ridden bed, overheard a servant impertinently reply to guests who complained of a night spent scratching themselves that 'the only bugs in the beds were the ones they had brought with them'; and the Comte de Caylus described the reportedly best inn at Modena as 'unspeakable' and the one at Narni as 'infamous'.

At an inn north of Florence, so Catherine Wilmot reported:

Over sloppy stones, in an atmosphere heavy with indescribable stenches, I felt rather than saw my way to the foot of a stone staircase; this I ascended, and on the floor above found a dusky room, where tableclothes and an odour of frying oil afforded some suggestion of refreshment. My arrival interested nobody; with a good deal of trouble I persuaded an untidy fellow, who seemed to be a waiter, to come down with me and secure my luggage. More trouble before I could find a bedroom; hunting for keys, wandering up and down stone stairs and along pitch-black corridors, sounds of voices in quarrel. The room itself was utterly depressing – so bare, so grimy, so dark.

Faced with the prospect of spending a night in places such as these, travellers eagerly welcomed invitations to stay in a private house. Yet accepting private hospitality could be as expensive as staying in a hotel, since the payment of vails to servants was almost universally expected. In London at the beginning of the eighteenth century, tipping servants was also what one foreign visitor described as a 'considerable expense'. 'If you take a meal with a person of rank, you must give every one of the five or six footmen a coin when leaving. They will be arranged in file in the hall, and the least you can give them is one shilling each, and should you fail to do this, you will be treated insolently the next time.' Later in the century, however, the custom began to die out, and by 1771 was said not to be suffered 'in any genteel families'. But it was long afterwards continued in Italy, where not only was a tip solicited by the servants after a meal but in some houses was demanded by 'a multitude of domestics' from guests who had not been offered so much as a drink. In Rome, Montesquieu complained, 'You go to see a man: immediately his servants come to ask you for money, often even before you have seen him. Men better dressed than I have often asked me for alms. In short, all this rabble is constantly after you.'

Nor was it only servants who were constantly demanding tips. 'You cannot find a man who does not ask you for money,' Montesquieu continued in Verona. 'A shoemaker asks for alms after selling you a pair of shoes; a man who has sold you a book asks for the *buonamano*; the man who tells you the way or a piece of news asks for a reward.' A bargain already struck did not preclude a subsequent request for further payment: 'A man with whom you have made a bargain for a *louis* would find it very odd if he was not given an *ecu* for a tip when he carried it out.' Having tipped some porters a guinea with which they seemed perfectly well satisfied, Edward Gibbon was afterwards asked for an additional payment by one of them because he had lent him a pair of gloves. Nowhere did tips, or rather bribes, change hands more frequently than in custom-houses and frontier posts whenever the slightest irregularity, real or pretended, was discovered in a passport or a proscribed article in a trunk.

In France travellers who removed from their trunks and portmanteaux 'such linen and necessaries' as they might have occasion for upon the road, and had their heavy baggage 'sealed with lead' as they were advised to do at their port of arrival, were usually 'exempted from further visitation'. But in Italy where there were so many independent states, kingdoms, republics and duchies this was not possible; and the traveller was likely to have all his belongings tumbled about repeatedly unless he were sufficiently generous with his *'buona mancia per il signor ufficiale della dogana'*.

As for passports, the tedious and complicated formality of obtaining one to pass from one state or town to the next was matched by the tiresome delays while they were checked and examined by officials who hinted that the whole process might be indefinitely delayed were the customary bribe not to be forthcoming. Nugent cautioned the tourist:

In travelling thro' Italy you should be careful not to be without the passport of some prince, ambassador, or cardinal, by which means you will pass unmolested thro' every city and fortified town. . . . Another advantage of these passports is that on the confines of neighbouring states they are looked upon as a bill of health. . . . It is to be observed, however, that those who have not a passport must take a bill of health at Bologna to enter the Grand Duke's territories, otherwise they will be obliged to return to Bologna.

As well as a passport signed or stamped in the name of an Italian authority, it was advisable also to have one issued by a British consul such as that which William Gunn obtained in 1785 from John Birkbeck, 'his Britannick Majesty's Consul General for Nice', and which requested 'all whom it may concern to permit the bearer hereof . . . an English Gentleman . . . to pass from hence to Genoa and Leghorn'. But no passport was a certain guarantee of uninterrupted passage and regulations were, in any case, constantly changing, particularly in times of war, many towns having ordinances peculiar to themselves. 'When any person arrives here [in Genoa] he must either go himself, or send his own servant [to the town hall], to give in his name, country and station of life. He then receives a billet without which the people of the inn cannot [let him] lie in their house.' A similar regulation applied in Ferrara. Nor did a passport issued in one city necessarily entitle the holder to return to it: a Neapolitan passport, for example, was required to go from Rome to Naples, and another document, to be procured at Naples, in order to return.

Most cities required bills of health in addition to passports, Venice being 'extraordinarily precise herein'. 'When you depart from a city', one experienced traveller advised, 'you must be sure to take a bill of health out of the office that is kept everywhere for that purpose, without which you can hardly get to be admitted into another city, especially if it be in the territory of another prince or state. If any one comes from an infected or suspected place, he is forced to keep his quarantain (as they call it) that is, be shut up in the Lazarette or pest-house forty days.'

With his bill of health and his passport in order, his letters of credit and introductions, the tourist set off from Turin on his *giro d'Italia*. He might, perhaps, make first for Venice, hoping to arrive there while the carnival was still in progress, and going by way of Milan, Bergamo, Brescia, Verona, Vicenza and Padua.

Although there were 'a great many excellent paintings to be seen' there, in the words of Thomas Nugent who proceeded to list two full pages of Titians, Baroccis, Leonardos, Raphaels, Caraccis, Gallitias, Bassanos, Ceranis and Renos, Milan did not detain the tourist long. He was expected to see the theatre, of course (the largest in the world), the Brera Palace and the Ambrosian Library with its huge collections of books and manuscripts, its medals, antique sculpture and the mechanical drawings of Leonardo da Vinci, who had settled in Milan in 1482. And even the most perfunctory sightseer would at least stroll through the Gothic Cathedral – the largest church in Europe after St Peter's and the cathedral in Seville – work on which had started in 1386 and was still not finished five centuries later.

This cathedral, built of 'white polished Marble both inside and outside', struck Catherine Wilmot as being more beautiful than anything she had seen in her life, though she thought the gullible friar who acted as guide – relating the 'most extravagant miracles' of a saint, one of whose teeth, set in diamonds and framed in gold and mother of pearl, was set above the altar of his silver-panelled chapel – was a perfect specimen of a 'wholesale camel-swallower'. Also, the splendour of the interior was much diminished by the crowds of importunate beggars swarming around the foreigners, pestering them with the same relentless persistence as the pimps who, offering 'women of whatever colour and country you want', loitered in every square in the city as well as in the grounds of the Palazzo Sermonetta, where numerous tourists went to hear the famous echo which obliged Addison by repeating the sound of his pistol shot fifty-six times and Boswell by repeating *his* fifty-eight.

50 The Ponte delle Navi spanning the Adige at Verona, by Bellotto.

While he was in Milan, Boswell went to the opera where the singers 'seemed slovenly' and he was disgusted to see the 'blackguard boys' who held the sweeping trains of the ladies letting them go from time to time so that they could scratch their heads or blow their noses. He was thankful to get away to Piacenza where he was amused to see in the market place sparrows sitting and chirping on the fiercer of 'two equestrian statues of Dukes of Parma' and where he was impressed by 'one fine street, a new elegant church by Vignola, and the Cathedral' in which he found 'many good pictures'.

Neither Bergamo nor Brescia elicited much comment from most tourists; nor did Verona which they hurried through, even though Mrs Piozzi thought it the gayest town she had ever lived in. But then came Vicenza where the great Andrea Palladio had worked and died, and here, perforce, the good tourist took careful notice of all he saw. Captain John Northall, who arrived here in the 1750s, provided a short, pedestrian description which may be taken as typical:

On the third June we came to Vicenza a small town but very populous, the manufacture of silk being very considerable here. The townhouse was built by Palladio and here is a beautiful piece of architecture by the same, a theatre built after the antique manner. Near this town is a famous country seat [the Villa Rotonda] belonging to the Marquis of Capra by Palladio.

The work of Palladio and of Vincenzo Scamozzi had by then been long admired by cognoscenti in England, by Inigo Jones, who had travelled widely in Italy where he threw himself deeply into the theory and philosophy of the classical style, and by Inigo Jones's near-contemporary, John Evelyn, who, on his visit to Vicenza in 1646, wrote enthusiastically of the master's works, of the Teatro Olimpico – of its kind 'the most perfect now standing in all the World' – and of the 'well built Palaces' with which this 'sweete Town' was better supplied than any other 'of its dimensions in all Italy'. 'I would now very faine have visited a Palace call'd the Rotunda,' Evelyn lamented, 'but one of our Companions hasting to be gon, and little minding anything save drinking & folly, caused us to take coach sooner than we should.'

After Evelyn's day no Grand Tour was considered complete without a visit to Vicenza to see the works of Palladio, and to his villas along the Brenta, which were to have so profound an influence on the architecture of England and the United States. When the third Earl of Burlington, the eighteenth century's leading patron and high priest of Palladianism, set out upon his first continental tour in 1714 neither Colen Campbell's *Vitruvius Britannicus* nor Nicholas Dubois's translation of Leoni's *The Architecture of A. Palladio* had been published; and Burlington passed through Vicenza in a hurry without spending a single night there. But while he was abroad both the translation of Leoni's book and the first

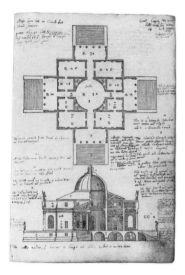

Veduta del Palazzo del N.H. Grimani.

51 (Left) Inigo Jones's annotations on his copy of Palladio's Quattro libri dell' architettura. *Inigo Jones, who travelled widely in Europe in the late sixteenth and early seventeenth centuries, introduced the Palladian style to England.*

52 (Right) The palace of the Grimani family overlooking the Brenta between Venice and Padua.

volume of Campbell's appeared, and soon after Burlington's return Campbell – whose book strongly advocated a return to 'antique simplicity' in the manner of Inigo Jones – was called in to replace James Gibbs in the reconstruction of Burlington House, Piccadilly to designs based upon the Palazzo Porto at Vicenza.

While work was still in progress on Burlington House, Burlington left for Italy again, this time specifically to study the buildings of Palladio in Venezia and to buy whatever drawings and manuscripts of the master might be on the market, as well as to bring back musicians from Italy for an academy of music which he intended to inaugurate in London with Handel as first director and Paolo Rolli as librettist. By November 1719 Burlington was back in Vicenza, where he bought one of the several copies of Palladio's *Quattro Libri dell' Architettura* (1570) later to be found in the library at Chiswick House, the villa which Burlington, strongly influenced by both Palladio and Scamozzi, built to display his works of art and to entertain his friends.

While he was in Vicenza, Burlington carefully examined the Villa Capra, which was to have so pervasive an influence on Palladian houses in England, and was deeply moved by the 'ornaments and exquisite taste that is in the most minute part of it'. He also studied in exact detail the Villa Foscari, now the Malcontenta, on the right bank of the Brenta, the Palazzi Chiericati and Iseppo di Porti, and the Palazzo Thiene of which he wrote, 'If any of Palladio his designs, can claim a preference to the rest, this in my opinion has the best rule in it, it is certainly the most beautiful modern building in the world.'

Burlington's enthusiasm was both infectious and influential, and his patronage was decisive in transforming the taste of those English gentlemen whom he taught, in the words of his protégé, William Kent, to turn their backs upon 'that damned gusto that's been for this sixty years past'. He arranged for the publication of Kent's designs of Inigo Jones, he himself published a widely read edition of Palladio's *Fabbriche Antiche*, and he made it impossible for the conscientious tourist to race through Vicenza as he himself had done on his first visit to the town. He did not, however, command universal agreement. The young Scottish architect, Robert Adam, considered Palladio vastly overrated. 'I walked out to see the different buildings of Palladio with which [Vicenza] abounds and of which I am no admirer,' he wrote. 'He is one of those fortunate geniuses who has purchased reputation at an easy rate. I am now fully satisfied that I have it in my power to say that I have seen his works here, but by no means incline to spend more time on him.' Adam himself was, in later years, to have a profound influence on English taste when the rage for Palladianism had abated.

Although there was another fine example of Palladio's work at Padua, the church of S. Giustina, which Evelyn described as 'incomparable', Padua did not much recommend itself to eighteenth-century tourists, few of whom even bothered to look at Giotto's frescoes, having little interest in mediaeval art. In the sixteenth and seventeenth centuries there had always been numerous Englishmen in the town, many of them attending the university. Fynes Moryson, himself one of its students, had been happy in Padua and spoke well of the inhabitants' kindness and honesty:

The Hostesse dresseth your meat in the bargaine for your chamber, and findes you napkins, tablecloths, sheetes and towels; and either in your chest or her owne, will lay up the meat and the very bread you leave. . . . And little boyes attend in the market with baskets, who for a *soll* will carry home the meat you buy, and dare not deceive you though you goe not with them.'

The Scottish traveller William Lithgow, however, found Padua far less attractive. Indeed, it was, in his opinion, the 'most melancholy city in Europe'. As for the university, the students were notorious not only for their violence but also for 'beastly Sodomy', which was as 'rife here as in Rome, Naples, Florence, Bologna, Venice, Ferrara, Genoa, Parma not being excepted, nor yet the smallest village of Italy: A monstrous filthiness, and yet to them a pleasant pastime, making songs, and singing sonnets of the beauty and pleasure of their *Bardassi*, or buggered boys.' Later commentators do not mention Padua's reputation for homosexuality. In fact, despite the reputation that Italy had in England as a hotbed of sodomy, the English traveller seems rarely to have noticed much evidence of it anywhere; and the case of Richard Cresswell, a former Member of Parliament, who was arrested in Genoa in 1716 for thirty-eight homosexual offences 'in his own house, the streets, in porches of Churches and Palaces', was a rare one indeed. Eighteenth-century tourists were, though, almost universal in their condemnation of Padua, whose university had lost its reputation, noting the grass growing in the streets, the crumbling stonework, the peeling paint. 'It is badly built,' wrote the Comte de Caylus, dismayed by its 'very poverty-stricken appearance'; 'its houses lack any trace of beauty and it is extraordinarily badly paved'. In the late eighteenth century it was celebrated for its bullfights, but these were usually depressing spectacles.

The eleven-year-old Elizabeth Wynne recorded in her diary in February 1791:

Papa had bought a window for to go to see the Bull fighting. I went their was about ten oxen for which they send the dogs after than they cut the head of a poor Oxen very badly indeed, however after come a Bull wich killed two dogs on the spot and all the others were slew, all this was very cruel. . . . Today we had an example of poverty and misery which are at Padua. Whilst at our lessons we heard a lamentable voice, we ran to the window and saw a little boy who was naked but for a little petticoat. He cried for the cold. We gave him some clothes.

Most tourists were as thankful as the two young daughters of Richard Wynne were to turn their back on the town and, with mounting excitement, to step aboard the *burchio* to go down the Brenta to Venice.

53 The Brenta Canal at Padua in about 1740 by Canaletto.

CHAPTER 7

*

VENICE

*

'The brothel of Europe'

TO GLIDE INTO THE LAGOON IN THE EVENING and to see the city illuminated by the dying rays of the sun was to 'enter another world'. The rich William Beckford, stretched beneath the awning of a gondola, passed smoothly over the waters one August evening in 1780, looking across at the distant domes and towers. The air was still, the sky cloudless, a light wind rippled the surface of the sea as it lapped gently against the steps of a chapel on an island shaded by a garden wall overhung with pines and fig-trees:

We were now drawing very near the city, and a confused hum began to interrupt the evening stillness; gondolas were continually passing and repassing, and the entrance of the canal Reggio, with all its stir and bustle, lay before us. Our gondoliers turned with much address through a crowd of boats and barges that blocked up the way, and rowed smoothly by the side of a pavement, covered with people in all dresses and of all nations. Leaving the Palazzo Pesaro . . . we were soon landed before the Leon Bianco [the celebrated hotel where many English stayed at great expense] which being situated in one of the broadest parts of the Grand Canal, commands a most striking assemblage of buildings. I have no terms to describe the variety of pillars, of pediments, of mouldings, and cornices, some Grecian, others Saracenical, that adorn these edifices, of which the pencil of Canaletti conveys so perfect an idea as to render all verbal description superfluous. At one end of this grand scene of perspective appears the Rialto; the sweep of the canal conceals the other.

The rooms of our hotel are as spacious and cheerful as I could desire. . . . [From the balcony I observed] as well as the dusk would permit, the variety of figures shooting by in their gondolas. As night approached, innumerable tapers glimmered through the awnings before the windows. Every boat had its lantern, and the gondolas moving rapidly along were followed by tracks of light, which gleamed and played upon the waters. I was gazing at these dancing fires when the sounds of music were wafted along the canals, and as they grew louder and louder, an illuminated barge, filled with musicians, issued from the Rialto . . . the gondoliers, catching the air, imitated its cadences, and were echoed by others at a distance. . . . I retired to rest, full of the sound; and long after I was asleep, the melody seemed to be in my ear.

Before five o'clock the next morning, Beckford was awakened by a loud din of voices and by sounds of splashing beneath his balcony. Looking out, he saw

54 (Opposite above) The fourth Earl of Manchester arrives in Venice in 1707, by Luca Carlevaris, a precursor of Canaletto.

55 (Centre) The entrance to the Arsenal by Guardi, c.1758.

56 (Below) Canaletto's view of the Campo SS Giovanni e Paolo with Verocchio's statue of the condottiere Bartolomeo Colleoni and the Scuola di San Marco to the left of the church.

57 *A courtesan by Fuseli, one of many 'dressed in the gayest colours,*
with their breasts open, and their faces bedaubed with paint'.

*58 The Piazza San Marco with the Basilica and the Doge's Palace on the right
as portrayed by Canaletto from the Bacino.*

the Grand Canal so entirely covered with fruit and vegetables, on rafts and in barges, that he could scarcely distinguish a ripple of water. 'Loads of grapes, peaches and melons arrived, and disappeared in an instant, for every vessel was in motion; and crowds of purchasers, hurrying from boat to boat, formed one of the liveliest pictures imaginable.' Among the crowds he noticed several figures 'whose dress and carriage announced something above the common rank' and was later told that these were 'noble Venetians, just come from their casinos, and met to refresh themselves with fruit, before they retired to sleep for the day'.

Beckford himself bought some grapes and bread, hired a gondola and was rowed under the Rialto and down the Grand Canal to the marble steps of Baldassare Longhena's lovely church of Santa Maria della Salute which had been built on 1,156,627 wooden piles driven into the mud to commemorate the end of a plague in 1630. From there he was 'wafted across the waves to the spacious platform' in front of Palladio's church of San Giorgio Maggiore, which he thought 'by far the most perfect and beautiful edifice' had had ever seen.

Putting up an umbrella, he then lay in its shade to savour the view towards the Doge's Palace, the tall columns at the entrance of the Piazza San Marco, 'the arcades of the public library, the lofty Campanile, and the cupolas of the ducal church, one of the most striking groups of buildings that art can boast of'. Along the Riva degli Schiavoni gondolas bobbed about in the water, their vermilion oars and shining ornaments in striking contrast to the black paintwork; and senators and magistrates in long black robes walked up and down between the crowds in their more colourful clothes as 'aged devotees [crept] to their devotions'.

For the next few days, Beckford wandered happily about Venice, enjoying the incomparable delights that the city had to offer, venturing into the most 'curious and murky quarters of the city', down alleys and canals, prying through porches and into doorways, contemplating the gardens of the Giudecca, visiting Murano, Burano and Torcello and the other islands, walking round churches and finding SS. Giovanni e Paolo, 'a church to be held most holy in the annals of painting', decorated for a festival, its huge Gothic pillars covered with red damask and its shrines of saints glimmering with tapers. He inspected the paintings of Titian, of Tintoretto and Veronese, he was taken around palaces and he visited 'the Mendicanti, one of the four *conservatorios*, which give the best musical education conceivable to near one hundred young women' – the others being the Incurabili, the Ospedaletto, and the Pietà where Vivaldi had been *maestro di cappella* until shortly before his death in 1741, all of them orphanages for female foundlings and centres of Venetian musical life.

He crossed the Bridge of Sighs, his fancy 'haunted by horrors and dismal prospects'; he refreshed himself with the 'cool air and cheerful scenery' of the Fondamente Nuove; he admired the 'bronze and gold horses that adorn the chief

59 (Left) The colonnade of the Procuratorie Nuove, with the Basilica San Marco and the campanile, *by Canaletto.*

60 (Right) Acrobatic gondoliers performing on a raised platform during a festival in the Piazzetta.

portal' of San Marco, and Scamozzi's 'exquisitely wrought' range of the Procuratie Nuove which he attributed to Sansovino who did, indeed, design the library which adjoins it at the angle of the Piazzetta; he climbed the steps of Palladio's masterpiece, the church of the Redentore, 'a structure so simple and elegant' that he thought himself 'entering an antique temple and looked about for the statue of the God of Delphi'; he was 'struck with awe' on looking up at the Campanile, and enchanted by the beauty of the building that decorated its base, 'the Loggetta which serves as a guard-house during the convocation of the Grand Council'; and he explored the Doge's Palace and the Cathedral from which he was driven out into the piazza by the 'vile stench' which emanated 'from every recess and corner of the edifice' and which the incense from all the altars could not subdue.

That was the trouble with Venice, most tourists had to agree. It was variously described as 'a stinkpot, charged with the very virus of hell', as 'more noisome than a pigstye', as 'filthy' (by Gibbon and Goethe), as 'poisonous' (by Charles de Brosses), and as cursed by 'nauseous air' (by Walpole). John Howard, the prison reformer, with thoughts of gaol fever in mind, advised a young man who was staying in the same house as himself not to remain in Venice longer than four days. 'The very stairs are like a sink,' wrote Baron von Archenholz of the Doge's Palace. 'Go where you will, you will find whole rills of stinking water, and smell its noxious exhalations. The nobles, who honestly contribute their share, never regard these nuisances, and paddle through them with uplifted gowns.'

61 A concert given by the girls of one of Venice's foundling hospitals where they had 'the best musical education conceivable'.

62 (Opposite) A young Venetian lady painted in her domino and tricorne by Tiepolo, c.1760.

63 (Left) A portrait painter at work in about 1750, by Pietro Longhi, master of Venetian genre.
64 (Right) A masked reception in a courtyard in 1755 by Longhi.

The Cathedral, castigated by James Edward Smith as 'perhaps the most dirty place of public worship in Europe, except the Jews' synagogue at Rome', was also condemned for its architecture, its 'barbarous, inelegant style'. It was generally considered to be 'much too dark and dismal', to have 'nothing to recommend it but its great antiquity and the vast riches of the building'; it was constructed in an 'absurd old Gothic style', yet not really 'what we call Gothic nor regular'.

It is a church in the Greek style [wrote Charles de Brosses, expressing the general view], low, inpenetrable to the light, in wretched taste both within and without, surmounted by seven domes covered with gold mosaic which makes them seem far more like cauldrons than cupolas. . . . One can see nothing so pitiable as these mosaics. Happily the workmen had the wise precaution to inscribe on each subject what they wished to represent.

Indeed, apart from its Arsenal – and even that was now but a shadow of the exciting, noisy, bustling place that John Evelyn had admired – Venice was usually then enjoyed not so much for its treasures and architecture (Palladio's, Scamozzi's and Sansovino's work apart) as for its people. The city itself, in Gibbon's estimation, consisted of 'old and in general ill-built houses, ruined pictures and stinking ditches . . . a fine bridge [the Rialto] spoilt by two rows of houses upon it, and a large square decorated with the worst architecture [he] ever saw'. Richard Pococke described it in his simple way as 'a city you know as it were in the sea, an odd place'. He did not like the look of it. The 'Plazza at St Mark [was] the only pleasing thing that's obvious'.

The cosmopolitan crowds to be seen thronging every *calle* in the centre of the city were, however, irresistible.

In the evening [wrote John Moore] there generally is on St Marks place, such a mixed multitude of Jews, Turks, and Christians; lawyers, knaves, and pick-pockets; mountebanks, old women and physicians; women of quality with masks; strumpets barefaced; and, in short, such a jumble of senators, citizens, gondoliers and people of every character and condition, that your ideas are broke, bruised and dislocated in the crowd, in such a manner that you can think, or reflect on nothing, yet this being a state of mind which many people are fond of, the place never fails to be well attended and in fine weather numbers pass a great part of the night there. When the piazza is illuminated and the shops in the adjacent streets are lighted up, the whole has a brilliant effect; and, as it is the custom for the ladies, as well as the gentlemen, to frequent the casinos and coffee houses around, the place of St Mark answers all the purposes of either Vauxhall or Ranelagh.

65 (Left) The marble Scala dei Giganti in the Doge's Palace, 'a lovely though foetid stairway' leading from the courtyard to the council chambers and apartments of the Doge.

66 (Right) Rosalba Carriera's portrait of Horace Walpole, who was twenty-one when he embarked on his Grand Tour in 1739.

William Beckford, who enjoyed the sights of Venice far more than most of his contemporaries, also delighted 'in the strollers and the mountebanks, singing and scaramouching in the middle of the square', the Orientals, the Turks and Arabs muttering in every corner, the Armenian priests and jewellers, the Dalmatians, the Russians, Greeks and Slavs mingling with the Italians. 'Had St Mark's Church been the wondrous tower, and its piazza the chief square of the city of Babylon,' he thought, 'there could scarcely have been a greater confusion of languages.' Among the minstrels and rope-dancers, the fortune-tellers and magicians, strolled the Venetians themselves – the Doge, wearing purple silk trimmed with ermine, a cloak of cloth of gold, horn-shaped hat, jewelled belt and painted sandals; the nobles in their silk and fur-lined ankle-length togas, coloured black, red, cream or violet according to their rank; the ladies, no longer wearing those enormously high clogs, described by Evelyn as 'great scaffolds' that made them half as tall again as other passers-by, yet still with long, scented hair, streaked with unnatural colours, or in wigs, their painted faces almost entirely concealed by veils, their bejewelled breasts thrown forward by high, tight stays, their fingernails very long. Walking past them were workers on their way to lace shops, glass factories and places where they made furniture, metalwork and pottery; and courtesans 'dressed in the gayest colours', as Nugent described them, 'with their breasts open, and their faces bedaubed with paint'.

In such crowds as these it was never necessary for a stranger to ask the way, for as Fynes Moryson discovered, and as visitors find four hundred years later, 'if hee will follow the presse of people hee shall be sure to be brought to the market place of Saint Marke or that of Rialto'. The crowds were as thick by night as by day. J.B.S. Morritt, the rich young owner of Rokeby Hall in Yorkshire, who was in Venice in 1794, told his brother how much he enjoyed gliding about in the skilfully manoeuvred gondolas, 'the nicest lounging carriages possible, though, from their all being black, they look a good deal like hearses laid on a long canoe'. But the hours of the Venetians' amusements were 'insufferable'. 'We find it a great bore to go to the opera, which does not begin till eleven and lasts till three or four; and what do you think must be the spirit of the public balls which are given after the opera sometimes? Now I could forgive people's turning water into land, but when they come so completely to turn night into day they make too great a change in the old system.'

Venice was never more crowded or more lively, or more 'infested with English', as Lady Mary Wortley Montagu put it, than it was at the time of the carnival when the city was crammed with thirty thousand visitors, when a tourist wearing

67 (Opposite) Distinguished guests at a banquet on 9 September 1755 in a Venetian palazzo, the Casa Nani.

S.A.R. Clemente Augusto Elettore di Colonia

Questa si rara e nobil disfata Cena
Dier i Veneti Cuori al Colono,
Nella gloria e stupor d'Adria, il Pare,
E alta sua il più inmaginosi ripeta

Atti 9 Servitio entro nel Palazzo

Nani alle Gondeze

68 Rowlandson caricatures a group of tourists in conversation in Venice in the 1790s.

a white or black mask was welcome almost anywhere, when there were bullfights and acrobatic displays in the Piazza San Marco, boxing and wrestling tournaments, wild beast shows and ceremonial processions; when there were dances, fireworks and gambling parties in the evenings; and at all times masquerades at which the inhabitants 'forget all marks of distinction, and resign themselves up to joy and liberty, frequently attended with folly and great disorder'.

Indeed, the carnival had changed little since the middle of the seventeenth century, when John Evelyn described it thus:

The Women, Men & persons of all Conditions disguising themselves in antique dresses, & extravagant Musique & a thousand gambols, & traversing the streetes from house to house, all places then accessible, & free to enter: There is abroad nothing but flinging of Eggs fill'd with sweete Waters, & sometimes not over sweete; they also have a barbarous costume of hunting bulls about the Streetes & Piazzas, which is very dangerous, the passages being generally so narrow in that City: Likewise do the youth of the severall Wards & parishes contend in other Masteries or pastimes (fighting each other on the bridges) so as tis altogether impossible to recount the universal madnesse of this place during this time of licence: Now are the greate banks set up for those who will play at Basset, the Comedians have also liberty & the *Operas* to Exercise: Witty pasquils are likewise thrown about, & the Mountebanks have their stages in every Corner: The diversion which chiefly tooke me up, was three noble *Operas* which I saw, where was incomparable Voices, & Musique.

69 The parlatorio *of one of Venice's convents, some of which were regarded more as finishing schools than religious institutions.*

In Venice with their parents in 1790, Elizabeth and Eugenia Wynne also enjoyed the opera to which they went almost every day. 'Went to the opera at St Benetto,' Elizabeth recorded in her journal on 15 February, 'and run about the boxes always masked in the Italian fashion. They made a great furore for Mrs Banti they throwed verses in her praise, Peacocks, Pols, Pigeons and golden rain was thrown to. They made us a present of three pigeons.' Her twelve-year-old sister's diary records for that same day:

Dressed very soon [as] a Shepherdess. Stoped very long for our *Cavalier Servants* which are the sons of the Embassador of france. Walked in the place of St Marc. . . . Papa was dressed in weomen's clothes. . . . There was a great quantity of people. . . . We see a little girl with to faces and behind she is as well formed as any child can be she has got to legs a coming out from her breast for the rest she is very well shaped. . . . There is a man that comes down from the top of the Campanil on St Marc on a rope and gieves a nosguay to the Doge and then they make some very good fireworks.

During the carnival the gambling rooms were as crowded as the piazza and the opera houses, and, so Nugent warned, far more dangerous:

Their gaming houses are called *Ridotti*, apartments in noblemen's houses, where none but noblemen keep the bank, and fools lose their money. They dismiss the gamesters when they please, and always come off winners. There are usually ten or twelve chambers on a floor with gaming-tables in them, and vast crowds of people; a profound silence is observed, and none are admitted without masks. Here you meet ladies of pleasure, and married women who under the protection of a mask enjoy all the diversions of the carnival, but are usually attended by the husband or his spies. Besides these gaming-rooms, there are others for conversation, where wine, lemonade, and sweetmeats are sold. Here the gentlemen are at liberty to rally and address the ladies, but must take care to keep within the bounds of decency, lest they meet with bravoes or assassins.

While foreigners in masks were welcome to these apartments during the carnival, and at other times when they were clearly prepared to lose money, their noble owners were otherwise rarely lavish with their hospitality, not knowing what it meant to offer a meal, complained Charles de Brosses who attended a *conversazione* 'at the Procuratress Foscarini's, a house of enormous wealth', where he discovered that the only refreshments offered were small cups of coffee and a large sliced water-melon, 'a detestable dish if ever there was one'.

At more raffish houses than the Foscarini's the entertainments were less dull than this, yet even the most libertine *ridotti* were not so entertaining as the squares and *calli*, 'the resort of pleasure and dissipation', where, in Beckford's words, anything like restraint seemed 'perfectly out of the question' as parties of revellers and party-goers walked about the pavements, flirted in the porticos, sipped at coffee and sorbets, or engaged in noisy conversations; where courtesans strolled cheerfully and boldly about between the bridges as the city 'grew gayer and gayer as the day declined'; where even the priests wore dominoes and abbés strolled abroad in highly polished shoes with red heels and glittering silver buckles.

Venetian churchmen, indeed, were often as attentive to their dress as laymen, concerned to appear attractive to the ladies who wrote them love letters after listening impatiently to a sermon or after attending a highly theatrical Mass during which they gossiped with each other in their *décolleté* dresses. For religion was never to be taken too seriously: as Pope Gregory XIII said, 'I am Pope everywhere except in Venice.' Papal protests against the conduct of life in convents were, for example, constantly ignored. Nuns were considered to make delightful lovers. The Venetian-born Casanova certainly found them so. One nun he met in the city was a deliciously sensual creature, who enjoyed the bodies of women as well as those of men, and who gave him as much excitement as any girl he had ever

70 (Opposite above) Tiepolo portrays the carnival, a time of great excitement in Venice when the city was 'infested with English'.

71 (Below) Masked visitors to a ridotto, *with gamblers in an inner room, by Guardi.*

known. Another nun fought a duel with an abbess over a mutual lover. A third, Maria da Riva, fell in love with the French ambassador with whom she had so torrid an affair that the Inquisition in Venice, usually readier to find excuses than to condemn, forbade her to see him any more. The prohibition had no effect, so she was exiled to Ferrara where she soon married someone else.

The Inquisition was equally ineffectual in its occasional efforts to prevent Venice's convents from becoming finishing schools for the daughters of wealthy families who could be seen at Mass behind grilles, as Charles de Brosses saw them, laughing and chatting to each other, pretty and animated. They were given lessons, but none too demanding, and they waited for the day when they could catch the eye of a suitable man who would ask an older nun about her and then perhaps take her away to marry her.

Charles de Brosses found the courtesans of Venice as attractive as the nuns. He believed that 'fairies and angels combined' could not have produced such beauties, and he himself made love to at least eight of them. In the early seventeenth century there had been as many as twenty thousand courtesans in the city, Coryate had estimated, 'where of many [were] esteemed so loose that they [opened] their quivers to every arrow'; and in the eighteenth there were still so many of them prepared 'to receive all comers' that Venice had the reputation of being 'the brothel of Europe, the place where you had to beware of 'the four Ps': the *pietra bianca*, the slippery white stone of the steps of the 450 bridges; the *prete*; the *pantaleone*; and, above all, the *putana*, the whore. To protect their sons from 'contracting distempers with common harlots', rich mothers made bargains with poor neighbours whose daughters could be hired as bedfellows for their sons, but this was an arrangement which could scarcely be made by tourists who had to take the risks that Boswell took if they found it impossible to resist the temptations of women who were, in Captain Northall's opinion, the 'most insinuating' and had 'the most alluring arts of any in Italy'.

Having 'wearied of travelling continually by water, shut up in those lugubrious gondolas', having failed to take to bed Chiara Michieli, an attractive middle-aged lady who told him light-heartedly that she would no sooner choose to take a lover for a mere fortnight than a good cook, Boswell's 'fancy was roused by the glittering tales [he] had heard of the Venetian Courtesans'. He 'went to see them' and was proud to record, quoting Horace, that he 'fought, not without glory'. But the wounds of previous campaigns were 'barely healed' when he received fresh ones. 'What is worse,' he told Rousseau, 'my Lord Mountstuart [the young son of the Prime Minister, the Earl of Bute] was of the party. He saw that I was excited and asked what I was up to. I told him I was going to take a look

72 (Opposite) Guests, with masks in hand, waiting to go to a ball.

at the girls, to taste the pleasures and get to know the world, but I begged him not to go. As you can well imagine, we went together. A pretty dancer was our common flame, and my lord catched a Tartar as well as I. A fine piece of witless behaviour. . . . Behold now the steady young man who was to help Lord Mountstuart to improve himself.'

Boswell met Chiara Michieli at the *palazzo* of John Murray, the English Resident, who was almost as compulsive a womaniser as Boswell himself. Casanova said that he looked like a picture of Bacchus by Rubens, while Lady Mary Wortley Montagu maintained that he was 'such a scandalous fellow in every sense of the word' that he was 'not to be trusted to change a sequin'. He had started life as a smuggler and was 'always surrounded with pimps and brokers who [were] his privy councillors'. He had certainly induced his sister to marry Joseph Smith, the retired Consul in Venice, when Smith was over eighty with a view, so it was alleged, of getting his hands on the old man's magnificent collection of books and pictures, sculptures, medals and cameos. Boswell also met John Udney, Smith's successor as Consul, who had once been the lover of John Wilkes's lustful mistress, Gertrude Corradini, and on 14 July 1765 he called at Smith's 'elegant villa' and was introduced to the 'curious old man' himself, then aged ninety-one.

Smith had lived in Venice since he was eighteen and had been appointed Consul in 1744. 'A most lively and entertaining companion', though far from popular, he had entertained a whole generation of English tourists at his *palazzo*, now the Mangilli-Valmarana, opposite the Pescheria on the corner of the Grand Canal and the Rio dei Sant' Apostoli, which, first leased then purchased from the Balbi family, had been rebuilt for Smith to the designs of Antonio Visentini, Canaletto's engraver. Although dismissed by Walpole as 'the merchant of Venice' who knew no more of the books he collected than their title pages, Smith was a discerning virtuoso. He was the patron of Francesco Zuccarelli, of the portraitist Rosalba Carriera (who painted a fine picture of the Earl of Middlesex in Venice in 1737 wearing his mask on his hat), of the brothers Marco and Sebastiano Ricci and, above all, of Canaletto for whom he arranged numerous commissions. He hung examples of his artists' work on the walls of his palace, arranging for travellers to visit their studios and for the artists themselves to visit London, and he did his best to ensure that commissions were completed satisfactorily and on time.

With Canaletto these arrangements were not easily made. Ever since the artist had sold a picture to his first recorded patron, the future second Duke of Richmond, in the early 1720s, Canaletto's pictures were far more widely admired and eagerly sought after than those of his elderly rival, Luca Carlevaris, formerly the most popular depicter of the Venetian scene, who painted from his studio rather than, as Canaletto did, on the spot. And the more successful Canaletto became, the less easy he was to deal with. 'The fellow is whimsical,' the Irish impresario, Owen McSwiny, told the Duke of Richmond in 1727, 'and vary's his prices every day; and he that has a mind to have any of his work, must not seem to be too fond of it, for he'l be ye worse treated for it, both in the price and the painting too. He has more work than he can do in any reasonable time.' This 'covetous, greedy fellow' was so spoiled by the English – who were, according to Charles de Brosses, prepared to pay three times more than he asked – that it became virtually impossible for any other would-be owners of his work to do business with him, and even rich and extravagant Englishmen often found it difficult to obtain the pictures they wanted without Smith's help.

'At last I've got Canal under articles to finish your 2 pieces within a twelvemonth,' runs a characteristic letter from Smith to one English collector. 'He's so much follow'd and all are so ready to pay him his own price for his work (which he vallues himself as much as anybody) that he would be thought in this to have much obliged me.' These two pictures were eventually supplied, and now hang at Tatton Park. Numerous others followed them to England, including the series of twenty-two small and two large canvases now at Woburn Abbey and the pictures from Smith's own collection which were bought by King George III for the Royal Collection.

The tourist who had neither the money nor the patience to buy a Canaletto might purchase a picture by the then less popular Francesco or Gianantonio Guardi. He might also acquire a *veduta* by Canaletto's nephew and assistant, Bernardo Bellotto, or a canvas by a lesser known artist such as Bartolomeo Nazzari, perhaps, as well as books, pieces of glass and silk. And then, having made arrangements to send these purchases home, he continued his journey south.

73 (Above) The Tower at Pisa was as 'perfectly awry' as anyone had a right to expect, but the cathedral, in the Pisan Romanesque style, and the Baptistry were not much admired by the eighteenth-century tourist.

74 (Below) A panoramic view of Florence by Thomas Patch, who lived in the city from 1755 until his death in 1782.

CHAPTER 8

*

ACROSS THE

APENNINES TO

FLORENCE

*

'*A scene of enchantment,
a city planted in a garden*'

TOURISTS WHO HAD GONE STRAIGHT TO Venice from Turin usually left for Florence by way of Ferrara and Bologna and across the Etruscan Apennines; but some chose to visit Venice on their journey home, to cross the Ligurian Apennines to Genoa and then to take the coast road through La Spezia, Viareggio and Pisa, perhaps visiting Lucca, Pistoia and Leghorn on their way to Florence. The journey across the Ligurian Apennines was not, however, to be recommended, certainly not by Charles Burney:

Such bridges! Such rivers! Such rocks! . . . Two days and two nights we were clambering up and sliding or tumbling down these horrid mountains . . . the road always on the very ridge of the mountain and the sea always roaring beneath, with a strong loud wind, which I often thought would have carried me, mule and all, into it. . . . However, at length, about eleven at night, we arrived at a wretched inn or pigsty, half stable and half cowhouse, with a fire but no chimney, surrounded by boors and muleteers, all in appearance cut-throat personages, with no kind of refreshment but cold veal and stinking eggs.

Nor, having crossed the Apennines, did the tourist find much on the coastal route to appeal to him.

Genoa, with its magnificent harbour and fine palaces luxuriating in the shade of orange trees, was admitted to be beautiful. It was 'not without reason', so Smollett thought, 'called *La Superba*'. He praised its stately buildings, its bread, the 'best and whitest' he had ever tasted anywhere, the 'juicy and delicious' meat, the well-stocked shops and markets. The Albergo di Londra was a particularly good hotel, 'a great large-looking house and many attendants'. Matthew Todd and his master 'got very magnificent apartments' there, as 'superb as ever anyone witnessed'. On asking for 'a Temple of Ease' they were 'conducted to a most magnificent one . . . beautifully clean [though] not much calculated for cold weather, as it was entirely of white marble'. In the morning they had a very good breakfast of coffee and eggs, and for dinner, which was 'well served up', they had 'soup with cheese in it, boil'd fowl, roasted potatoes, beefsteak and fried potatoes and onions, green peas, a lobster, some small birds, an apple pie and 5 or 6 plates of fruit'. The next day, having looked around the town and had another excellent meal including rice soup, beefsteaks, sweetbreads, roast chicken, trout, veal cutlets, 'green peas and a large sausage, apple pie and several dishes of fruit', Todd concluded that 'the houses and streets of this town far surpass Paris as well as the living'.

75   The Tribuna in the Uffizi gallery by Zoffany who, beneath the array of paintings on the walls, portrayed numerous English tourists who were in Florence in the 1770s. Sir Horace Mann, the British Minister, is seen wearing a star beside Titian's 'Venus of Urbino'. Sitting down beside him is the Hon. Felton Hervey; holding the picture is Thomas Patch; George, third Earl Cowper, stands at the far left beside 'Cupid and Psyche'. Next to him, wearing a star, is Sir John Dick, British Consul at Leghorn; to his left is the sixth Earl of Plymouth; and, looking round Raphael's Madonna, Zoffany himself. Sitting on the stool is Charles Loraine-Smith, and bending down behind him, Richard Edgcumbe. On the far right, standing with his arms behind his back beneath the 'Venus de Medici', is James Bruce, the African traveller. Standing immediately beneath the right arm of the 'Satyr with the Cymbals' is George Legge, Lord Lewisham.

76 'The Golden Asses', Thomas Patch's largest group painting of Grand Tourists in Florence, 1761.
He painted himself astride the statue of a golden ass on the right.

Walpole and Gray were also much taken with Genoa, where there was no lack of pleasant company, it being much favoured by both French and English as a winter resort. 'We find this place so very fine that we are in fear of finding nothing finer,' Walpole wrote. 'We are fallen in love with the Mediterranean sea, and hold your lakes and rivers in vast contempt.' There was so much to see that Lady Craven wished she could have spent three months here examining the pictures alone. Yet this would have been unwise, some guide-books warned, for the air, like that of Pisa, was 'unwholesome and noxious to strangers', while a prolonged stay might lead to a tourist acquiring an unfortunate accent, since James Howell's

Instruction for Forreine Travel maintained that 'the very worst Italian dialect [was] spoken here'. Furthermore, being a city in decline, Genoa was so crowded with beggars that walking the streets could be an ordeal. 'You are likely,' Mrs Piozzi discovered, 'to feel shocked at having your knees suddenly clasped by a figure hardly human, who, perhaps, holding you forcibly for a minute, conjures you loudly by the sacred wounds of our Lord Jesus Christ to have compassion on his wounds.'

Pisa was also in decline and had about it an air of decay, though it was not, so Smollett said, 'absolutely dilapidated'. The tower was as 'perfectly awry' as Beckford and other visitors had expected, but they had not been adequately prepared for the Pisan Romanesque style of the late eleventh-century cathedral, the most 'curious edifice' that Beckford's eyes had 'ever viewed'. 'Don't ask of what shape or architecture,' he wrote. 'It is almost impossible to tell, so great is the confusion of ornament. The capitals of the columns and carving of the architraves, as well as the form of the arches, are evidently Grecian design, but Gothic proportions. The dome gives the mass an oriental appearance which helped to bewilder me; in short I have dreamed of such buildings, but little thought they existed.'

The strangeness of the building was compounded by the camels that lumbered through the piazza transporting water from door to door, and the atmosphere of desolation in the town by the number of empty houses and the grass growing in the streets through cracks in the pavement. 'In its present state, chameleons only can inhabit this city,' wrote one tourist who had thought of settling there in 1754 but had soon changed his mind. 'Horses indeed may graze and fatten in the streets. Human creatures, unless they are Italians, cannot find lodgings or subsistence.'

Lucca was considered equally depressing. Beckford was thankful that its surroundings were so lovely because he defied 'almost any city to contain more ugliness within its walls'. 'Narrow streets and dismal alleys,' he commented; 'wide gutters and cracked pavements; everybody in black, according with the gloom of their habitations which, having all grated windows, convey none but dark and dungeon-like ideas.'

Similar sentiments were expressed about both Leghorn and Pistoia. Indeed, in Pistoia, so Misson advised in his *New Voyage to Italy*, there was nothing that deserved either the trouble or charge of going out of the way to see. Charles de Brosses dismissed the cathedral as having 'the air of a village church', and Captain Northall discovered 'ruin, desolation and indolence' upon every side.

Those who travelled to Florence through Ferrara and Bologna were less disappointed, although Ferrara itself was as strongly denounced as anywhere, its canals – choked and abandoned – covered with swarms of mosquitoes, its streets looking so poor and being so deserted that Baron von Archenholz suggested that the authorities put up a notice on the gates announcing, 'This Town is To Be Let'; and Mrs Piozzi said that she might have commended the streets for their cleanliness had she not reflected that there was no one to make them dirty, not even a single beggar – 'a bad account of poor Ferrara'. Misson thought the place so pathetic that it could not be viewed without compassion, while Sacheverell Stevens complained that its provisions were not only 'excessive dear' but what was 'still worse, very bad'.

Bologna, however, was by contrast a delight, 'one of the handsomest cities in Italy', in Nugent's opinion, and in that of another author, 'the finest and most wealthy city in the whole ecclesiastical state'. John Moore went so far as to say that 'next to Rome itself there is perhaps no town in the world so rich as Bologna'.

The food here was in general excellent: the sausages, although Gibbon heard they were 'made of ass-flesh', were superb; the pasta delicious. The opera, in the judgement of the Earl of Essex in 1723, was 'the finest that ever was heard'; the machines on the inn tables for driving away the flies the 'most useful inventions'. There was much to see: the basilica of San Petronio; the lovely Fontana del Nettuno by Giovanni da Bologna; the churches of Santo Stefano, San Giacomo Maggiore, San Francesco and San Domenico; the remarkable fifteenth- and sixteenth-century palaces in the square which were approached from the several sanctuaries of Santo Stefano; the Piazza di Porta Ravegnana; the embalmed body of S. Katerina di Vigri in the church of Corpus Domini.

As for the pictures, Bologna 'next to Rome [boasted] the most capital paintings in the world', according to *The Gentleman's Guide in his Tour through Italy* of 1787. 'The Caraccis and their scholars having carried this art to the summit of perfection.' Although not so highly esteemed today, the pictures by Guido Reni and Guercino, as well as by the Caraccis, which were scattered about the churches and palaces of the town, were then considered as fine as any works of art in Italy. Mariana Starke, for example, considered one of Annibale Caracci's pictures could 'vie with the finest productions of Raffaele, while it [surpassed] them all in beauty of colouring'.

Even the road over the Apennines from Bologna to Florence, which Beckford and Gibbon found so dreary and melancholy, was generally considered one of Italy's better ones, although it was certainly advisable not to make the journey in severe weather when carriages had to be abandoned for mules, or to spend a night *en route* in such a grim village as the one from which two hags stalked forth with lanterns and fearful grins to invite Beckford to a dish of mustard and crows' gizzards, a dish that he was half afraid of tasting, lest it should transform him into 'some bird of darkness, condemned to mope eternally on the black rafters of the cottage'.

But soon Beckford 'bade adieu to these realms of poverty and barrenness and entered a cultivated vale' where the voices of peasants could be heard singing under the cypress trees' and 'all nature seemed in a happy tranquil state' as he came down to catch sight of Florence, 'surrounded with gardens and terraces rising one above another'.

Despite the 'mediaeval gloom' of so many of its sombre palaces, nearly all Beckford's contemporaries liked Florence, as English travellers had done for generations. 'I live in Florence,' wrote one of them in 1608, 'in an excellent coole terrene, eate good melons, drink wholesome wines, looke upon excellent devout pictures, heer choyse musique.'

A few years before, Fynes Moryson had written with comparable delight of the

Florentine inns which, unlike so many of which he had experience elsewhere, were 'most neate', their tables invitingly spread from morning to night with white cloths, glasses of 'divers coloured wines' and dishes of fruit, all gaily decorated with flowers and fig leaves. 'At the Table they touch no meate with the hand, but with a forke of silver or other metall, each man being served with his forke and spoone, and glass to drinke,' Moryson continued. 'And as they serve small peeces of flesh (not whole joints as with us), so these peeces are cut into small bits, to be taken up with the forke. . . . In Summer time they set a broad earthen vessel full of water upon the Table, wherein little glasses filled with wine doe swimme for coolenesse.'

In the middle of the eighteenth century the inn to which most English travellers made their way was the one on the left bank of the Arno, opposite the Palazzo Corsini, kept by a convivial Englishman, Charles Hadfield, a man from Manchester whose daughter married the miniaturist Richard Cosway. It was a well run and moderately priced inn. 'Almost all the English live in this house,' Sir Lucas Pepys told his brother in 1767, 'and considering all things we do not pay very extravagantly. Everybody pays 2s 6d a day for his apartment, not quite 4s for his dinner, 8d his breakfast or tea, 1s fire, and if any chooses supper it is 1s 6d. This is very reasonable considering noblemen and all live in the same manner.'

It was here at Carlo's that Gibbon stayed in June 1764, and, judging by the supper he was given on his first night, he considered that Hadfield well deserved the reputation his fellow-Englishmen had given him. The next morning several of the inn's habitués called to welcome the new arrival, including Lord Fordwich who had become 'almost a Florentine', though not on this occasion Thomas Lyttleton (later 'the wicked' Lord Lyttleton), who, unlike Gibbon – a visitor to the Uffizi gallery on at least fourteen occasions – took a perverse pride in boasting in his garrulous way that he saw no point in bothering with the place himself, or, indeed, with art or antiquities at all. Soon afterwards Gibbon made himself known to Sir Horace Mann, who had been appointed successor to Charles Fane as British Resident in Florence in 1740 and was to remain there, becoming increasingly Italian in his manners, for over forty years. He lived at the Palazzo Manetti on the Lungarno near the Ponte di Santa Trinità, where he good-naturedly dispensed sound advice and generous hospitality to an unending succession of English tourists, warmly recommending to them all the works of his friend Thomas Patch, who had hurriedly left Rome in 1755 when his homosexuality had landed him in trouble and had come to Florence, where he painted both caricatures and views of the city and became an authority on Masaccio and early Florentine art.

Mann was the best and most obliging person in the world, Thomas Gray thought; while Gibbon described him as 'an agreeable man, quiet and polished,

77 (Left) The third Duke of Roxburghe caricatured by Patch with the dome of the cathedral and the campanile in the background.

78 (Right) A wayside inn on the road to Florence in 1791.

but somewhat wrapped up in a round of important trifles'. He obligingly arranged for a good seat from which Gibbon could watch the celebrated horse-race through Florence's narrow main thoroughfare, the Corso; he also arranged for him to see the ceremony of homage to the Grand Duke of Tuscany in the Piazza Signoria and the Palio de' Cocchi, and the chariot races in the Piazza Santa Maria Novella. He took him and his other young acquaintances, friends and charges to rather dull receptions in Florentine palaces, where Gibbon practised the Italian he was taught during the day; he invited them to his box at the opera which was always full of 'the nation', as Gibbon always referred to the English, who amused themselves 'with anything other than the performance'; and in August he gave a grand party of his own which put those of the native aristocracy to shame.

Unless led into one by Mann, the English tourist was as unlikely to be entertained in a private house as he was in Turin or in Genoa, where to 'give one a meal is unheard of', so one disgruntled visitor complained. 'You would not believe how far the parsimony of these princes goes.' They seemed equally parsimonious in Florence. No one 'ever received guests for dinner' there, Arthur Young wrote. Marquis Riccardi had forty servants in his palace, many of whom had their own servants to wait upon them, but an invitation to dinner there was very rare. 'The Ranuzzi,' Young continued, 'are even richer and more people live at their expense; but there are no dinners, no parties, no equipages and no comfort.'

Fortunately there was much else to do and to see. Guide-books listed the 152 churches, the 89 convents, the 84 fraternities, the 18 halls belonging to merchants, the 160 public statues, the 17 palaces, the 6 columns, the 2 pyramids. There was the Cathedral to visit, an 'extraordinary' structure, as Captain Northall described it, though 'one of the masterpieces of Gothic architecture'; there were the numerous churches, 'some built in the Gothic taste and fine in their way', others 'more modern and built in a good taste'; there were the Boboli gardens, the Palazzo Medici and the mausoleum of the Medici family in the chapel of San Laurenzo with its sculptures by Michelangelo; there were the paintings by Fra Angelico at San Marco, the pictures in the Grand Duke's Gallery at the Pitti Palace and the treasures in the Uffizi, whose Tribuna was painted by Zoffany with portraits of Mann and of numerous English tourists studying the works of art on display, including the Medici Venus which Joseph Spence went to see about a hundred times. There were meetings of the Accademia della Crusca to attend; drives on the Cascine to buy baskets of carnations, mignonettes, yellow roses and orange blossom; days spent riding in the beautiful countryside outside the town, up to Fiesole or along the Arno valley beside the rows of mulberry trees; evenings walking in gardens where cypress and ilex cast shadows in the moonlight across crumbling statues; nights at the opera where, in the 1770s, in drunken sleep in the corner of his box, might be seen Charles Edward Stuart, the Young Pretender – the exiled, self-styled King Charles III of England.

There was also so much to buy in Florence apart from paintings and copies of paintings, books, coins, medals and leatherwork. There were vases and chimney pieces, *pietre dure* cabinets, *scagliola* table tops by Lambert Gori or Enrico Hugford, copies of antique statues by Francis Harwood, even seeds such as the melon and broccoli seeds that Lord Nuneham sent home in 1756.

All but the most captious critics were captivated by Florence, where good meals were not expensive and, in Mariana Starke's words, 'noble houses, un-furnished, may be hired by the year for, comparatively speaking, nothing'. Florence, wrote Dr Sharp, 'will be preferred to all the other cities of Italy as a place of residence'. And Smollett, although 'much disappointed in the chapel of St Lorenzo', unimpressed by the Cathedral – 'a great Gothic building, encrusted on the outside with marble' and 'remarkable for nothing but its cupola' – and not so taken with either Ghiberti's Baptistry doors or with the Venus de' Medici as his contemporaries were, decided that Florence was, nevertheless, 'a noble city that still retains all the marks of a majestic capital, such as piazzas, palaces, fountains, bridges, statues, and arcades. I need not tell you that the churches here are magnificent, and adorned not only with pillars of oriental granite, porphyry, jasper, *verde antico*, and other precious stones; but also with capital pieces of painting by the most eminent masters.'

He continued:

That part of the city which stands on each side of the river, makes a very elegant appear-ance, to which the four bridges and the stone quay between them, contribute in a great measure. I lodged at the widow Vanini's, an English house delightfully situated in this quarter. The landlady, who is herself a native of England, we found very obliging. The

79 (Above) A nocturnal concert in a palatial villa outside Florence, by G.M. Terreni.

80 (Below) A dinner party at Sir Horace Mann's, c.1763–5 by Thomas Patch. Mann is the tall figure standing on the left, and also appears in the caricature portrait on the wall.

lodging rooms are comfortable; and the entertainment is good and reasonable. There is a considerable number of fashionable people at Florence, and many of them in good circumstances. They affect a gaiety in their dress, equipage, and conversation; but stand very much on the punctilio with strangers. . . .

With all their pride, however, the nobles of Florence are humble enough to enter into partnership with shop-keepers, and even to sell wine by retail. It is an undoubted fact, that in every palace or great house in this city, there is a little window fronting the street, provided with an iron knocker, and over it hangs an empty flask, by way of signpost. Thither you send your servant to buy a bottle of wine. He knocks at the little wicket, which is opened immediately by a domestic, who supplies him with what he wants, and receives the money like the waiter of any other cabaret. It is pretty extraordinary, that it should not be deemed a disparagement in a nobleman to sell half a pound of figs, or a palm of ribbon or tape, or to take money for a flask of sour wine; and yet be counted infamous to match his daughter in the family of a person who has distinguished himself in any one of the learned professions.

Tourists disinclined to spend much time sightseeing, or bored by such entertainments as the Florentine nobility were prepared to give, had no need to look far for congenial fellow-countrymen with whom they could happily pass the time. When James Boswell arrived in Florence in the summer of 1765, he soon encountered Lord Beauchamp; Earl Tylney; Colonel Isaac Barré; the Hon. Peregrine Bertie, a younger son of the Earl of Abingdon; the Hon. Keith Stewart, a son of the Earl of Galloway; Baron Wallmoden, reputedly a natural son of King George II by his German mistress, the Countess of Yarmouth; Lord Hertford's cheerful chaplain, Dr James Traill, a future Bishop of Down and Connor; and Earl Cowper who, having fallen in love with a married Marchesa, had been languishing in the city for years.

When Walpole and Gray had arrived some years earlier there were fewer Englishmen in Florence, but they were both delighted with the pleasures that the city had to offer, and Walpole, who was to maintain a correspondence with Sir Horace Mann for forty-five years, had never been more happy anywhere else on the Continent. Florence was 'infinitely the most agreeable of all the places [he] had seen since London'. He was not over-conscientious in his sightseeing. 'Except pictures and statues, we are not very fond of sights,' he admitted. 'Don't go a-staring after crooked towers and conundrum staircases. . . . I recollect the joy I used to propose if I could but once see the Great Duke's Gallery [the Uffizi]. I walk into it now with as little emotion as I should go into St Paul's . . . I have left off screaming Lord! this! and Lord! that!' 'Instead of being deep in the liberal arts, and being in the Gallery every morning,' he continued in a letter to Richard West, 'we are all in idleness and amusements of the town. For me, I am grown so lazy, and so tired of seeing sights, that, though I have been at Florence six months, I have not seen Leghorn, Pisa, Lucca or Pistoia; nay not so much as one of the Great Duke's villas.'

Yet he enjoyed himself to the full:

I have done nothing but slip out of my domino into bed, and out of bed into my domino. The end of the Carnival is frantic, bacchanalian; all the morning one makes parties in masque to the shops and coffee-houses, and all the evenings to the operas and balls. *Then I have danced, good Gods! how have I danced!* . . . The freedom of the Carnival has given me opportunities to make several acquaintances.

Half a century later he still recalled those 'delicious nights on the Ponte di Trinità', wearing his linen dressing-gown 'and a straw hat, with *improvisatori*, and music, and the coffee-houses open with ices'. And he remembered too the lovely Elisabetta, Marchesa Grifoni, whose *cavaliere servente* and, no doubt, lover he became.

Other tourists certainly found mistresses, though in 1767, when the last Medici Grand Duke had died and Florence had become a mere appendage of the Austrian Empire, Charles James Fox wrote that 'there had been a woman of fashion put in prison lately for fucking (I suppose rather too publickly) a piece of unexampled tyranny! and such as could happen in no place but this.' Fox himself, as he told a friend the following year when he was nineteen, was a long time on the Continent before he 'could get a fuck'. 'But in recompense for my sufferings,' he wrote, 'I have now got the most excellent piece that can be allowed. . . . There is a Mrs Holmes here, an Irishwoman more beautiful than words can express, and very agreeable into the bargain. Now it so happens that tho' this woman is exquisite entertainment for Charles, yet, as she is chaste as she is fair, she does not altogether do for Carlino so well. There is also . . . a silversmith's wife who is almost as fair as Mrs Holmes, but not near as chaste and she attracts me thither as regularly in the evening as the other does in the morning. . . . This has led me to make verses and you shall soon have a poem of my composing upon the pox in Latin.'

As in Turin, Boswell was disappointed in the responses of the women he met in Florentine society whom he deemed cold and calculating, and, 'quite furious', he dashed off to one of the city's bridges to find a prostitute. He found two, contracted gonorrhoea again, and was obliged to send for Dr Tyrrell, the Irish physician who, for well over twenty years in practice in Florence, had been treating Englishmen similarly afflicted after encounters with these 'poor craiturs' of the bridges. Having been told by the doctor that he was infectious and could honourably indulge in no more gallantries, Boswell decided to tell the man he wanted only 'little advice' and then dismiss him. He also decided, however, that he must ask for 'condoms for Siena'. In Siena he was to be more fortunate in his affairs.

81 *St Peter's and the Vatican by the light of fireworks from the Castel Sant' Angelo in about 1776 by Joseph Wright of Derby.*

CHAPTER 9

*

FROM SIENA

TO

ROME

*

'One cannot walk fifty paces without observing some remains of its ancient grandeur'

IN THEIR ANXIETY TO REACH ROME, FEW tourists remained longer in Siena than it took to look round the cathedral which John Durant Breval described as 'of a Gothic style indeed, but very beautiful in its kind, and would be still more so in my opinion, were the Marble all of one Colour'. It was admittedly an 'attractive little city' noted for the 'purity of the Italian tongue which [was] spoken here', so Nugent said, 'without that gutteral pronunciation so disagreeable in the Florentines'. Yet there were rarely more than a few English tourists staying here. Edward Gibbon for one had 'not the slightest anxiety to stay' in Siena, having been to an assembly there and found the women 'so ugly and the men so ignorant'.

Boswell was an exception. When he was there in 1765 he found himself the only foreigner in the city, but he was perfectly content, eating well, enjoying the local wine, sleeping in a pleasant apartment, practising his Italian, taking lessons in singing and the flute, paying court to the wife of the Grand Duke's chamberlain, with whom Lord Mountstuart had had a brief affair, and making overtures at the same time to Girolama Piccolomini, the wife of the Capitano di Popolo by whom she had had four children. 'I lied to her certainly no fewer than a hundred times a day,' he confessed. '*My valet de place*, a lout who could neither read nor write, was sent off with his face turned to the east to carry a letter to Signora A in his right-hand pocket and a letter to Signora B in his left.' Signora Piccolomini succumbed to his blandishments sooner than he had expected and, while he had not felt in the least attracted to her at first, he soon grew fond of his 'dear little mistress' who had unashamedly fallen deeply in love with him before he went on his way.

As they approached Rome, the 'great crown of their travels', as one of them called it, English travellers 'must needs be conscious of mounting excitement'. Yet their first experiences of the city were commonly disappointing and often exasperating. As elsewhere, the custom-house officials were a pest, tumbling 'the things about under a pretence of searching to the bottom for contraband goods' and 'ceasing their activities only on the offer of presents'. Then, outside the custom-house, the coaches of the new arrivals were 'surrounded by a number of *servitori di piazza* offering their services with the most disagreeable importunity', and clambering onto the vehicles even when forcefully informed that the occupants had no occasion for their services.

The Piazza del Popolo by which the visitor from the north entered Rome was admitted to be fine enough, even 'noble' and 'august', despite the goats wandering

82 (Left) A conversation piece in Rome by Nathaniel Dance: the seated figure is Thomas Robinson, later second Lord Grantham, holding an elevation of the Temple of Jupiter Sator.
83 (Right) Pier Leone Ghezzi's caricature of English tourists Lutin and Charlemont in a Roman coffee-house.

about, the one-storey hovels of washerwomen on its circumference and the seedy lodgings of prostitutes in the side alleys beyond. But the principal street that led out of it to the centre of the city was 'much too narrow for its length', in the opinion of Charles de Brosses, 'and was made still more so by the *trottoirs* for the use of pedestrians' who were almost suffocated by the dust thrown up by the everlasting drive of carriages along it. It was also very badly paved, his fellow-countryman Father Labat had already complained, and 'extremely dirty' as well as dusty. In the evenings a few carts were trundled about by men who swung from side to side leather tubes attached to water barrels, but Romans did not really 'know what sweeping means, they leave it to Providence. Heavy rain showers act as brushes in Rome.'

A man on his first arrival at Rome is not much fired with its appearance [Dr Sharp maintained]. The narrowness of the streets, the thinness of the inhabitants, the prodigious quantity of monks and beggars, give but a gloomy aspect to this renowned city. There are no rich tradesmen here . . . All the shops seem empty, and the shopkeepers poor; not one hackney coach in so large a town.

Other disgruntled arrivals commented upon the multitude of lackeys offering their unwanted services with tiresome persistence, and upon the far larger number of beggars, particularly in the streets around the Piazza di Spagna, many of them supplied with begging-letters by the scriveners who could be seen sitting beneath

84 (Left) Sir Sampson Gideon and a companion painted in 1767 by Pompeo Batoni, the most in demand of all portrait painters working in Rome, though 'uncommonly dear'.
85 (Right) A caricature done in Rome by Joshua Reynolds in 1751: the fastidious Lord Bruce (left) stands talking to his companions.

umbrellas in every square. These mendicants, hovering at the doors of palaces, sitting on the steps of churches, waiting in the streets at dusk with lanterns, were constantly approaching tourists to offer some unwanted service, to propose employment as guides, to recommend an inn, to open a door, to brush a coat, indeed to perform any unnecessary task or to impart any unsolicited information which could be deemed worthy of a reward. Those who did work never seemed to work hard. The hours of the siesta were long, and during those hours, so Father Labat said, the only living creatures to be seen in the streets were dogs, lunatics and Frenchmen. Even before and after the siesta, the 700 workshops of the masons and smiths, the painters and engravers, wood-carvers and potters were frequently closed and shuttered. Feast days and festivals were so common that almost every other day was a holiday; there were 150 religious festivals at the beginning of the century and only 30 less than this by 1770. On working days the greater part of the population appeared to be intent upon doing 'absolutely nothing', living on charity and the money which found its way to Rome from all over Christian Europe. There was 'no agriculture, no commerce, no manufactures', and it was not in the least uncommon to be told in a shop, with complacent equability, that the goods required were available but rather awkward to get at, so would the customer please come back another day.

Charles de Brosses was driven to the conclusion that a quarter of the population of Rome were priests, a quarter statues and a quarter people who did nothing. He added that a large proportion of the hundreds of visitors were English, 'most of them very rich'. Other visitors complained of the 'uncomfortableness and danger of passing through the streets after sunset', for there was 'not the least provision for lighting them'; of the 'almost uninterrupted succession of narrow, vulgar-looking streets, where the smell of garlick prevails over the odour of antiquity'; of the Tiber, 'in comparison with the Thames, no more than an inconsiderable stream, foul, deep and rapid'; of the Piazza Navona which, while 'adorned with three or four fountains one of which [Bernini's] is perhaps the most magnificent in Europe', was 'almost as dirty as West Smithfield where the cattle are sold in London'; of palaces 'disgraced with filth', their 'corridors, arcades, and even staircases depositories of nastiness and [smelling] in summer as strong as spirit of hartshorn'; of the 'numberless' English tourists, 'school-boys just broke loose', as Walpole described them, 'or old fools that are come abroad at forty to see the world'; of their stupid and knavish tutors, who, in combination with the 'folly of British boys' had, so Lady Mary Wortley Montagu said, 'gained us the glorious title of Golden Asses'; of the standard of such lodgings as those unwillingly occupied by Thomas Jones which had

a brick floor rougher than that of many of our English stables – the walls hung round with dirty dismal pictures of Weeping Magdalens, bloody Ecce Homos, dead Christs and fainting Madonas – by my bedside was fixt a kind of little Alter with a Crucifix – My Curtainless bed consisted of a large bag of Straw and Mattress, placed on a few boards, which were supported by two iron benches. In this melancholy Chamber, or rather chapel, I retired to rest, and lulled to sleep by the pattering of the rain against the windows, sometimes dreamt of the many enjoyments I had left behind me in London.

To escape from these dismal surroundings Jones flew to the English coffee-house which was patronised by many of the English artists who studied and worked in Rome, including Joshua Reynolds who had a room on the third floor in 1750. Jones discovered the place to be

a filthy vaulted room, the walls of which were painted with Sphinxes, Obelisks and Pyramids, from capricious designs of Piranesi, and fitter to adorn the inside of an Egyptian Sepulchre than a room of social conversation. Here, seated round a brazier of hot embers placed in the centre, [he and his companions] endeavoured to amuse [themselves] for an hour or two over a cup of coffee or glass of punch.

Outside, in the Piazza di Spagna, the English ghetto as it came to be known,

86 (Opposite above) The Piazza del Popolo in Rome by Pannini showing the twin churches of S. Maria di Monte Santo and S. Maria dei Miracoli on either side of the Corso.

87 (Below) Carriages parading around the flooded Piazza Navona, in the centre of which stands Bernini's 'Fountain of the Four Rivers'.

88 (Left) David Allan depicts a young traveller and his suite arriving during the carnival in the Piazza di Spagna, the 'English ghetto'.

89 (Right) The interior of a coffee-house by David Allan, who lived in Rome from 1764 for about thirteen years.

groups of tourists gathered, breathing what Captain Northall considered to be 'the worst air in Rome, mixed with clouds of dust, pestered with beggars, and incommoded by coaches which press forward without observing rank or order'.

'This is the first impression,' said Dr Sharp, whose criticisms had been among the most severe, 'but turn your eye from that point of view, to the magnificence of their churches, to the venerable remains of ancient Rome, to the prodigious collection of pictures and antique statues . . . and, with a very few grains of enthusiasm in your composition, you will feel more than satisfied.' 'We have been ten days at Rome,' wrote Lady Knight in March 1728, 'and have already seen enough of it to make us think it the finest city of the world.'

There were tourists who by now had seen all the magnificent churches, venerable remains, pictures and antique statues that they had patience to see, who, wanting no guide 'to go prattling from fragment to fragment', proposed to wander about, like Beckford, 'as the spirit chuses', or who agreed with Walpole that in a hundred years' time Rome would not be worth seeing, that it was less worth seeing 'now than one would believe: All the public pictures are decayed or decaying; the few ruins cannot last long; and the statues and private collections must be sold, from the great poverty of the families'. There were those, too, like Lord Baltimore, who rushed round the Villa Borghese in ten minutes, and Dr John Moore's young acquaintance who, having a severely limited interest in art and architecture, considered two or three hours a day far too much to spend on 'a pursuit in which he felt no pleasure, and saw very little utility', and who

90 (Left) Tourists being shown a statue of dubious authenticity by an antiquary in Rome in 1788.
91 (Right) Johann Winckelmann, the Prussian cobbler's son who became Chief Supervisor of Antiquities in Rome in 1763.

consequently ordered 'a post-chaise and four horses to be ready early in the morning, and driving through churches, palaces, villas and ruins with all possible expedition, fairly saw, in two days, all that we had beheld during our crawling course of six weeks'.

There were also tourists who, wandering aimlessly about the city, found little of interest to record other than its oddities, imperfections and incongruities, who mentioned the Palatine, only to draw attention to the weeds that overran it and the 'few tattered ropemakers working in the shade of a foot or two of ancient wall', who mentioned the Arch of Septimius Severus only to point out that part of it was used as a barber's shop, the Capuchin church of S. Maria della Concezione only to dwell upon the grinning skulls and clothed skeletons in the chapels of the crypt, the Forum only because a market was held there twice a week, the Theatre of Marcellus because its arches were filled in and occupied by poor families, the Baths of Caracalla because they were smothered in foliage, and the Colosseum because it was occupied by animals and a hermit and 'several portions [were] full of dung'.

This last comment was Boswell's, but he at least was one of those who took the trouble to visit the sights in the company of a knowledgeable antiquary. There were numerous self-styled antiquarians in Rome who were far from knowledgeable, who, as Captain Northall said, offered themselves 'to strangers of quality to serve them as guides in surveying the curiosities of the place . . . who will make such novices believe a copy to be an original of Raphael, Angelo, Titian or some other great master which they purchase at an extravagant price'. Some of these

*92 The Pantheon, here
depicted by Canaletto in
1742, a painting acquired
by George III from
'Consul' Smith.*

*93 The interior of the
Pantheon in about 1740
by Pannini: 'at the top
is a hole without any
covering which is the
only light to the church'.*

94 Thomas Patch shows English antiquaries in conversation at Pola on the Adriatic coast, 1760. Among them is the fifth Earl of Stamford, who brought the picture back to England.

95 *(Left) A tourist inspecting the Albani Antinous in the Capitoline Museum.*
96 *(Right) One of Rome's principal guides, the Scotsman James Byres, and his family.*

tricksters and dealers were English, Smollett warned, and peculiarly skilful in imposing upon their fellow-countrymen who, since they were reputed to have money to throw away, were constantly being urged to part with it for worthless pictures and antiques. For genuine, if often extremely expensive antiquities, the tourist was recommended to approach Cardinal Alessandro Albani, the celebrated collector who usually had items for sale, or Thomas Jenkins, the art dealer and banker, or Gavin Hamilton, the neo-classical painter turned excavator and dealer, who discovered in the ruins of Ostia, Rome's ancient seaport, the lovely Venus which was sold to Charles Townley for £700 and which, like other items excavated by Hamilton, was smuggled out of Italy because an export licence would certainly have been refused by the papal authorities.

Few tourists were fortunate enough to find or buy so exquisite an antiquity as the Townley Venus, but those content with lesser treasures had much to choose from. J.B.S. Morritt wrote home that:

I have at last wound up by buying two most beautiful cameos this morning, which were part of a Roman collection, now selling off. The one is a very well cut head of Brutus with the dagger, and the other a most superb gem of a Medusa, in full face and very high *rilievo*, upon which I mean to establish my fame. These I shall sport as rings when I dine at Sedbury or in places of the sort, and expect to show them off with no small *éclat*. I have bought a picture or two likewise in Rome, so that if I get clear away before I ruin myself, you may think me well off; for, to say the truth, I cannot resist temptation. I shall have something good at least to show for my money, I hope, and so shall content myself, as a good many people spend theirs without.

97 The ruins of the Roman Forum painted by Bernardo Bellotto in the 1740s.

Once a reliable antiquary had been found, he could be relied upon, in Dr Moore's estimation, to conduct a tourist on 'a regular course' of Rome, occupying about three hours a day for six weeks, although the highly conscientious, twenty-year-old Earl of Carlisle was 'out on this business seven or eight hours a day' in 1768. Ideally this guide in the first half of the eighteenth century would be Francesco di Ficoroni, author of *Le Vestigia e Rarità di Roma*, or the English artist James Russel, who had arrived in Rome in 1740. After Russel's death two Scotsmen, Colin Morison and James Byres, became known as the city's principal *cicerones*; but no guide was as authoritative as Johann Winckelmann, a Prussian cobbler's son who made himself Europe's leading authority on classical art and was appointed Chief Supervisor of Antiquities in 1763. Infectiously enthralled by his subject, he was also, in the opinion of John Wilkes, one of those for whom he acted as mentor, 'a gentleman of exquisite taste' and tact. When showing Wilkes and his mistress, Gertrude Corradini, round Rome, he pretended not to notice their absence when, overcome by lust, they disappeared for a few moments to make love behind a convenient ruin. 'This was the more obliging,' Wilkes commented, 'because he must necessarily pass such an interval with the mother of Corradini who had as little conversation as beauty.'

Although Wilkes's friend James Boswell met Winckelmann, who took him round Cardinal Albani's villa (now Villa Torlonia) where he was librarian, Boswell's guide in Rome was his fellow-Scotsman, Colin Morison. Under Morison's tutelage, Boswell embarked upon 'a study of antiquities, of pictures, of architecture and of the other arts' in Rome which might well have served as a model for every

98 *The interior of the Colosseum by Louis Ducros, who had a studio in Rome in the 1770s and '80s.*

99 *A view of the Tiber by Vanvitelli with the Ponte Sant' below the dome of St Peter's and the Castel Sant' Angelo on t*

100 (Left) The tomb of Arruncius in 1756, after Piranesi, whose vedute *of Rome were much sought after by tourists.*

101 (Right) David Allan portrays the Cardinal Duke of York, the soi-disant *King James III, at prayer.*

other young eighteenth-century tourist. He inspected the Sistine Chapel and the Vatican library; he went over the Baths of Diocletian and studied the antiquities in the Campus Martius; he visited Santa Maria sopra Minerva, where he saw Pope Clement XIII give his blessing to the congregation who knelt before him and kissed his slipper; he walked round Santa Maria Maggiore where he admired the oriental marble columns, and San Pietro in Carcere where he saw the remains of the 'famous Tulla prison of which Sallust gives so hideous a picture'; he attended a 'superb high Mass' in St Peter's; he visited the Borghese Palace and the Belvedere, surveyed Michelangelo's 'superb' statue of Moses, the 'supreme' Laocoön and the 'beautiful' Apollo; he viewed the Forum and experienced 'sublime and melancholy' emotions as he thought of all the great scenes which had been enacted there; he went to the Colosseum, which presented 'a vast and sublime idea of the grandeur of the ancient Romans', and he found it 'hard to tell whether the astonishing massiveness or the exquisite taste of this superb building should be more admired'; he climbed the Palatine hill on which cypresses seemed to mourn for the ruin of imperial palaces, and there saw a statue which so resembled Cicero that he resolved to speak Latin for the remainder of his stay; he also walked up Michelangelo's *cordonata* to the Capitol where, from the roof of the modern Senate, so Boswell recorded, 'Mr Morison pointed out ancient Rome on its seven hills. He showed me a little map of it, and read me a clear summary of the growth of this famous city to its present extent.'

A few months before, in October 1764, Edward Gibbon had also been on the Capitol; and in the gloom of that fateful evening, as barefooted friars were

102 (Left) Tourists were expected to bring home sketch-books from their tour as well as diaries: a drawing by Hubert Robert, who left Paris for Rome in 1754.
103 (Right) A Roman lady and her duenna painted by John Brown.

chanting their litanies in the Church of Santa Maria d'Aracoeli, he 'conceived the first thought' of what was to become *The Decline and Fall of the Roman Empire*. Once he had awakened from those 'dreams of antiquity' which intoxicated him as he trod, with 'lofty step, the ruins of the Forum' – marking 'each memorable spot where Romulus stood, or Tully spoke, or Caesar fell' – Gibbon, like Boswell, descended to 'a cool and minute investigation' of the city.

Most of the earnest young Englishmen who set out upon similar investigations, armed with maps and plans, magnifying glasses, mariner's compasses, pencils, sketching pads, notebooks and guide-books, wrote far more prosaic accounts of what they saw than Gibbon was to do. Assured by Nugent that 'no place in the universe affords so agreeable a variety of ancient and modern curiosities' and that one could not walk 'fifty paces without observing some remains of its ancient grandeur', the conscientious tourist strolled around the churches and palaces, the columns, arches and obelisks, the squares and bridges, fountains, villas and temples, lamenting that so much was lost beneath crumbling medieval wells and the debris of centuries, and dutifully recording his impressions.

'All the remains we see of Ancient Rome are very grand,' wrote Richard Pococke in one characteristic passage. 'I was in the Pantheon [described by one of his contemporaries as looking like 'a huge cockpit open at the top']. There is a fine Portico to it, with vast Pillars of one piece of granite within there are pillars of Jallo antique that go up about two thirds towards the spring of the arch – in the middle of the Arch at the top is a hole about 12 feet diametre, without any covering which is the only light to the church. The outside is brick.' 'We went into the catacombes which go a mile towards Tivoli cut out of this rock just high enough to walk in,' the same tourist wrote in another passage like scores of others. 'Both sides are cut out in holes 1 foot deep from 2 to 6 long, when bodies were put in they were closed with tiles of marble plastered round as we saw and in some that were broke down we saw bones lie in their proper order very rotten and viols set in mortar within 'em in which they say they put the blood of the martirs.'

Some tourists could not disguise their boredom as they gazed at F.M. Misson's enumeration of 'fourty-eight classes of objects' that the visitor to Rome should endeavour to view, his lists of '107 most notable palaces' and of seventy-one more of less distinction. Lord Baltimore, 'wearied of everything in the world', was pleased with nothing except St Peter's and the Apollo Belvedere, and 'finally got so unbearable' that Winckelmann 'told him what he thought of him' and would have 'nothing more to do with him'.

Lord Webb, as J.B.S. Morritt discovered, became equally bored and lethargic.

There are at least eighteen or twenty houses, of which each has a rich picture gallery, and many fine collections of statues [Morritt wrote]. Add to these the antiquities, and the modern artists in all ways that deserve attention, and you will suppose how busy our mornings are. But before I left I began to be a good deal like my Lord Webb, who asked me one day at Rome, 'Sir, are there any fine pictures in this house?'

'No.'

'God be thanked. Nobody will plague me to look about me.'

For those with no patience for 'minute investigation', Rome offered numerous spectacles both entertaining and exciting or gruesome and pathetic. There were the long ceremonies in the convents where young girls took the veil and, with crucifixes by their side, had their dresses, ornaments and hair cut off, their temples bound with sack cloth and their heads crowned with thorns. At one such ceremony, so Catherine Wilmot reported, not only the women, but 'many of the young Englishmen were also in indignant tears . . . and one Englishman instinctively laid his hand upon his sword, swearing that such heart-rending superstitious cruelties ought to be extirpated from the face of the earth'.

Then there were the public punishments and executions to witness, and there were few tourists who returned home without having seen at least one of these during their travels. In the sixteenth and seventeenth centuries English travellers had frequently witnessed torture as well on the Continent. While he had been in

104 (Opposite above) Pannini's 'Ancient Rome', the walls of an imaginary gallery covered with pictures of the city's most famous ancient monuments.
105 (Below) Pannini's 'Modern Rome', the city of the Renaissance and the Baroque. The two pictures were painted in 1757.

Paris, John Evelyn had gone to the Châtelet prison to see a suspected robber's naked body

drawn at length in so extraordinary a manner as severed the fellow's joints in miserable sort. . . . In this Agonie confessing nothing, the Executioner with a horne (such as they drench horses with) stuck the end of it into his mouth, and pour'd the quantity of 2 [buckets] of Water downe his throat, which so prodigiously swell'd him, face, Eyes ready to start, brest & all his limbs, as would have pittied & almost affrited one to see it; for all this he denied all was charged to him.

In the Piazza San Marco in Venice, Evelyn later witnessed the execution of a 'wretch who had murdered his master, for which he had his head chopped off by an axe that slid down a frame of timber'. It was also in Venice that Fynes Moryson had seen two young men, the sons of senators, beheaded after their hands had been cut off, and their tongues ripped out at the place where they had sung blasphemous songs; and no sooner had William Lithgow landed in that city than he perceived 'a great throng of people, and in the midst of them a great smok'. A Venetian told him 'it was a grey Friar burning quick at St Mark's pillar for begetting young Noble nuns with child, and all within one year'. 'I sprang forward through the throng,' Lithgow recalled, 'and came just to the pillar as the half of his body and right arm fell flatlings in the fire.'

In Rome in the eighteenth century miscreants were still punished by being tied face downwards on the *cavalletto* while blows were struck at their spines with a bull's penis; and more serious crimes were punished with the *martello*,

which is to knock the malefactor on the temples with a hammer while he is on his knees, and almost at the same time to cut his throat and rip open his belly. Lesser crimes are frequently punished by the gallies or the *strappado:* the latter is hanging the criminals by the arms tied backwards, and thus bound they are drawn up on high, and let down again with a violent swing, which, if used with vigour, unjoints their backs and arms.

Lord Byron compared the drama and excitement of an Italian execution with the squalor of an English hanging.

The ceremony, including the *masqued* priests; the half-naked executioner; the bandaged criminals; the black Christ and his banner; the Scaffold; the soldiery; the slow procession; and the quick rattle and heavy fall of the axe; the splash of blood, and the ghastliness of the exposed heads – is altogether more impressive than the . . . dog-like agony of affliction upon the sufferers of the English sentence.

During the Roman Carnival the drama of execution became a grotesque comedy with the headsman disguised as *Pulcinello* and the audience expected to play their parts as at a pantomime. The Carnival – held every year for eight days just before Lent and heralded by the ringing of a bell on the Capitol which was otherwise sounded only for the death of a pope – was a festival of wild tumultuous revelry in which tourists joined enthusiastically, wearing masks and strange disguises, throwing streamers through the air, singing and dancing, joining the Roman crowds at tournaments in palace courtyards, at the races of the riderless Barbary horses which, filled with oats and often with stimulants, thundered down the sand-covered Corso into the Piazza Venezia, the blood streaming down their flanks from the nails which were roped to their backs to act as spurs. At night the revellers poured into the streets again, carrying tapers, jostling and pushing, trying to blow out each other's flickering flames while keeping their own alight, climbing onto the tops of carriages as fireworks exploded in the sky and in their 'beauty, invention and grandeur' exceeded anything Robert Adam had ever seen or indeed could conceive. In his opinion,

What was the grandest part of the operations – 'were the thousands of rockets which are sent up at one time, which spread out like a wheatsheaf in the air, each one of which gives a crack and sends out a dozen burning balls like stars . . . illuminating the landscape, the castle of Sant' Angelo, the river Tiber and the crowds of people, coaches and horses which swarmed on all sides, and appeared to me the most romantic and picturesque sight I have ever seen.

At times less hectic than those of the Carnival there were parades and displays, water jousts and mock naval battles to see in the Piazza Navona, which was 'filled with water about half the depth of the horses' legs'; local processions, fêtes and fairs in which each district of the city bid to outdo the next in the magnificence of its decorations, the loudness of its band and the originality of its floats and fancy dresses; wild football matches with teams of up to thirty on each side; mountebanks and acrobats, astrologers and puppeteers; the *trattorie* in the dark, cramped, garlic-flavoured alleys of the Trastevere; the gardens on the Quirinal; the wine shops on Monte Testaccio; the theatres and opera houses where people went as much to meet their friends, to eat ice cream, enjoy a picnic or to gamble as to watch the performances. 'Instead of listening to the music,' wrote one English visitor, 'they all laugh and talk as though they were at home.' Servants stumbled about with wine and refreshments, and the rowdier members of the audience threw rotten fruit at the performers who responded in kind until the house fell into silence at a favourite aria.

The voices of the singers playing female parts were those of *castrati*, many of whom were undistinguishable from women. 'They have hips, buttocks, bosoms and plump round necks,' a French visitor wrote. 'You could mistake them for real girls.' Indeed, according to Montesquieu, an Englishman did mistake one of them, a transvestite *castrato* from the Capranica, for a girl and fell 'madly in love' with him. Emasculated when children in such surgeries as that near the Vatican

106 (Above) William Drake of Shardeloes with his tutors, Dr Townson and Mr Holdsworth, in his apartment in Rome, 1744.

107 (Below left) The fifth Earl of Stamford and Sir Henry Mainwaring by Teresa Mengs.

108 (Below right) Batoni's 'Portrait of a Young Nobleman' with suitable books, including Lives of the Painters *and* Rome Ancient and Modern, *on the table.*

109 (Opposite) Colonel the Hon. William Gordon in flamboyant pose by Pompeo Batoni in 1766.

Genl the Hon.^{le} John William Gordon

whose services were advertised by a signboard proclaiming, 'The Pope's Chapel Singers Castrated Here', *castrati* were to be found in many a fashionable café where, so an English tourist thought, 'they looked as pretty and tempting as may be'.

Boswell preferred the company of young girls, and in search of these he 'sallied forth of an evening like an imperious lion', remembering the 'rakish behaviour of Horace and other amorous Roman poets' and thinking that he might well allow himself 'a little indulgence in a city where there were prostitutes licensed by the cardinal-vicar'. He had no trouble in finding them, even though he decided to have a 'girl every day' and, according to his accounts, exceeded his resolve. One day he found a '*fille charmante*', the sister of a nun, near Cardinal Colonna's palace and recorded 'much enjoyment'; later he became a customer of a small brothel run by three sisters named Cazenove; he also recorded an adventure, 'quite brutish', with an old woman, a '*monstre*', whom he paid five shillings. The younger, prettier girls were more expensive, but only slightly so: he never seems to have paid more than fourteen *paoli*, about 7s, and sometimes had more than one girl for less than that.

Rome, indeed, as most tourists agreed, was comparatively cheap in other respects as well. Admittedly there were certain places which the improvident traveller was well advised to avoid, such as the Albergo Londra, the Golden Mountain and the Black Eagle, where Thomas Coke and William Kent stayed in 1716; and it was only the rich who could afford the best of the elegant apartments at Casa Guarneri near the Spanish Steps. But there were numerous other places which were much more reasonable, as, for instance, the Palazzo Zuccari on the Pincian Hill, which had been divided into apartments, originally for artists. Reynolds moved there from the English coffee-house in 1751, and Joseph Vernet, the French artist whose work was eagerly sought after by English collectors, also had rooms there.

In the 1750s lodgings with marvellous views over the city could be had in the Palazzo Zuccari for as little as £6 a year. For his nearby lodgings, 'a decent first floor and two bed-chambers on the second', Smollett paid 'no more than a *scudo* (five shillings) per day'. His 'table was plentifully furnished by the landlord for two and thirty pauls, or eighteen pence'; he hired a 'town coach at the rate of seven shillings a day; and a *servitore di piazza* for eighteen pence', the coachman costing him an additional shilling a day. Although 'the *vitella mongana*, the most delicate veal' he had ever tasted, was very dear at a shilling a pound, provisions in the city were otherwise 'reasonable and good', while the wines were more varied than anywhere else in Italy, from the 'rich wines of Montepulciano, Montefiascone and Monte di Dragone' to the Orvieto, a 'small white wine of an agreeable flavour', which he usually drank at meals. Lady Knight had 'eight rooms, besides a very good kitchen and cellar' for which she paid about £12 10s a year: 'in London they would cost at least two hundred pounds per annum'. 'And when I tell you,' she wrote in 1778, 'that beef is only three-halfpence a pound, a fine turkey not quite fifteen pence, that I can have a coach for six hours for three and six-pence, you will think how differently I must be in England.'

Robert Adam was equally content with a pleasant apartment, and the services of a cook, valet, coachman and footman, which cost him only twelve shillings a day. And the poorer Scottish architect, Robert Mylne, managed to provide both for himself and his brother on little more than ten shillings a week. Moreover, there were in Rome, unlike many another Italian city, several palaces where English visitors were welcomed, some of them owned by their fellow-countrymen like that of the Dukes of Dorset. Circumspect Protestants steered clear of the Cardinal Duke of York, second son of the Old Pretender, the *soi-disant* King James III, who was born in Rome and became Bishop of Frascati in 1761. Indeed, the British government employed spies to keep an eye on tourists suspected of Jacobite tendencies, one of these spies in the earlier years of the century being the collector and connoisseur Baron von Stosch, who lived in Rome for several years. But by the 1760s a visit to the Palazzo Muti-Papazzurri, where the aged, sickly Old Pretender lived in seclusion, was not likely to get a tourist into trouble provided he did not see the old man himself and avoided talk of politics.

It was not, however, a lively place, and the tourist in search of an entertaining evening would rather make his way to the Borghese Palace which was filled most evenings with English people, though some of them agreed with Charles de Brosses that it was more like an art gallery than a home since 'all the great compartments', which were 'so vast and so superb', were 'only there for foreigners'.

The masters of the house cannot live in them [Charles de Brosses wrote of the grander Roman palaces in general], since they contain neither lavatories, comfort nor adequate furniture; and there is hardly any of the latter even in the upper storey apartments which are inhabited. . . . The sole decoration in the rooms consists of pictures with which the four walls are covered from top to bottom in such profusion and with so little space between them that to tell the truth they are often more tiring than attractive to the eye. On top of this they spend hardly anything on frames, the majority of them being old, black and shabby, and, for all the tremendous number they crowd in, they have to mix a fair quantity of mediocre works with the beautiful ones.

Tourists who could afford to do so bought pictures in Rome to take home with them, paintings of Roman scenes or ruins by Panini, perhaps, or by the Swiss artist Louis Ducros, who had a studio in the 1780s in the Strada della Croce, or etchings by Giovanni Battista Piranesi whose *Vedute di Roma* were published from 1745, or a genre scene by the Scottish artist, David Allan, who moved from Naples to Rome in 1773. Few could afford the prices paid by Lord Burlington,

110 (Above) Tourists sometimes had themselves painted in groups as well as individually, usually with some Roman monument in the background.

111 (Below) The 'supreme' Laocoön in the Museo Pio Clementino in the Vatican.

112 (Opposite) Thomas Patch, a fine landscape artist as well as caricaturist, depicts the beauties of Tivoli.

113 (Left) Sir Watkin Williams-Wynn, Thomas Apperley and Captain Edward Hamilton by Batoni.
114 (Right) Peter du Cane by Anton von Maron, the Viennese pupil of Anton Raffael Mengs.

who as well as commissioning the beautiful bronzes of the four seasons by Massimiliano now in the Royal Collection, bought while in Rome four Madonnas by respectively Pascoline, Carlo Maratta, Domenichino and Pietro da Cortona, two paintings by Viviano, 'The Temptation of St Anthony' by a follower of Annibale Carracci and 'Noah Sacrificing' by Maratta. But most English tourists did at least have their portraits painted while they were in the city, preferably against the background of one or other of its notable antiquities, a kind of souvenir made popular in the 1740s by artists like Angelo Trevisani, Antonio David, Masucci and Imperiale, and later produced for English sitters by the German artist Anton Raffael Mengs, his Viennese pupil Anton von Maron, the Englishman Nathaniel Dance and, most in demand of all, Pompeo Batoni.

Batoni's prices were high, though. 'Went to Pompeii Batoni's, the best modern painter very fat,' recorded Robert Harvey in 1773. '[He was] working at several English portraits which are well done but uncommonly dear. Sixty sequins (about £30) ye least, then 75 and for a whole length 200.' Earlier, Trevisani, who painted Thomas Coke, Earl of Leicester, in Rome, and Carlo Maratta, who made a fine chalk drawing of Sir Andrew Fountaine, had both charged comparably high prices. So had Rosalba Carriera, who painted Coke as well as Burlington and the Earl of Middlesex. And so, indeed, did many others of the numerous artists working in Rome in the eighteenth century, who, said John Patteson of Norwich, charged thirty guineas for portraits that could have been as well done for ten or fifteen in London. An exception was the young artist George Willison, a Scottish student in Rome who painted in Batoni's manner but charged far less: his excellent portrait of his fellow-Scot James Boswell, now in the National Portrait Gallery of Scotland, cost about £15.

While Willison was completing his portrait, Boswell set off for Tivoli, as nearly all Englishmen did before leaving Rome, to visit the site of Horace's Sabine farm, which so filled him with 'classical enthusiasm' that, on seeing the celebrated *Fons Bandusiae*, he recited Horace's ode on the spot. Some years earlier Richard Pococke had been there and had been less impressed. 'We saw considerable ruins Horaces villa,' he recorded in his prosaic way. 'Two arched apartments remaining we saw the round temples of the Sybils and of modern things the Gardens d'Este belonging to the Duke of Modena with great water works and an extended prospect – nothing extraordinary . . .'

Even the least impressionable tourist, if similarly unimpressed by Tivoli, was delighted by the prospects yet to come.

*115 James Boswell painted in Rome by the Scottish student, George Willison,
a portrait for which the sitter paid about £15.*

CHAPTER 10

*

NAPLES AND
THE BURIED
CITIES

*

*'There cannot in all respects be a
more agreeable place to live in'*

IN THE SUMMER WHEN THE WIND WAS FAIR the sea voyage south to Naples could be a delight; but delays caused by foul weather and the threat of pirates led to most tourists going by land. This was the way recommended by Nugent, who in the 1740s advised those of his readers who had little time to spare to book a fifteen-day trip with a *vetturino* who would undertake to provide eight meals on the journey south, another eight on the way back, pay for all ferry charges at river crossings, for five nights' accommodation in Naples and day excursions to Vesuvius and Pozzuoli for an inclusive charge of five crowns. After Nugent's time *vetturini* also included excursions to the huge 1,200-room palace at Caserta between Rome and Naples which, designed by Luigi Vanvitelli for the King of Naples in the 1750s, was not completed until over half a century later. Its splendid staircase was considered the most magnificent in all Italy; its gardens and cascades were compared with those at Versailles; its aqueduct was 'prodigiously beautiful'.

Travelling by land south from Rome through Caserta could, however, be a most unpleasant experience. William Beckford was caught in a violent thunderstorm which cast the road into darkness at four o'clock in the afternoon.

We lighted torches, and forded several torrents almost at the hazard of our lives. The plains were filled with herds, lowing most piteously, and yet not half so much scared as their masters who ran about cursing and swearing. . . . For three hours the storm increased in violence, and instead of entering Naples on a calm evening, and viewing its delightful shores by moonlight; instead of finding the squares and terraces thronged with people and animated by music, we advanced with fear and terror through dark streets totally deserted, every creature being shut up in their houses; and we heard nothing but driving rain, rushing torrents, and the fall of fragments beaten down by their violence. . . . All night the waves roared . . . and the lightning played clear in my eyes.

The next morning, however, peace was restored; the sun shone in a cloudless sky and, from the large window of the bedroom of his inn, Beckford looked across to the white buildings on the Island of Capri, to the smooth waters off the cape of Sorrento, and towards Vesuvius 'with all that world of gardens and casinos scattered about its base'. The street below was 'thronged with people in holiday garments, and carriages, and soldiers in full parade'.

116 (Opposite) Naples, Lord Macaulay wrote, 'overflows with life', a painting of the bay by Pietro Fabris with Vesuvius in the background.

117 'Some guests of the Marquis play billiards all afternoon', wrote Lord Macaulay.

Beckford's enjoyment of this Neapolitan scene was shared by almost everyone from the Frenchman, Stendhal, who thought the Strada di Toledo the 'gayest street in the world', to the German, Goethe, who considered the city 'a paradise' in which everyone lived in 'a sort of intoxicated self-forgetfulness', and the Englishman, Lord Macaulay, who thought it the only place in Italy which had the same sort of vitality as great English ports and cities: 'Rome and Pisa are dead and gone; Florence is not dead but sleepeth; while Naples overflows with life.' Nugent confirmed this:

'Tis generally allowed that Naples is the pleasantest place in Europe. The air is pure, serene, and healthful; it is scarce ever cold in winter, and in the summer they have refreshing breezes both from the mountains and the sea. . . . The neighbouring country is the richest soil in Europe, abounding with corn, wine and oil, which are excellent. . . . Their wines particularly are the best in Italy, among which their Lachrymo Christi is reckoned the most delicious. . . . In fine, there cannot in all respects be a more agreeable place to live in.

Robert Adam was 'never more pleased and surprised with anything' than with the thousands of Neapolitans who took to the streets on a Sunday night,

dancing along to music of all different kinds in the most antique and Bacchanalian manner [he] ever saw, whilst others were assembled in gardens, at the doors of their houses, in drinking, eating and gaming. These multitudes of men, women and children, their gay dresses and active spirit, formed a most delightful scene. The infinite number of chaises also astonished me. All ranks of people use these light chairs drawn by a single horse, which with difficulty holds two people and is driven by a man who stands on the board behind and with a long whip makes these little machines go like the wind. The town is a perfect beehive, swarming with coaches, chariots, shays and people and, though very large, is in confusion from morning to night. Let it suffice to say it is infinitely the most crowded place I ever beheld.

With a population of three hundred thousand, it was the biggest town in Italy and the third biggest in Europe. There were said to be ten thousand prostitutes, much to the pleasure of Boswell who, 'truly libertine', so he told Rousseau, 'ran after girls without restraint', his blood 'inflamed by the burning climate' and his 'passions violent'. There were also forty thousand *lazzaroni* who strolled half naked through the streets by day, picking pockets when opportunity offered, going down to the sea to bathe, then 'walking and sporting on the shore perfectly naked', and, in the evening, swarming into the taverns until thrown out into the street by waiters.

The streets were 'dreadfully dirty'. Not only the *lazzaroni* and the hundreds of hawkers and porters, not only the 'little brown children', whom Gray described as 'jumping about stark-naked, and the bigger ones dancing with castanets', 'relieved themselves whenever they felt the urge', but 'even people in carriages', so P.-J. Grosley said, 'often got out to mix with the pedestrians for the same purpose, each citizen taking the same liberty in other peoples' houses as he would have done in his own'. Yet, if some of the houses and palaces of Naples were as dirty as the streets, few complained of their owners' lack of hospitality.

Exceptionally generous were Gaetano Filangieri, author of *La Scienza della legislazione* and his delightful sister, the Principessa Ravaschieri di Satriano, and the Duke of Monte Leone who, according to Charles de Brosses, held 'the largest and most magnificent assembly in the town, which costs him, so they claim, more than fifty thousand francs in candles, ices and refreshments'. The Prince of Francavilla's entertainments were even more lavish. He frequently had young English gentlemen to splendid dinners, taking them to the casino afterwards and getting his pages, 'all sweethearts of the Prince', to dive into the sea. When one of his guests remarked that he would have preferred to see girls rather than boys, the Prince agreed to give another party the next day when a marble basin in his garden was 'filled with ten or twelve beautiful girls who swam about in the water'.

Evening entertainments at court were not so pleasant. The King from 1759 until his death in 1825 was the Bourbon Ferdinand I who, though 'exceedingly civil', looked to one tourist like 'an overgrown ass' and to William Beckford as though he had succeeded in prolonging his childhood into maturity: he seemed to 'see nothing but the end of his nose, which [was] doubtless a capital object'. His Austrian Queen was a 'sturdy looking dame' who gave the impression of a housewife bustling about after her poultry; while the Prince danced about like a cow, 'kicking up his hoofs and making a noise like the braying of an ass'.

Beckford was thankful when his presentation was over 'to return to Sir W.'s and hear Lady H. play'. Sir William Hamilton, a grandson of the third Duke of Hamilton, and, in Robert Harvey's opinion, 'a much more sensible though not so amiable a man as Sir Horace Mann', had been British Envoy in Naples since 1764 and had married, as his first wife, Catherine Barlow, daughter of Hugh Barlow of Lawrenny Hall, Pembroke. A woman of delicate health, plain, kind and retiring, she was a harpsichord player of exceptional talent; and she made her husband's official residence in Naples, the Palazzo Sessa, a veritable Accademia di Musica where musical assemblies were held every week. The palace was also a treasure trove of antiquities, as were Hamilton's two country villas just outside the city. His collections of Greek vases were renowned and many of these, together with bronzes, specimens of ancient glass, coins, gems and ivories were eventually acquired by the British Museum. But none of these treasures was considered more valuable than his second wife, the lovely Emma Hart, a Cheshire black-smith's daughter who had been the mistress of his nephew, Charles Greville. They lived most amicably together, so his wife told her former lover, and Sir William did 'nothing all day but look at [her] and sigh'. 'We have company almost every day,' she continued. 'They are all very much pleased with me, and poor Sir William is never so happy as when he is pointing out my beauty to them. He thinks I am grown much more ansome than I was.' As well as playing to entertain her husband's guests, she adopted what she called her 'attitudes', *poses plastiques* representing classical figures, clothed in diaphanous draperies or barely clothed at all. J.B.S. Morritt saw one of her performances and was duly impressed:

In her attitudes she exceeds herself, and joins every grace that ever was united to the greatest beauty of face and person. Such is Lady Hamilton and as we knew her story you may conceive we did not expect so much. She was perhaps designed by Dame Nature for the stage, as, besides her wonderful talent for attitudes, she has that of countenance to a great degree. I have scarce known her look the same for three minutes together, and, with the study she has made of characters, she mimics in a moment everything that strikes her, with a versatility you have not a notion of. After this you may suppose her entertaining to a degree . . . seeing her only can give you an adequate idea of what she is, as you may suppose from the reason given by her husband for marrying her, namely, that she only of the sex exhibited the beautiful lines he found on his Etruscan vases.

Every man has a reason for marrying, and this is certainly a new one, though perhaps as good a reason as most others. If one may judge from effects, the case is so indeed, for

118 (Above) The music room in the Neapolitan villa of Lord Fortrose, one of several foreigners who had homes in the city.

119 (Below) View of the first discovery of the Temple of Isis at Pompeii in 1765 from Hamilton's Campi Phlegraei.

120 (Left) 'From Sir William Hamilton's collection', a caricature of 1801 by Gillray, depicting the art collector and vulcanologist in the shape of a vase from his collection.

121 (Right) A shop in Naples, frequented by collectors of antiquities, with Sir William Hamilton, the British Envoy, third from the right, 1798.

no creature can be more happy or satisfied than he is in showing her off, which he does exactly as I have seen a wax figure exhibited, placing you in the most favourable lights, and pointing out in detail before her all the boasted beauties of his *chère moitié*, and, luckily for him, without any more bad effects upon her than would happen if she were a wax figure.

If not at the Hamiltons, the English tourist might well have been found at Posilipo, where the Irishwoman Sara Goudar, a former barmaid, lived with her French husband who ran their villa as a casino. She was also 'exquisitely beautiful', in Casanova's judgement, and 'sang with the voice of a syren'. And, if not at the Goudars', the English tourist was likely to be with the expatriate Sir Francis Eyles, whose villa was known as 'the English Coffee-house'; or he might have been encountered at one or other of those palaces where guests enjoyed themselves until five o'clock in the morning while their servants slept on the marble tiles of the baroque halls until it was time to escort their masters home; or, if at none of these places, he was probably at the opera.

The Neapolitan opera, in Lady Mary Wortley Montagu's opinion, was 'by far the finest in Italy'. But others complained that, unlike the opera in Paris, it was generally impossible, as elsewhere in Italy, to hear the performance above the chatter of the audience, the laughter, the shouts of excited gamblers, and the noisy greetings and kissings as parties moved about, upstairs and downstairs and from box to box. 'It would not only be the most fruitless, but the most vulger thing in the world,' so Morritt said, 'to attempt listening to the opera.'

122 (Left) Hamilton's second wife, Emma, the lovely daughter of a Cheshire blacksmith.
123 (Right) 'Poor Sir William,' his wife told her former lover, 'is never so happy as when he is pointing out my beauty.'

When Beckford entered the 'enormous edifice [of San Carlo], whose six rows of boxes blazed with tapers', a 'tolerable silence was maintained, the court being present; but the moment his Majesty withdrew (which great event took place at the beginning of the second act) every tongue broke lose, and nothing but buzz and hubbub filled up the rest of the entertainment. . . . Every lady's box is the scene of tea, cards, cavaliers, servants, lapdogs, abbés, scandal and assignations.' Even when the performance could be heard, 'for want of dancing,' so Charles Burney said, 'the acts are necessarily so long that it is wholly impossible to keep up the attention so that those who are not talking or playing usually fall asleep'.

Sleep was out of the question during the wild festivities and celebrations after the liquefaction of the blood of San Gennaro on the first Sunday in May and on 19 September. When the miracle was delayed the people 'grew quite outrageous', wrote John Wilkes who witnessed the ceremony in 1765. Since the failure of the dried blood to liquefy in its phial was a portent of disaster, 'the women shriek'd hideously, beat their breasts, and tore their hair. The men seemed equally frantic. They began the most frightful yelling, and several were cutting themselves with knives.' But then the 'cursed saint' relented; the miracle was performed as usual; and the wild celebrations began with shouting, kissing, laughter and the dancing of the tarantella to the beating of tambourines, instruments played long ago by their ancestors, 'as it appears', so Henry Swinburne noted, 'by the pictures of Herculaneum'.

When Swinburne's *Travels in the Two Sicilies* was published in 1790, the excavations at Herculaneum had not long since begun. Although the existence of a buried city beneath the vineyards and mulberry fields in the shadow of Vesuvius had long been known, it was not until 1738 that the search for it began at the suggestion of Ferdinand I's mother, who had been intrigued by the amount of classical statuary lying about in the palace gardens. By the end of that year various bronze statues, marble busts and painted columns had been uncovered; and in June 1740 Horace Walpole wrote to West, 'We have seen something to-day that I am sure you have never read of, and perhaps never heard of . . . perhaps one of the noblest curiosities that has ever been discovered. It was found out by chance about a year and a half ago. . . . They have found among other things some fine statues, some human bones, some rice, medals and a few paintings extremely fine.'

In December that year Lady Mary Wortley Montagu also visited the site and, like so many other observers, was appalled by the haphazard way in which the digging was being conducted.

Since the first discovery no care has been taken. And as the ground has fallen in, the present passage to it is, as I am told by everybody, extremely dangerous. . . . Probably great Curiositys might be found there, but there has been no expense made either by probing the Ground or clearing a way into it, and as the Earth falls in daily, it will possibly be soon stopp'd up as it was before. . . . I have taken all possible pains to get information, and am told 'tis the remains of the ancient city of Hercolana, and by what I can collect there was a Theatre entire with all the Scenes and ancient Decorations. They have broke it to pieces by digging irregularly.

The excavations continued haphazardly, however, and in April 1755 Robert Adam

viewed with great pleasure and much astonishment the many curious things that have been dug out, consisting of statues, busts, fresco paintings, books, bread, fruits, all sorts of instruments from a mattock to the most curious Chirurgical probe. . . . We traversed an amphitheatre with the light of torches and pursued the tracks of palaces, their porticoes and different doors, division walls and mosaic pavements [Adam continued]. We saw earthern vases and marble pavements just discovered while we were on the spot and were shown some feet of tables in marble which were dug out the day before we were there. Upon the whole this subterranean town, once filled with temples, columns, palaces and other ornaments of good taste is now exactly like a coal-mine worked by galley slaves.

By then excavations had also begun at Pompeii, and thereafter no Grand Tour was complete without a visit to both sites and to the various collections in Naples

124 (Opposite above) The excavations were at first carried on in a most haphazard manner.

125 (Below) The eruption of Vesuvius in 1774, depicted by Philipp Hackert.

126 *Antiquities from Herculaneum being transported ceremonially to the museum in Naples, with the King and Queen watching in the box to the left.*

where objects discovered could be inspected. So profound were the consequent effects upon taste that Sacheverell Sitwell suggested that the excavations might be accounted the second wave of the Renaissance. Coming so soon after Palladio's works had made so deep an impression, they destroyed any leanings the English aristocrat might have had towards rococo, and were responsible for the taste in interior decoration associated with the brothers Adam. The uncovering of Pompeii and Herculaneum was also largely responsible for late eighteenth-century taste in both furniture and decorative pottery. The 'Etruscan' pottery made famous by Josiah Wedgwood and the style of certain pieces of furniture associated with the names of Sheraton and Hepplewhite are directly derived from these discoveries. Indeed, one of Sheraton's chair designs which reproduced various classical *motifs* recovered from the excavations was actually called 'The Herculanium'.

While a visit to Pompeii and Herculaneum became *de rigueur* for the tourist after 1740, the ascent of Vesuvius, difficult as it was, always had been so. Sir William Hamilton, a learned vulcanologist, had climbed it twenty-five times within four years. Few tourists enjoyed the experience. Boswell laconically recorded, 'On foot to Vesuvius. Monstrous mounting. Smoke; saw hardly anything.' It took five men to get John Wilkes up, two in front whose belts he clung to, and three behind to push. He lay down at the edge of the crater and, peering in at the 'ragged mountains of yellow sulphur', was 'almost suffocated by the smoke'; and then descended 'with great difficulty, sometimes almost up to the knees in ashes'. Yet the masses of burned stone, the enormous cinders and clouds of sulphurous smoke were undeniably awe-inspiring, especially when fire poured out of the crater, spouting forth red hot stones and cinders that fell down in showers. 'Your views were converted into the most Hellish solemnity,' Robert Adam thought, 'whilst the view of nothing but sulphur, burnt rocks and ashes all around augmented the savage prospect.'

By the time they had returned to Naples from Vesuvius most tourists were making preparation for their journey home, planning the route so that they could visit towns they had missed on the journey south, making final purchases. They were unlikely to have bought as much as Lord Burlington, who returned home with 878 pieces of luggage; but there were few tourists who had not bought some work of art in addition to the mementoes, the clothes, prints and books that nearly every traveller accumulated on his journey.

As well as paintings, statues, objects of virtu, bas reliefs and a huge bust of the Emperor Lucius Verus, Thomas Coke, for instance, bought several valuable manuscripts in Venice and, in Padua, a large part of the library of the Canons Regular of San Giovanni in Verdara which had been in their possession since the fifteenth century. In addition to the paintings he had acquired in Rome, Lord Burlington bought a diamond ring there for 1,350 crowns, as well as a marble table, some porphyry vases and twelve miniatures by Rosalba Carriera. Among other items he also purchased a brass viol, two harpsichords and a set of silver dessert baskets in Paris (not to mention books and fourteen pairs of gloves); and, when he returned to Burlington House, he brought back with him the sculptor Giovanni Battista Guelfi, who was probably responsible for much of the garden statuary at Chiswick House, and Pietro Castrucci, who was to become first violin in Handel's operatic orchestras. The influence of Italy on Burlington had been decisive. Its influence on future generations was yet to be seen.

127 Rowlandson portrays a disapproving custodian showing foreign visitors round the 'Museum of ancient Paintings in Palace of Portici'.

CHAPTER II

*

SWITZERLAND,

GERMANY

AND THE

LOW COUNTRIES

*

'A vast variety of prospects'

'AFTER THE VARIOUS TOILS OF A FATIGUING journey,' so tourists were advised, they could not choose a 'more agreeable place of repose' than Geneva: 'the goodness of the air, the mildness of the government, and the plenty of all things, together with the conversation of the inhabitants, who are sprightly and polite, make this a most agreeable city to live in; insomuch that it is styled the court of the Alps.' To be sure, the 'utmost decorum' had to be observed during the hours of divine service on a Sunday, but as soon as the churches were empty 'the usual amusements' began, packs of cards were produced to play games prohibited by law in other parts of Switzerland where the precepts of Calvin were more rigorously observed, and families left the city for drives in the country until summoned to return by the beating of drums on the ramparts which gave warning of the imminent closure of the town gates.

No visit to Geneva was considered complete in the 1760s and early 1770s without a visit to Ferney, four miles outside the city, where Voltaire had bought an estate in 1758. 'You do not approach so close to Mecca without making the pilgrimage,' one visitor wrote. 'Ferney attracts more of the truly devout today than the Vatican.' Crowds of people gathered outside the house merely to get a glimpse of the great man 'as though it were a king passing', although, much as he relished the flattery, Voltaire grew to find such attention exasperating. 'Well, gentlemen,' he once burst out to a group of gaping Englishmen, 'you now see me; and did you take me to be a wild beast or a monster that was fit only to be stared at, as a show?' And to an English lady who managed to view the *philosophe* after many disappointments in 1776, he remarked gloomily, before immediately disappearing again, that he had obliged her by briefly emerging from his tomb.

Before he became a hypochondriacal recluse, however, English visitors were delighted by his welcome and hospitality, even though some, like Sir James Macdonald, confessed that they wished they could stop their ears when he made one of his blasphemous remarks, while others agreed with John Conyers that in 'talking to ladies he was inclined to be rather indecent and was too apt to be ludicrous'. James Boswell was at first rebuffed by a message from one of Voltaire's footmen that his master, who was still in bed, was 'very much annoyed at being disturbed', and when Voltaire did appear he did not seem much inclined to be

128 (Opposite) Boating parties on the lake in front of the Schloss *at Nymphenburg in about 1761 by Bellotto.*

gracious: an observation by the flustered visitor that the Academy of Painting in Glasgow had not proved a success, elicited the reply, 'No. To paint well it is necessary to have warm feet.' A subsequent enquiry as to whether his host still spoke English, brought forth the response, 'No. To speak English one must place the tongue between the teeth, and I have lost all my teeth.' A comment about Boswell's forthcoming tour of the Hebrides with Dr Johnson prompted the short exchange: 'Very well. But I shall remain here. You will allow me to stay here?'

'Certainly.'

'Well then go. I have no objection at all.'

Boswell was asked to stay for dinner, however, as were other guests, and although their host did not join them he did so when Boswell called on another occasion and after dinner 'some sat snug by the fire, some chatted, some sung, some played the guitar, some played at shuttlecock'.

It was rarely that there were no guests staying or dining in his house. When Gibbon called in 1763 and was entertained by a performance of *L'Orphelin de la Chine*, the 'whole company' was invited to 'a very elegant supper of a hundred covers' followed by a 'ball for a hundred people'.

Voltaire also had a house in Lausanne; and this place, too, seemed to one visitor 'as overrun with English as Geneva'. Gibbon had been sent there by his father and lived in the rue Cité-derrière with a Calvinist minister and his 'ugly, dirty, proud, ill-tempered and covetous wife'. He had not been happy at first, but he soon made friends with other Englishmen in the town, among them Lord Huntingdon, the Earl of Blessington and John Baker Holroyd, later Lord Sheffield, who described the pleasures of its assemblies, its balls, its parties with their games of cards and blind man's buff, its picnics in the summer.

If not as lively as Lausanne, other Swiss towns were considered quite as agreeable. Admittedly there was little exciting to do after dark; in some places sumptuary laws were still in force; in Zurich certain classes of people were forbidden to keep carriages; in Basel servants were not allowed to run behind them and the women inside them were condemned by Karamzin as being universally ugly. But most places were considered as pleasant as Berne, 'a beautiful city' with good shops, sparkling fountains and streets kept clean by gangs of men and women who not only swept the pavement, cleared up all the rubbish but even dusted the gates and rails. Most tourists, however, kept as clear as they could of the mountains, sharing Misson's view that it was 'matter enough for astonishment that anyone should venture', unless compelled to do so, among such 'dismal cliffs and precipices'. The wild and terrible chaotic beauty of Alpine scenery made little appeal to the early eighteenth-century eye, trained to appreciate the nice regularities of controlled forms and more responsive to pastoral scenes, to artificial ruins and cascades, and to trees cut into the shapes of peacocks than it was to the reckless grandeur of the wilderness. Thomas Gray was virtually alone among his contemporaries in sharing the enthusiasm which Ruskin was later to express for the beauty and grandeur of mountain scenery.

It was not until the middle of the eighteenth century that the tourist first began to be persuaded that the Alps might perhaps offer something more than a frisson of horror. In 1744 there appeared *A Letter from an English Gentleman giving an Account of the Glaciers or Ice Alps in Savoy*, which described an expedition to Chamonix undertaken by William Windham and seven companions. Twenty years later muleteers were organising excursions up the Alpine paths at a price of three shillings for a day's trip which included magnificent views of waterfalls and ice-capped summits. In 1765 an inn was opened at Chamonix to which John Moore and the Duke of Hamilton climbed merely for the sake of the scenery. Fifteen years later there were inns also at Grindelwald and Lauterbrunnen; and there were as many as thirty visitors a day to the Montanvert, most of them English. By the end of the century tourists were regularly making excursions to the Mer de Glace, the Glacier des Bossons, and to the source of the Aveyron, taking with them kettles to boil water in order to determine heights, as well as handbooks of Alpine plants. In 1789 William Coxe published his *Travels in Switzerland* in which he wrote of his leaving his party to 'enjoy interrupted, and with a sort of melancholy pleasure, these sublime exhibitions of Nature in her most awful and tremendous forms'. In 1790 Wordsworth walked for pleasure in the Swiss mountains.

Even then, however, the majority of tourists preferred to keep to the lowlands where the people were friendly and hospitable – often inviting travellers to share their simple meals – and where the inns were neat and welcoming.

This could not be said of the inns of Germany. These, indeed, though admittedly cheap, were frequently little better than barns in which, as Nugent warned, the traveller was tumbled pell-mell to sleep with 'landlord and landlady, men and servants, and passengers of both sexes, cows, sheep and horses'. In some of them broken shutters served the purpose of windows, straw took the place of beds, and, where beds were provided, these were likely to be 'little wooden boxes or troughs', as cold as they were uncomfortable. Sacheverell Stevens was obliged to put up at one such dreadful place in 'a dirty little village' in Westphalia. It

consisted of only one large room; at that end next the fire place were several little places, like cloaths presses, or closets with folding doors, in each place was a bed, to which you ascended by a little step-ladder; you are obliged to undress before the landlord and landlady, who see each passenger to his respective bed, and then shut the folding doors; but I begged to have mine left open for fear of being suffocated. At about ten yards from me, on one side of the room, there were several cows in their stalls, and on the other hogs in little pens. I never had so disagreeable a lodging.

129 'The splenitive Englishman travelling in Germany' by Bunbury, 1770. German postilions were widely condemned as the laziest, slowest, most drunken and intractable in Europe.

Boswell, having been offered a straw-covered table at an inn in Vellinghausen, was shown into a barn at Mameln in Hanover which was already occupied by eight or ten horses, four or five cows, a cock, several hens and an immense mastiff, growling most horribly and rattling his chains. He might well have felt grateful for the presence of the mastiff, since, as more than one guide-book counselled its readers, 'safety ought always to be suspected' in German inns: it was advisable to have your servants sleep in the same room as yourself, to keep a candle burning all night, to push the furniture against the door to prevent attack by 'needy assassins', and to show the landlord 'your firearms and to tell him, with a courageous look, that you are not afraid of a far superior number of enemies'.

This landlord was likely to be an uncivil fellow such as the one 'wrapt in a great coat, with a red worsted cap on his head and with a pipe in his mouth' who stalked before the door of the inn where Ann Radcliffe once stopped. 'He makes no alteration in his pace on perceiving you, or, if he stops, it is to eye you with curiosity; he seldom speaks, never bows, or assists you to alight; and perhaps stands surrounded by a troop of slovenly girls, his daughters, whom the sound of wheels has brought to the door.'

The food provided in such places was likely to be limited to greasy black sausage with *Sauerkraut* and gingerbread, or to 'miserable pumpernickel' or 'half raw bacon', while the beer offered was often deemed undrinkable, although German guests drank so much of it that a sofa was commonly placed near the dining-room table for the benefit of those too drunk to sit up.

If German landlords were surly and difficult, German postilions were even less helpful, 'insolent beyond measure and dreadful cheats', guilty of the 'most heinous impositions'. Karamzin found them 'insufferable'. 'They stopped at every tavern for beer, and the unfortunate travellers had either to put up with this or bribe them to go on.' The post-wagons they drove were scarcely distinguishable from peasants' carts, bumping and creaking along at three or four miles an hour over roads which in bad weather, so the *Traveller's Guide to Germany* warned, were 'a perfect misery', axle-deep in mud or wet sand. On his way to Berlin, Charles Burney's postilion lost his way in the dark and led his horses 'into a bog on a bleak and barren heath'. Catherine Wilmot was thrown into a ditch when the springs of her carriage broke, then, after rattling and screeching over 'such roads or rocks' that she felt she would never survive the journey, she was flung out of the vehicle again as one of the wheels flew off. She arrived at her destination 'more dead than alive', without strength to take off her clothes.

Uncomfortable as it so often was, travel in Germany was not cheap, and the tourist was constantly being called upon to pay extra charges above his *Postgeld* and *Wagengeld*. There was *Schossegeld* to pay at the turnpikes, *Schwargargeld* to pay the postilion, *Schmiergeld* for greasing wheels, *Barriergeld* at the toll-gates, and *Trinkgeld* for the ostlers' drinks. There were also the dues, both official and irregular, to be paid at the custom-houses in frontier towns, where, as in some Italian towns, baggage was searched with a slowness which Mariana Starke thought would be impossible to conceive by anyone who had not been through this ordeal. Charles Burney, shivering with cold in wet clothes after three hours' detention at the barrier outside Berlin, was detained for more than two hours at the custom-house while everything was taken out of his trunk and writing box and examined with a thoroughness equalled only by that displayed by the officials at Potsdam, whose examination could not have been more thorough had it been conducted at the postern of a town besieged. 'Name, character, whence, where, when, to whom recommended, business, stay,' and several other particulars were demanded, to which 'the answers were all written down'.

Germany had its compensations, though. A few of its inns were as good as the best in Switzerland and in the larger towns there were hotels as comfortable as any in Europe, the Three Kings at Augsburg, the Emperor and the Red House at Frankfurt, the Stockholm at Cassel, the Darmstadt Hof at Karlsruhe and the Hôtel de Pologne at Dresden all having international reputations and providing food which, strange as it sometimes looked, was excellent. *Schnitz*, for example, 'a dish of bacon and fried peas', had the appearance of an 'infamous mess', but, on tasting, proved to be 'better than passable'. Moreover the hospitality offered in private houses was, so Nugent said, as generous as it was unreserved: 'a single letter of introduction is sufficient to produce a person an agreeable reception among the Germans, which can hardly be said of the inhabitants of any other country'.

The poor were quite as welcoming as the well-to-do, even in the 1760s when the effects of the Seven Years War were still to be seen on every side and large tracts of desolated country were only just beginning to be brought back into cultivation. There were difficulties over language, of course, since few tourists had any German, and those who did had difficulty in understanding the various local dialects which were scarcely intelligible even to people from neighbouring provinces. But 'talk was easily dispensed with', so one tourist remarked, when 'a smiling housewife brought in steaming plates of beef and dumplings, *Zuckerwert* and *Pflaumenmus* with cream and apricots'. William Beckford recalled delightedly a family in Bavaria at whose cottage he had 'begged some refreshment'. Immediately there was a contention amongst the children who should be the first to oblige him. A little black-eyed girl succeeded and brought him 'an earthern jug full of milk, with crumbled bread, and a platter of strawberries fresh picked from the bank'. He had never been 'waited upon with more hospitable grace'.

Also, while the roads of Germany were indisputably appalling, travelling by water was generally a pleasure – though not all tourists found it so. Charles Burney, who went down the Isar and the Danube from Munich to Vienna in 1772, recorded a dismal journey which was memorable for a frightening thunderstorm and a hot and stuffy cabin ankle-deep in rainwater and constructed of 'green boards which exuded as much turpentine as would have vanquished all the aromatics of Arabia'. When the raft was moored for the night his servant went to the nearest village to buy food, but returned with nothing more appetising than beer, 'black, sour pumpernickel', 'vile' cheese and 'bad' apples. In the shallows of the Isar, Burney was in a perpetual fear that the boat, a flat-bottomed raft of fir logs, would run aground; and in the swirling Danube he was even more alarmed by the roaring noise the waters made as they rushed past the projecting rocks. Nor did the landscape compensate for the alarm and discomfort. Beyond the banks of the Isar was a wretched view of gravel, willows, sand and sedge; beyond Linz the Danube was so wide that the banks disappeared from view in a thick fog. Encouraged by the sight of Vienna, Burney's spirits were immediately dashed again by the customs officers who confiscated his books.

Burney's experiences were, however, exceptional. Going up the Danube from Regensburg, Lady Mary Wortley Montagu travelled 'in one of those little vessels that they very properly call wooden houses, having in them all the conveniences of a palace, stoves in the chambers, kitchens, etc. They are rowed by twelve men each, and move with such incredible swiftness that in the same day you have the pleasure of a vast variety of prospects'. Travelling on the Rhine was particularly pleasurable. Mirror-smooth, it was the 'beautifullest river in Europe'. In the

*130 Peter Jacob Horemans's ' A Musical Gathering at the Court of the Elector Karl Albert of Bavaria',
1730, detail.*

summer passengers were served with trout and salmon, asparagus and strawberries and delicious Rhenish hocks; and in the winter, though they had to
huddle over 'a little smoking stove', the views of vineyards and neat farms, of
crumbling castles and small riverside towns at the foot of rocky, wooded hills
were a constant delight.

The tourist's route through Germany was often largely governed by the letters
of introduction he had to present at the various princely courts. There were some
sixty of these scattered about the country, some the courts of petty princelings
scarcely worth a detour, others centred upon grand palaces offering generous
hospitality, splendid displays of paintings and sculpture, musical performances
of magnificent virtuosity, impressive military parades and thrilling hunting. The
language spoken at court was normally French, so those who had acquired some
command of that language in Paris or Blois had no cause to regret their lack of
German. They also had little cause for dissatisfaction with the welcome accorded
them. 'Everywhere in Germany,' Henry Crabb Robinson was to write in the next
century, 'English travellers are treated as if they were noble, even at the small
courts where there is no ambassador. No inquiry is made about birth, title, or
place.'

James Boswell, who revelled in ceremonial and dressing up, in 'shows and gaiety and ribbons and stars', drove excitedly from court to court, styling himself Baron and delighting in the low bows which the uncouth peasants made to his coach as it passed. Only at Mannheim and Potsdam was he disappointed by his reception. At Mannheim the Elector Palatine, Karl Theodor, was 'very high and mighty' when 'Baron Boswell' was presented to him, while the 'much painted' Electress was also 'exceedingly lofty'. The Elector's court was the scene of magnificent entertainments, French comedies as well as operas and concerts. But strangers were seldom invited to dine by the 'unhospitable dog', so Boswell was obliged to take his meals at an ordinary 'amongst fellows of all shapes and sizes, which disgusted [him] sadly'. At Potsdam he saw Frederick the Great standing before his palace in the sunlight with 'an air of iron confidence', carrying a cane and wearing a blue suit with a star and a white, feathered hat. He felt that he would never forget this 'glorious sight' of the monarch who had 'astonished Europe by his warlike deeds'. He longed to be presented to him, but this he could not contrive, even though he appeared at a military parade with a most conspicuous Scots blue bonnet which he was convinced would attract attention. His biographer says that Frederick the Great was 'the only person Boswell ever set himself seriously to meet without meeting'.

Elsewhere Boswell was delighted by the attentions paid to him. At Brunswick he had a 'pretty long conversation' with the Duke, and sat next to the Duke's brother at dinner. He was 'absolutely electrified' and felt that he had been born to live among princes. At the court of Anhalt-Dessau he hunted and danced as well as dined; at Gotha, upon his appearance in a suite of flowered velvet of five colours, the Princess invited him to her table, exclaiming '*M. Boswell! Mais vous êtes beau!*' At Karlsruhe he was presented to the Margrave of Baden-Durlach, 'a grave, a knowing, and a worthy prince' who recognised his 'merit'. At Dresden he found the court of Saxony in mourning and, as he had no black coat, he put a cockade in his hat, tied a piece of crêpe round his sleeve, and presented himself as an English officer. 'Sir, that is not a uniform,' protested the Elector's Master of Horse. 'No, sir, not properly speaking,' Boswell replied, quite unperturbed. 'But in our country, if you have a red coat, you are an officer; it is enough.' He was admitted: it was a 'great palace'; the Elector was a 'sweet prince'.

J.B.S. Morritt was also admitted to court at Dresden but liked it less well:

Yesterday I dined at Court, which is a pretty awful ceremony. . . . A German dinner lasts about three hours and a half, for when you are all seated round the table it is conceived you are all much too great people to make use of your hands, or to carve; so every dish is cut up by the servants at a sideboard, and handed round on plates one after the other, an excellent contrivance for getting the meat perfectly cold and prolonging a great beastly party, when you have nothing to say.

As well as visiting courts, tourists went to the university towns of Gottingen, Heidelberg, Jena and Leipzig. Boswell was so taken with Leipzig that he regretted not having been at the university there himself and made a resolution – fulfilled thirty-one years later – to send a son there instead; while an illegitimate son of the first Marquess of Lansdowne passed the winter of 1786–7 *'extreamely well and agreably'* at Leipzig, overlooking the fact that the 'fine people [were] merchants, and [finding] their society very pleasing and on an easy footing'. Tourists also visited Germany's famous watering places – Baden, Carlsbad, Langensschwalbach, Cleves and Wiesbaden – to take the waters and to recuperate from the exertions of travelling, the debilitating life of the German courts or self-indulgence in the Italian sun. In these watering-places the inns were far more comfortable than those of the country and although naturally more expensive were not unreasonably so. At Cleves, for example, towards the end of the eighteenth century, 'to prevent any imposition', there was 'a set of regulations respecting the price of rooms, meals, wines etc. According to these, you may sleep comfortably for five guilders (about nine shillings per week); breakfast for sixpence, dine for sixteen; sup for twelve, have a bottle of decent Rhenish wine, containing three pints for eighteen, and of Moselle for sixteen.'

The larger towns of Germany were, however, rarely found as interesting or as inviting as those in France or Italy, while their architecture was commonly dismissed as worthless, as it was by Benjamin Tate's tutor, Thomas Dampier, who told William Wyndham, 'If you receive no more Pleasure in Germany than we did in ye Little we passed thro' of it, you will heartily repent of your journey. Gothicism sits triumphant upon every Building and Palace in ye whole country.' There were certain exceptions. Salzburg was reckoned 'very handsome' with a cathedral that Baron Riesbeck thought the most handsome building he had seen since leaving Paris. Strasbourg also had a magnificent cathedral, 'one of the wonders of Germany', with a tower believed to be the highest in the world. Frankfurt, for long a centre for booksellers, was 'a rich and cheerful town', though so behind the times that when Goethe arrived at Leipzig university with a suit he had had made in Frankfurt he found himself dressed in the style of an earlier generation. And although its great days were yet to come under Ludwig I and his successors, Munich was generally considered a delightful place. 'The splendour and beauty of its buildings both public and private and the magnificence of its churches and convents,' wrote Nugent, 'are such that it surpasses anything in Germany for the bigness.' The Elector's palace was magnificent, its furniture 'rich beyond imagination'; the Munich opera was superb; and the social life most agreeable and convivial.

Immediately after supper [Beckford recorded], we drove to a garden and tea-room, where all degrees and ages dance jovially together till morning. Whilst one party whirl briskly away in the valz, another amuse themselves in a corner with cold meat and rhenish. That despatched, out they whirl amongst the dancers, with an impetuosity and liveliness I little expected to have found in Bavaria. After turning round and round, with a rapidity that is quite astounding to an English dancer, the music changes to a slower movement, and then follows a succession of zig-zag minuets, performed by old and young, straight and crooked, noble and plebeian, all at once, from one end of the room to the other.

Yet for the most part, English tourists liked few German towns well enough to stay in them for long. Hamburg was a 'sad place', Wordsworth thought; and, in Fynes Moryson's day, its inhabitants were 'so unmeasurably ill affected to the English' that it was unsafe to walk the streets after noon when the inhabitants were 'warmed with drink'. Cologne, the ugliest town in Germany in Baron Riesbeck's opinion, was roundly condemned for its insolent beggars, its squalor, its dilapidated churches littered with tawdry ornaments, its dirty, smelly streets in which weeds grew through cracks in the paving, and its ill treatment of Jews who, as at Augsburg, were mostly obliged to live in villages outside the city walls and, as at Frankfurt, to wear a piece of yellow cloth when permitted to enter through them. It was a 'beastly place', Thackeray considered, expressing an opinion that an earlier generation would have fully endorsed: 'The cathedral unfinished, the weather hot beyond all bearing. I was consequently in my room a great part of the day, employing myself between sleeping, smoking, reading, eating raw herrings and onions.'

Mainz appeared to be in 'a perpetual state of decay and neglect'; Coblenz was 'dingy'; Bonn was rather less gloomy than it had been in Misson's day when it was 'a dirty little city' in which there was 'nothing to detain the visitor', but it still received few plaudits. So did Düsseldorf, whose celebrated art gallery was the one inducement to persuade strangers 'to stay a moment within its walls'. 'More crooked streets, more indifferent houses' than those of Düsseldorf one 'seldom met with'. Except by soldiers, the place seemed deserted. Nuremburg, where 'a frightful horn' sounded from the walls each evening to warn people to hasten home before the gates were locked, was even more depressing. Here there were several distinguished families, some very rich, yet so haughty, according to Nugent, that 'nobody visits them, and they scarce visit one another'. 'They are apt to ape the noble Venetians in everything,' he continued, 'and to tyrannize over the people. They wear pointed hats and monstrous bushy ruffs.' 'Conversation with the fair sex is under much greater restraints in Nuremburg than in most other large cities,' John George Keysler added a few years later. 'And although a foreigner be recommended to a Nurenberger in the strongest manner, he will very seldom invite him to his house if he has a wife or daughter, but is so mistrustful that he rather chuses to carry him to a tavern, and there do him the honour of a *rausche*, i.e. make him drunk.'

Rather than spend his time in such towns as these, the tourist was advised to stay in smaller places like Mannheim, 'one of the most handsome little towns of Europe' where, in Beckford's words, 'almost every window bloomed with carnations' and it was hardly possible to cross a street 'without hearing a german flute'. Or he was advised to make straight for Berlin, which was admitted to be 'certainly one of the most beautiful cities in Europe', as well as being one of the most lively. Some complained of the fearful smells arising from the canals, but Boswell, who stayed with a friendly, jolly family in the old part of the city, thought Berlin 'the finest city' he had ever seen. It was situated on 'a beautiful plain'; its streets were 'spacious', and its houses 'well-built'. He recalled with pleasure meals in the garden with his host and hostess after his fencing practice or riding lessons at the academy, romps with their children, rides in their chaise, evening strolls Unter den Linden, visits with friends to the Tiergarten where he had supper at 'a kind of little Vauxhall' and drank delicious cherry wine, a visit to a brothel, his adventure with the wife of the Potsdam guardsman.

Like Berlin, Vienna was considered an excellent place for an English tourist to settle for a time. There were fencing and riding schools, good libraries and theatres; the operas at the Burgtheater, founded by Joseph II in the Michaelerplatz, were as well produced and sung as anywhere else in Europe. And although Mariana Starke had harsh words to say of them towards the end of the century, it was generally accepted that, for those who could afford them, the larger inns, among them the Court of Bavaria, the Golden Crown, the Black Eagle and the Black Elephant, were all first class; while for those who had 'occasion to be careful in their expenses' private lodgings were available, if not always easy to find – one visitor ran about the city three whole days with his *laquais de place* before he found rooms to suit him.

Vienna, Martin Sherlock wrote, 'is perhaps the best city in Europe to teach a young traveller the manners of the great world; at his arrival he will be introduced into all the best houses; and, if he is an Englishman, he will meet with the most flattering reception'. 'Indeed, if an Englishman wore his shoes on his head,' Morritt thought, 'he would have imitators here, as we are in high vogue and received with great cordiality.' 'I imagine there is no city in Europe where a young gentleman after his university education is finished, can pass a year with so great advantage,' Dr Moore considered, 'because, if properly recommended, he may mix on an easy footing with people of rank and have opportunities of improving himself by the conversation of sensible men and accomplished women.'

The young and susceptible tourist had to be on his guard against falling into the extravagant and even dissolute ways of the city which, in atmosphere, was more French than German, in which French fashions prevailed, in which the French language was to be heard as often as German in the fashionable salons,

131 A view by Bellotto of Munich, regarded by many tourists as the most delightful town in Germany.

and in which, so Morritt believed, society was not only French in manners but also in morals, 'which are pretty licentious. No woman here loses her character in society for what would in England banish her from it even now.'

'In the short time I have been here,' reported Baron Riesbeck, whose *Voyages en Allemagne* was published in 1792, 'I have seen more splendid equipages and horses than there are in all Paris. Our fashions prevail here universally. Dressed dolls are regularly sent from Paris for the purpose of teaching the women how to put on their gowns and dress their heads. Even the men from time to time get *memoranda* from Paris, and lay them before their taylors and hairdressers.'

There is no place in the world where people live more luxuriously than at Vienna [Nugent had written a generation earlier]. Their chief diversion is feasting and carousing, on which occasions they are extremely well served with wine and eatables. People of fortune will have eighteen or twenty sorts of wines at their tables, and a note is laid on every plate mentioning every sort of wine that may be called for. Especially on court days one sees the greatest profusion and extravagance in this kind of pageantry, the servants being ready to sink under the weight of their liveries, bedawbed all over with gold and silver.

On winter nights when the Danube and its branches were frozen over, and the streets covered with snow, ladies in fur-lined velvet capes adorned with jewels drove about in horse-drawn sledges constructed to resemble tigers, swans, griffins or shells. The horses were caparisoned with ribbons, plumes and bells; footmen rode in front with flaring torches; and 'a gentleman sitting on the sledge behind [led] the direction of the horse'. One young Englishman who was taken for a ride in one of these sledges to a dinner party thought that the jingling bells, the night lights in the windows, the shadows on the snow, the laughter and music were sights and sounds he would never forget.

In summer the town presented a less romantic appearance. The streets were often described as being both 'dirty and narrow', only the Prat, which was 'frequented by people of quality as the Mall is in London,' being kept reasonably clean. There were 'hardly three squares or places' which made 'any figure at all', in Baron Riesbeck's judgement, while the Emperor's palace was an 'old black building [with] neither beauty nor stateliness'. Where the great promenades now delight the eye a shabby wall enclosed the narrow streets.

Beyond the wall, however, there were palaces of astonishing splendour: the Liechtenstein with its splendid gardens and notable picture gallery, the two magnificent, riotously decorated baroque Belvedere palaces built between 1716 and 1724 for Prince Eugen of Savoy by the Italian-born Lukas von Hildebrandt, and Schönbrunn, which was built by another master of Baroque who drew his inspiration from Italy, Johann Bernhard Fischer von Ehrlach. Here the Empress Maria Theresa brought up her sixteen children, including Marie Antoinette, who in 1755 was born in an armchair to which her mother had retreated from her desk when labour pains briefly interrupted her examination of state papers.

From Vienna tourists often set out for Prague by way of Dresden, a charming city with a world-famous picture gallery for which visitors paid 'monstrously dear' to see all the treasures. On the way they passed through a pleasantly hilly countryside, 'beautifully filled with vineyards', and in Prague they found a beautiful and wealthy city, though extensively damaged in the Seven Years' War. Its white stone houses, its copper-roofed churches, its many-arched medieval bridge spanning the Moldau, its ancient palace of the Kings of Bohemia overlooking the city from the heights, its fine Italianate buildings and Gothic cathedral all combined to make it, for one tourist at least, 'the handsomest city in Europe'. Moreover, the people were 'so handsome, the shops so good and everything [looked] so happy and delightful'. 'As to the company,' wrote another pleased visitor, 'there is no town in the empire that has a greater choice. There are assemblies in the houses of quality every night, where they divert themselves with gaming and crown the night with good cheer, as pheasants, ortolans, trouts, salmon and crayfish, with good wine.'

Tourists who now turned west to go home through the Low Countries were unlikely to see such assemblies on the Continent again. 'The gentility and nobility are not numerous,' wrote Nugent of the Dutch, 'many of their families having been extinguished in the Wars with Spain.' Those that remained were 'remarkable for their frugality and order in their expences'. Indeed, to many travellers it seemed that orderliness in the Low Countries was carried almost to excess. Several wrote with undisguised irritation of the obsessive passion for regularity, cleanliness and neatness displayed by the Dutch, their continued washing and scrubbing of floors and benches, their horror of seeing so much as a piece of orange peel in the streets, their habit of taking their shoes off before going upstairs, of offering visitors mats to wipe their boots on and straw slippers to wear before stepping on the spotless tiles of the *voorhuis*, the entrance hall which also served as a reception room. Sir William Temple, who was ambassador at the Hague for several years, recounted the story of a visitor who called at a house with a speck of mud on his shoes and was immediately seized in a fireman's lift by a hefty maidservant who carted him to the foot of the stairs, unloaded him on a lower step, and replaced the offending shoes with slippers before admitting him to her mistress's room.

After their experiences of inns in Germany, however, most tourists were thankful to find those in the Netherlands so tidy and spruce. Nugent commented adversely on Dutch innkeepers who reacted furiously if their bill was questioned and he recommended his readers to stay in English inns, which could be found in every large town and in which they would be accommodated very comfortably for five shillings a day, having their victuals dressed after the English manner. Certainly Dutch cooking was not to be recommended. Foreigners spoke disgustedly of the national dish, *hutsepot* – a stew of meat, vegetables and prunes, mixed with lemon juice and strong vinegar and boiled at length in fat and ginger. They also deprecated the Dutch habit of cooking huge amounts of food once or twice a week and then either reheating it or serving it cold with great quantities of bread, butter and cheese and gallons of beer. 'Butter, cheese and salt-meat are not foods that demand a great deal of attention,' the abbé Sartre commented. 'Their meat broth is nothing more than water full of salt or nutmeg, with sweetbreads and minced meat added, having not the slightest flavour of meat and showing quite clearly that it has not taken more than an hour to prepare.' Furthermore, as soon as the meal was over, and even between courses, Dutchmen lit up their pipes and blew smoke all over the table, occasionally spitting into the pots placed upon the cloth for that purpose. Grosley said that on opening the door of a small coffee-house he was almost blinded by the thick clouds emanating from hundreds of smokers inside.

Even so, the English traveller was readier to praise than condemn most of the large inns of the Low Countries, to comment upon their shining floors, their gleaming ornaments, their fresh linen and well-aired beds, and their reasonable prices, except in those places where the extravagance of rich Englishmen had induced the landlord to increase his charges, like the one who imposed upon Samuel Pratt by demanding for a plate of shrimps and a glass of milk and geneva four and a half times what he had seen a Dutchman pay.

132 A house in the Netherlands bordering a canal on which tourists could travel in the greatest comfort.

The inns at the Hague were unequivocally declared by one visitor to be without question the best in the world, yet one could live in them for as little as five or six shillings a day, whereas in London, at the King's Arms in Pall Mall or at Pontac's in the City, it required 'good economy to come off for fifteen shillings or a guinea a day'. The inns at Brussels were also said to be 'equal to any in Europe; and a stranger has this advantage, that for less than twentypence English, he knows where to dine at any time betwixt twelve and three on seven or eight dishes. The wines are very good and cheap.'

There was high praise, too, for the tree-lined main roads of both Flanders and the United Provinces. They were 'well worth the notice of a Traveller,' commented James Essex in 1773, 'being made through the most delightful enclosed country that can be imagined'. He singled out the Antwerp–Brussels road, which was 'paved in the middle as well as the best streets in London, and kept in better repair'. The road from Brussels to Ghent was equally good, 'all a fine causeway thirty miles long, broader than any street and well paved'.

The carriages were also far better than the German ones, the diligences, for instance, having separate chairs all facing the front and each having its own sash window through which the passenger could admire the views of the open countryside that seemed to Lady Mary Wortley Montagu like one large garden containing canals 'full of boats, passing and repassing', trim gabled houses with polished windows, windmills turning gently in the sun. Although irritated by the slowness of the carriage that crawled along so sedately that he believed a tortoise could have kept up with it without once being out of breath, William Beckford was at the same time captivated by the 'minute neatness of the villages, their red roofs, and the lively green of the willows' that shaded them, the 'innumerable barges gliding busily along', the storks 'parading by the water-side . . . and, as far as the eye could reach, the large herds of beautifully spotted cattle enjoying the plenty of their pastures'.

Beckford would have travelled even more slowly by water, but most tourists agreed that this was the way to get about in the Low Countries, being both comfortable and, at less than a penny a mile, very cheap. The most common conveyances were *trechschuits* which departed regularly from their landing places at the ringing of a bell, stopping 'at certain villages to give the passenger an opportunity of stretching himself, and taking a little refreshment in the inns'.

The boat is drawn by a horse and contains about twenty or five and twenty passengers [recorded one satisfied passenger]. It is very clean, and has a deck over it which covers them from rain. . . . They talk, read, sew, knit, as each likes best; and do not know they are going by water, except they look out, and see they are moving, the motion is so insensible. . . . Strangers are equally surprised and charmed by this way of travelling, as it is indeed far the most commodious, best regulated, and cheapest in Europe.

One *trechschuit* in particular, plying daily between Ghent and Bruges along a thirty-mile long canal, was described in the *Travellers' Guide through the Low Countries* as 'the most remarkable boat of the kind in all Europe; for it is a perfect tavern divided into several apartments, with a very good ordinary at dinner of six or seven dishes, and all sorts of wines at moderate prices. In winter they have fires in their chimneys, and the motion of the vessel is so small, that a person is all the way as if he were in a house.' The meal, which would almost certainly include pickled herrings, sausages and cheese, might also comprise soup, duck and salmon, veal, mutton or beef, vegetables and fruit, and would seldom cost more than 1s 6d. In 1773 James Essex paid 1s 3d for such a meal, which also included 'soals', 'biskits', 'crumplins' and filberts. The beer and bread were free.

Those who entered the Netherlands from Cologne and Düsseldorf usually made straight for Amsterdam through Arnhem, whose wholesome air attracted 'a great many persons of distinction'. At Amsterdam they would probably try to get rooms at the Queen's Head or the English Bible in Warmoes Street, and then set out to see this 'most singular looking town' in a canal boat, a screeching slide-carriage or a 'sporting cart', a small wooden vehicle whose wheels rattled and bumped over the cobbles and the planks of the bridges, through streets crowded with sailors and porters, coachmen and rope-dancers, puppeteers, street vendors, money-changers and musicians, with women in wooden shoes with pointed toes washing the streets, and hawkers at the ends of the bridges selling

133 *Isaak Ouwater's painting of the Prinsengracht in Amsterdam in 1782.*

fruit, making pies and frying pancakes. They went to see the warehouses on the islands of Bikkers and Realen, and the grandiose town hall, the Burgersaal, now the royal palace, finished in 1656 and built of stone imported from Germany in contrast to the surrounding brick, its foundations resting on almost fourteen thousand piles hammered into the mud. They visited the Exchange, modelled on that of Antwerp; the Weigh House in Nieuwmarkt Square, built as one of the city gates in 1488; the many churches, including the Zuiderkerk whose tower, so much admired by Christopher Wren, was said to have inspired some of his designs for his churches in the City of London, and was painted more than once by Rembrandt who had lived in a house opposite. They went to the Spin-House, where 'incorrigible and lewd women' were locked up and made to spin for the benefit of the poor, and where the custodians, though looking like 'grave and sober matrons', accepted payment to grant access to their charges 'on which occasions it is customary for these lewd women to entertain their visitors with such abominable discourses and indecent actions as are shocking to men of any sense of morality'.

Despite their reputation for strict respectability, there were also more women in Amsterdam who, provided they were not too closely tied to their families, were prepared to have liaisons with foreigners – sensual women in France were said 'to make love like a Dutchwoman'. And, while family life might appear to be eminently blameless, there were numerous cafés and dance-halls frequented by girls only too willing to take men home with them. There were hundreds of prostitutes in the streets by the docks, and in lodging-houses where their portraits were displayed on the doors.

From Amsterdam, the tourist might go to the Hague, universally agreed to be a most attractive city in which the houses and walks were 'exceedingly fine, and the air very good, which [made] it a most agreeable place'. 'The inhabitants are more genteel, conversible, and civil to strangers than those of the other cities of the provinces,' one commentator suggested. They were also far more taken up with fashions than were the people of Amsterdam, where in the cold weather, so Oliver Goldsmith said, 'the true Dutchman cuts the strangest figure in the world. He wears no coat but seven waistcoats and nine pairs of trousers. . . . The Dutchwoman wears as many petticoats.' The people of the Hague were also great gamblers, yet those 'who do not play are not thought so unfashionable and ill-bred, and consequently are not so much out of countenance as at Paris or London'.

Rotterdam, the birthplace of Erasmus, was also much admired. Peter Mark Roget, travelling tutor to the sons of a Manchester cotton merchant, who was enchanted by its rows of large trees and its 'fine canals filled with a variety of pretty sailing boats', described it as 'very beautiful'. To Lady Mary Wortley Montagu it presented yet another 'new scene of pleasure'. Both remarked upon its 'remarkable cleanliness'. Lady Mary – who was none too clean herself and once replied to a person who commented upon her dirty hands, 'If you call that dirty, you should see my feet!' – walked 'almost all over the town *incognita* in [her] slippers, without receiving one spot of dirt'.

All the streets are paved with broad stones [she continued], and before the meanest artificers' doors are seats of various coloured marbles, and so neatly kept. . . . You may see the Dutch maids washing the pavement of the street [more thoroughly] than ours do our bedchambers. . . . Here is neither dirt nor beggary to be seen. One is not shocked with those loathsome cripples, so common in London, nor teazed with the importunities of idle fellows and wenches, that choose to be nasty and lazy. The common servants and little shop-women here are more nicely clean than most of our ladies.

Similar compliments were paid to Scheveningen, than which there was not 'a pleasanter or more refreshing place anywhere for coaches, chaises, or people on foot on the sands, especially when the sea is out'; to Zutphen, 'a large, handsome, well-built town'; to Edam where those 'excellent cheeses that have a red crust' are made, and where a mermaid had been taught to spin and dress like a woman, though not to speak. Praise was also bestowed upon Nijmegen, Delft, Middelburg and the university towns of Utrecht, where James Boswell had studied, and Leyden where John Wilkes had spent two years in the 1740s – returning from 'that famous and much frequented seat of learning' with the 'tone and bearing of a scholar and gentleman' – and where, in the anatomy school, visitors were shown an assortment of curiosities ranging from a cat with wings and the dried skin of a Scotchman to a 'vegetable Priapus which is a curious plant' and 'a monster issued out of a hen's egg'.

Crossing the Rhine and the Maas, the tourist passed the frontier into the Austrian Netherlands and came to Antwerp, once one of the most prosperous and populous ports in Europe, but by the middle of the eighteenth century a neglected town of 212 streets and 22 squares in nearly all of which the grass grew in deep silence. It was a 'gloomy and lifeless' place in James Edward Smith's words; 'thinly inhabited' in Dr Roget's; and, in Beckford's, the quietest, dreariest place he had ever come across. 'There were no groups of squabbling children or talkative old women' to be seen when he arrived. 'The whole town seemed retired into their inmost chambers.' He kept 'winding and turning about from street to street, and from alley to alley without meeting a single inhabitant. Now and then, indeed, one or two women in long cloaks and mantles glided by at a distance; but their dress was so shroud-like, and their whole appearance so ghostly, that [he] was more than half afraid to accost them.'

Were any one to ask my advice upon the subject of retirement [he added], I should tell him: By all means repair to Antwerp. No village amongst the Alps, or hermitage upon

Mount Lebanon, is less disturbed: you may pass your days in the great city without being the least conscious of its sixty thousand inhabitants, unless you visit the churches. There, indeed, are to be heard a few devout whispers, and sometimes, to be sure, the bells make a little chiming; but walk about, as I do, in the twilights of mid-summer, and be assured your ears will be free from all molestation.

Beckford thought little of the other towns in Flanders he visited: Ostend was 'so unclassic a place! Nothing but preposterous Flemish roofs [and] mongrel barbers.' He was smoked out by the tobacco fumes and 'half poisoned with garlic', and, on entering a church in search of quiet and solitude, he found instead that 'half a dozen squeeking fiddles fugued and flourished away in the galleries, as many paralytic monks gabbled away before the altars, whilst a whole posse of devotees, wrapped in long white hoods and flanels, were sweltering on either side'. Ghent was not much better: 'a large, ill-paved dismal-looking city, with a decent proportion of convents and chapels, stuffed with monuments, brazen gates and glittering marbles'. Beckford did not extend his disapprobations to Bruges, but it was said by others that this had a 'decayed and mouldered aspect'. At every turn one saw 'traces of departed wealth and greatness', reflected in the still waters of its silent canals. Tournai seemed gloomy, too, as did Ypres and Namur, though the first two were worth visiting for their cathedrals and the last for its citadel, the medieval castle of the counts, high on a rock above the town.

Tourists wrote more favourably of Liège where, according to Nugent, the inns were 'very good', the provisions 'extremely cheap', good wine was available in great variety, and, in fact, a gentleman of small estate could live 'more comfortably than in any other place in the world'. But, if the traveller sought gaiety he was advised to go to Aix – where the waters and baths were said to be effective in the cure of all manner of disorders from gout and scurvy to rheumatism and sciatica, and 'where intrigues could be carried on with the ladies, as at Bath' – or, even better, he should go to Spa whose many inns had been frequented by foreigners since the sixteenth century. In the eighteenth century it was perhaps the most celebrated watering-place on the Continent, visited by royalty, including Joseph II and Peter the Great, and by numerous English tourists from Charles James Fox who had 'no difficulty in dissipating some of the paternal wealth' here, to the Earl of Carlisle who in August 1768 told George Selwyn, 'I rise at six; am on horseback till breakfast; play at cricket till dinner; and dance in the evening till I can scarce crawl to bed at eleven. This is a life for you.'

Brussels was even more lively as well as being regarded as 'one of the most brilliant cities in Europe'. Its inhabitants were affable and polite, its gardens and squares delightful, its fountains comparable with those of Rome. But few tourists stayed here long. If they were on their way home, as most of them were, they were anxious to set off for the Channel ports and to be back on the Dover road.

CHAPTER 12

*

WILDER

SHORES

*

'Some we steal, some we buy'

IN THE EIGHTEENTH CENTURY IT WAS UN-usual for an English traveller to venture into Portugal and Spain, to journey east into the Turkish Empire or to go south from Naples to Sicily and North Africa. When the second Duke of Richmond left for Spain in the 1720s, Lord Townsend could not 'conceive what curiosity should lead his Grace so much out of the usual road of travellers'. Even in the second half of the century, when travelling in the peninsula was not quite so uncommon, as many precautions had to be taken, so Thomas Pelham said, as if one were 'going into Arabia'. And those who did travel in these countries were usually such as could afford the attendants who accompanied Henry Swinburne to Spain in 1775 and to Sicily in 1777. When William Beckford arrived in Portugal in 1787 his attendants included a doctor, a chef, a tailor, a barber and over twenty servants who were able to ensure that their master escaped many of the discomforts that beset Robert Southey, who landed at Coruña in 1795 on his way to stay with an uncle in Lisbon. Southey was immediately apalled by 'the filth of the streets, so strange and so disgusting to an Englishman', by the dinner at his inn – 'a fowl fried in oil, and served up in an attitude not unlike that of a frog taken suddenly with a fit of the cramp, and an omelet of eggs and garlic, fried in the same execrable oil' – and by the misery of a restless night in which he was 'so flead' that a painter would have found him 'an excellent subject for the martyrdom of St Bartholomew'. Later, in Lisbon, Southey could not pass a street 'without being sickened by some huge tumour, some misshapen member, or uncovered wound, carefully exposed to the public eye'.

Beckford, too, rich as he was, could not avoid the bites of the fleas and mosquitoes of Spain, nor could he escape 'the human ephemera of Lisbon' who, 'the whole night long, frisk and dance and tinkle their guitars from sunset to sunrise. The dogs, too, keep yelping and howling without intermission; and what with the bellowing of litanies by parochial processions, the whizzing of fireworks, which devotees are perpetually letting off in honour of some member or other of the celestial hierarchy, and the squabbles of bullying rake-hells, who scour the streets in search of adventures, there is no getting a wink of sleep, even if the heat would allow it.' But, before long, Beckford moved out of the city to a *quinta* at Cintra where, in 'an ample saloon', he was able to lie down on a mat of the 'finest and most glossy straw', to contemplate 'the serene summer sky and the moon rising slowly from behind the brow of a shrubby hill'. Here he settled down with his books, his numerous attendants, and a flock of sheep sent out from Wiltshire, making occasional journeys into the surrounding countryside, listening to his musicians whom he concealed in groves of orange and bay trees, and visiting the Marquis de Marialva who lived in a feudal state which made his own household seem modest, with fifty retainers to wait at table, where dinners were served in thirty-five courses and entertainments were provided by 'swarms of musicians, poets, bull-fighters, grooms, monks, dwarfs and children of both sexes'.

When it was time to move on to Spain, Beckford departed by coach, riding off in as grand a way as he did in Italy where, with outsiders and relays of spare horses, he was mistaken for the Emperor of Austria. He had his own bed erected each night on the way and carpets spread around the room, and he arrived majestically in Madrid, passing through 'crowds of Mahogany-coloured hags, who left off thumping their linen to stare' at his retinue. As he approached the centre of the city he was much surprised by the neatness of the pavements, the loftiness of the houses and the cheerful, showy appearance of many of the shops. 'Upon entering the Calle D'Alcala, a noble street, much wider than any in London, I was still more surprised,' he wrote. 'Several magnificent palaces and convents adorn it on both sides. At one extremity, you perceive the trees and fountains of the Prado, and, at the other, the lofty domes of a series of churches. We have got apartments at the Cruz de Malta which . . . have the advantage of commanding this prospect.'

Travelling in South Italy and Sicily after Beckford's return to England, Craufurd Tait Ramage, tutor to the sons of the British Consul in Naples, enjoyed no such advantages. His experiences of journeys in the Kingdom of the Two Sicilies may be taken as characteristic. Soon after leaving Naples he found that a stranger in these remote parts of the peninsula was such an unusual sight that a band of peasant women took fright at his appearance, scampering 'off in the utmost confusion'; and when he approached Torchiara, whose inhabitants stared at him silently as he passed along, and entered a *locanda*, in which 'Salvator Rosa looking men' sat beneath hams and sausages, goats' cheese and dried fruit hanging in nets from the ceiling, everyone looked curiously up at him as he called for a flask of wine in the Italian upon which educated people in Naples had complimented him but which the landlord could not understand. 'The door was crowded, and they were climbing on each other's backs to look in at the windows. I was, no doubt, regarded as a great curiosity, as no Englishman had ever probably passed through their village before.'

On his travels Ramage usually had to be content with 'the everlasting sausage, coarse black bread and miserable wine', with occasional lumps of cheese so hard he could 'scarcely make any impression' upon them, with 'cold salted fish, swimming in vapid vinegar', and salads reeking of garlic. Sometimes he enjoyed a quail

134 One of the unpaved squares of Palermo, a town described by one tourist as 'apparently about to tumble into ruins' – drawn by Sir Richard Colt Hoare.

or a *beccafico*, a cup of coffee with a kind of liqueur, *rosolio*, made from figs, or an omelette, soup and a plate of macaroni in a monastery, but these were rare treats. At night he usually found himself in some such room as that in Calabria, where he was woken by 'a fearful uproar' from a number of chickens and ducks and two young pigs who took refuge with the insects in his bed, or the attic in Paestum containing a few boards to serve as a bed, a stool, a box, and a window with no glass and with shutters that did not fit. *En route* there were large black snakes to contend with, clouds of buzzing flies whose stings caused great pain, hornets, dogs that attacked him and had to be kept at bay with his tattered umbrella, bandits and such jacks-in-office as the well-dressed young man who, announcing himself as 'the Royal Judge of the District', peremptorily demanded 'in a loud and authoritative tone' who he was and what he wanted when Ramage sought hospitality at a monastery in Camerota.

He gave a sad picture of himself jogging along towards Taranto:

I am pretty well accustomed to the heat of this climate; to-day, however, was a fearful trial, and I was now convinced that my friends were right in warning me of what I had undertaken. . . . My umbrella was scarcely any protection, and my clothes would scarcely fit an Irish beggar. Perched on the back of my mule, which had an uneasy movement,

135 (Left) Lady Hester Stanhope in her habitual costume of an Arab chieftain, smoking her long pipe.
136 (Right) Lord Barrington arrayed in classical costume for his portrait painted by George Knapton for the Society of Dilettanti in the 1740s.

holding my umbrella over my head as I best could, I looked forward anxiously for the first view of Taranto. Our wine, too, was soon at an end. No water was to be found, and the pangs of thirst I never experienced so strongly before. Before we entered the city we had to cross the Tara, a very considerable stream, though it seems on the map to run only a short distance inland. Here we were all glad to bathe our throbbing temples; as the water was brackish, our thirst could not be slaked. The muleteers had some hesitation about crossing this stream, as they had heard of people being carried down to the sea. After consultation, one, who could swim, agreed to make the attempt, and entered the stream with his mule, while his companions and myself looked anxiously on. We expected every moment to see the mule floundering in the water; yet he got safely across, and, following his example, we reached the other side, though not without being thoroughly drenched. . . . In this dripping state I rode into the public square of Taranto, which was crowded with inhabitants, and my appearance evidently caused great amazement, as it was impossible for them to imagine how I should have got into such a state. I must have had much the appearance of a drowned rat. . . . I had been now quite twelve hours jogging on the back of a mile, and I need not tell you how thoroughly knocked up I felt. I proceeded straight to a man who was selling iced water, and, mingled a glass of it with *rosolio*, drank it off, setting at defiance all consequences. It is astonishing that my health should not have broken down under the fatigue and heat I have undergone.

For those with resources as slender as Ramage's, travelling in the Turkish Empire could be quite as much of an ordeal as in the Kingdom of the Two Sicilies. A

137 (Left) Thomas Bruce, seventh Earl of Elgin, whose acquisition of the marbles from the Parthenon aroused such anger in Lord Byron.

138 (Right) Byron in Albanian dress, which he thought the 'most magnificent in the world', portrayed by Thomas Phillips, c. 1813.

journey into Greece, which then formed part of the Turkish Empire, had never been part of the traditional Grand Tour, and few Englishmen had attempted to follow the example of Sir George Wheeler who, while in Rome in the 1670s, had been persuaded by a French archaeologist to venture further afield and had given an account of his subsequent travels in *Journey into Greece*. When the Society of Dilettanti was established in the 1730s with the object of 'encouraging at home a taste for those objects which had contributed so much to [the tourists'] entertainment abroad', one of its founder members, the fourth Earl of Sandwich, was considered highly adventurous when he embarked for Athens in 1738. A few years later two other young members of the Society, Nicholas Revett and James Stuart, also travelled to Greece.

The son of a Scottish sailor, Stuart had worked for a fan-painter in the Strand before leaving for Rome in 1741 to pursue his studies in art, walking for much of the way. In Rome he met Matthew Brettingham, the architect who was working with William Kent on the designs for Holkham Hall, as well as Gavin Hamilton, Charles Townley's agent, who spent most of his working life in Rome, and Nicholas Revett, the artist and draughtsman with whom Stuart sailed for Greece in 1751, intent upon compiling 'an accurate description of the antiquities of

Athens'. Stuart and Revett spent nearly four years in Greece, where they narrowly escaped being murdered, and in 1762 they published their widely influential *Antiquities of Athens*, which ensured Stuart's reputation as an authority on classical art and architecture and earned him the soubriquet of 'Athenian' Stuart. Thereafter he was inundated with commissions to build houses in the Grecian style and in 1763 was appointed painter to the Dilettanti Society, a post he held until succeeded in 1769 by Sir Joshua Reynolds who, it was hoped, would paint the portraits of its members which Stuart had failed to provide. Indeed, many of Stuart's clients found it difficult to get him to produce drawings for work he had agreed to do: Mrs Elizabeth Montagu, who had employed him to design a house for her in Portman Square, constantly complained of his unreliability and carelessness. The house he built for Thomas Anson at 15 St James's Square, the temples at Hagley in Worcestershire and at Shugborough in Staffordshire, as well as the neo-classical furniture in Kedleston and Spencer House were, however, pioneering works in the Greek Revival style, that 'Gusto Greco' which was by then so generally admired in England, despite the harsh judgements of Sir William Chambers.

Enthusiastically as the 'Gusto Greco' was welcomed in the 1760s, it was not until the Napoleonic Wars brought the Grand Tour to a halt that Englishmen began to consider the possibility of travelling in Greece and the Levant as an alternative to France and Italy. A few decided to go for the sheer adventure of travel, others as artists and architects, one or two as botanists or geologists, yet others with the intention not so much of viewing antiquities as of acquiring them and taking away some such prize as the Venus de Milo, which was acquired for France by the Vicomte de Marcellus.

One of these collectors was Edward Daniel Clarke, who went to Greece by way of Scandinavia, Russia, the Holy Land and Cairo. Having acquired numerous coins and cases, he set his heart upon bringing back to England a huge statue of Kristophoros which Sir George Wheeler had come across at Eleusis. Several vain attempts had been made to carry this statue off, but it was not until 1801 that Clarke, who claimed to have found it buried up to the ears in a dunghill, was able, in exchange for a telescope, to obtain a firman from the Turkish authorities in Athens permitting him to take it away and to have it carried to a merchantman; this sailed away with it on the beginning of a long journey that was eventually to end at the Fitzwilliam Museum in Cambridge.

While Clarke's negotiations were in progress, agents of the seventh Earl of Elgin, who had been appointed Ambassador in Constantinople in 1799, were busy in Athens making use of a firman Elgin had obtained to 'take away any piece of stone with old inscriptions or figures' from the Parthenon and the Erechtheum.

139 The Acropolis and the Hymettos in Athens in the time of Byron and J.B.S. Morritt, when there was an antique statue 'over almost every door' in the small town.

Day after day over three hundred men laboured to dismantle these marbles, and, when Lord Elgin arrived in Athens with his wife in April 1802, he was able to write contentedly to his mother-in-law, 'It would be sacrilege to speak hastily of such wonders, and the justice done to them. All I can say is, to express a belief, that the object has been attained, and that when all arrive safely in England, I shall be able to show a compleat representation of Athens.' Elgin's actions were as severely criticised at the time as they have been since. He was castigated as a vandal and despoiler, accused of dishonesty, berated by Byron in the *Curse of Minerva*:

> Be ever hailed with equal honour here
> The Gothic monarch and the Pictish peer:
> Arms gave the first his right, the last had none,
> But basely stole what less barbarians won.

Until their merit was recognised by Canova and others, the marbles were dismissed as of little artistic merit; and it was suggested that, while Elgin's action might well have saved them from further deterioration in Athens, it served him right that the £35,000 which was recommended by a parliamentary committee as the price to be paid for their acquisition for the nation was less than half the sum which he had expended on them.

Yet few collectors acted any more scrupulously than Elgin. When Charles Robert Cockerell, then an architectural student, five hundred of whose drawings made in Greece are now in the British Museum, was carrying out excavations at the fifth-century Temple of Aphaia on the island of Aegina with three companions, one of the workmen they had employed struck the marble head of a warrior which lay buried in the earth together with the pieces of fourteen other statues. The authorities of the island pleaded with the foreigners not to carry the statues away for fear lest some disaster befell them all. Cockerell dismissed their protestations as 'a rubbishy pretence of superstitious fear', 'a mere excuse to extort money', but to quieten their objections he and his friends agreed to pay about £40, knowing this to be but a fraction of the real worth of their discoveries which, when pieced together, were sold at auction for £4,500 to an agent acting for Prince Ludwig of Bavaria.

J.B.S. Morritt, so he confessed to his sister, did not always even offer money for his acquisitions in a country which he described as 'a perfect gallery of marbles', stealing them as often as he could. When he did offer money, he gave very little.

It is very pleasant to walk the streets [he wrote from Athens]. Over almost every door is an antique statue or *basso-rilievo* . . . Some we steal, some we buy, and our court is much adorned with them. I am grown, too, a great medallist, and my collection increases fast, as I have above two hundred, and shall soon, I hope, have as many thousands. I buy the silver ones often under the price of the silver, and the copper ones for halfpence.

Whether travelling as a collector or as a botanist, like John Sibthorp – who came back from Greece with over eight hundred packets of seeds – or as a classical scholar like John Tweddell – who employed a French artist in Athens to help him draw and copy 'not only every temple and every archway but every stone and every inscription with the most scrupulous fidelity' – or for the excitement and therapy of travel like the intrepid and attractive Elizabeth, Lady Craven – who roamed about with two 'most excellent little pistols' stuffed into her girdle – a journey in Greece was not undertaken lightly, and careful preparations had to be made and discomforts and dangers faced. More medicines were considered necessary than on the Grand Tour, and more clothes, including some sort of uniform to impress local officials, preferably with a smart blue coat with scarlet and gold accessories such as that worn as part of the Windsor uniform at the English court. A mosquito net was essential; so were horses; so were weapons; and so, often, were guards of soldiers, brigands being a menace both in the

Peloponnese and in Thessaly, where Albanian gangs operated under the protection of the despot Ali Pasha. The painter Hugh William Williams, 'Grecian Williams', who returned from his travels in 1818, provided an additional list of 'indispensable articles':

A small camp-bed, with a bear-skin, sheet, and blanket; a small canteen; a tea-kettle, tin tea-pot and canisters; a silver cup; a pocket knife and fork. The French or English dress is most respected. Two or three pairs of shoes will be absolutely necessary. Few clothes will be sufficient, but they ought to be strong and good. . . . A cap lined with an additional piece of leather will be found extremely useful, to protect the head from the heat of the sun. English saddles may be dispensed with, as the mules and horses are apt to be restive under them. . . . As vessels not unfrequently sail from London for Corfu, it may be advisable to forward the luggage to that island, consigned to a merchant of respectability.

Without a servant who can speak the Italian and Romaic (Greek) languages, the traveller will be exposed to much inconvenience and trouble. Such servants may be procured in Rome, in the islands of Corfu or Zante, and are occasionally to be met with in London; their usual charge is a dollar a-day. The English consul generally recommends a janizary.

In the inns, which were nowhere easy to find, and, when found, were 'such as you have no idea of', the sleeping quarters above the stables had often to be shared with other travellers or various members of the innkeeper's family, and always with bugs.

I can give you no idea of the severe hardship and privation of the present Grecian travel [Benjamin Disraeli wrote to his father in 1830 when he was on his way with two companions to Constantinople and the Holy Land]. Happy are we to get a shed for nightly shelter, and never have been fortunate enough to find one not swarming with vermin. My sufferings in this way are great. . . . Our food must not be quarrelled with, for we lived for a week on the wild boar of Pentelicus, and the honey of Hymetus, both very good . . . but the want of sleep from vermin, and literally I did not sleep a wink the whole time I was out, is very bad, as it unfits you for daily exertion.

In Athens, however, there were clean rooms usually available at the Capuchin Convent and – in the days of J.B.S. Morritt and Edward Clarke who both stayed there – in the house in Aghias Thealas Street of the British Vice-Consul, Procupius Macri. Prepared for the worst, English gentlemen travellers, or G.T.'s as they came to be known, were not as critical of the food or the wine as their predecessors had been on the Grand Tour; but their servants seem to have been less tolerant than were their masters of the meals provided, of the resinated wine and of the general disagreeableness of travelling in Greece. Byron's discontented servant, William Fletcher, spoke for most of them when asked by the captain of a boat in which they were sailing why his master chose to travel through such a wild country.

'Bless you!' Fletcher replied. 'There is very little country. It's all rocks and robbers. They live in holes in the rocks and some come out like foxes. They have long guns, pistols and knives. We were obliged to have a guard of soldiers to go from one place to another.' To a subsequent question, 'How did you live?' Fletcher replied in evidently rising indignation, 'Like dogs, on goat's flesh and rice, sitting on the floor in a hovel, all eating out of one dirty round dish; no knives, and only one or two horn spoons. They drink a stuff called wine, but it tastes more of turps than grapes, and is carried about in stinking goat-skins, and everyone drinks from the same bowl; then they have coffee which is pounded, and they drink it, dregs and all without sugar. They are all smoking when not sleeping; they sleep on the floor in all their clothes and shoes; they never undress or wash, except the ends of their fingers, and are covered with lice and fleas.'

Byron overheard this conversation and commented, 'Those that look at things with hog's eyes can see nothing else. What Fletcher says may be true but I didn't notice it.'

He and his friend John Cam Hobhouse, the future statesman Lord Broughton, sailed in July 1809 from Falmouth to Lisbon. Byron was very seasick on the voyage, which took four and a half days, but on arrival he reported himself as 'very happy here, because I loves oranges, and talks bad Latin to the monks, who understands it, as it is like their own – and I goes into society (with my pocket pistols), and I swims the Tagus all across at once, and I rides on an ass or a mule, and swears Portuguese, and have got diarrhoea and bites from the mosquitoes'.

From Portugal he and Hobhouse rode into Spain, covering seventy miles a day at 'a gentle gallop', eating eggs, drinking wine and sleeping in hard beds, passing through Seville – which Byron praised as a 'large and fine city' with a magnificent Gothic cathedral, though he thought topographical description 'disgusting' – and going to a bullfight in Cadiz, 'the prettiest town in Europe'. They went on to Gibraltar, 'the dirtiest and most detestable spot', where Byron bought a splendid uniform, sailed to Malta, where he fell in love with a Mrs Spencer Smith, and then to Greece in a naval vessel.

With a large train of horses, four big and three smaller trunks, three beds with bedding and two bedsteads, the two friends now made their tour in the Turkish Empire. They rode through a landscape of wild beauty towards Janina to see the celebrated Ali Pasha, and on the way, as domes and minarets glittered through the gardens and the groves of lemon and orange trees, and the smooth waters of the lake reflected the steep sides of the mountains, they passed a tree outside a butcher's shop and saw something hanging from a branch. They thought at first it was a piece of meat exhibited for sale but as they approached they saw it was a man's arm torn from his body and suspended by a piece of string tied to one of the fingers.

Ali Pasha, who was presumably responsible for this punishment, was not at Janina but campaigning in what his secretary described as a 'little war', so the

140 Travelling in the Turkish Empire: the road to Janina.

travellers went to Tepelene which they entered at five o'clock one afternoon as the sun was going down to witness a scene which Byron thought he would never forget:

The Albanians, in their dresses (the most magnificent in the world, consisting of a long white kilt, gold-worked cloak, crimson velvet gold-laced jacket and waistcoat, silver-mounted pistols and daggers), the Tartars with their high caps, the Turks in their vast pelisses and turbans, the soldiers and black slaves with the horses . . . two hundred steeds ready caparisoned to move in a moment, couriers entering or passing out with the despatches, kettle-drums beating, boys calling the hour from the minaret of the mosque.

Here his homesick and disgruntled servant, Fletcher, spent a long time delousing Byron's shirt, ignorant of the method advocated in Leake's *Travels in Northern Greece* in which the garment is held over a fire so that the lice therein, 'intoxicated by the smoke, may fall into the fire, when a crackling announces the success of the operation'. And here he was received by the fat, ingratiating Pasha who complimented his visitor on his aristocratic appearance and superb uniform and sent him almonds and sugared sherbet, fruit and sweetmeats 'twenty times a day'.

On his return to Janina, Byron began to write *Childe Harold's Pilgrimage*, the poem in Spenserian stanzas which describes the travels and reflections of a pilgrim who makes the journey that Byron made and laments the bondage of Greece, 'Fair Greece! sad relic of departed worth! Immortal though no more; though fallen, great!'

On Christmas Day 1809, Byron and Hobhouse arrived in Athens, a small town then with a population of no more than about ten thousand people, many of whom lived in wretched houses in the shade of the Acropolis. For two months he rented part of the house belonging to Procupius Macri's widow, where he met her delicious daughter Teresa, whom he celebrated in his poem 'Maid of Athens':

> Maid of Athens, ere we part,
> Give, oh give me back my heart!
> Or, since that has left my breast,
> Keep it now, and take the rest.

Their lodgings, so Hobhouse said, 'consisted of a sitting-room and two bed-rooms, opening into a courtyard, where there were five or six lemon trees, from which during our residence in the place was plucked the fruit that seasoned the pilaf and other national dishes served up at our frugal meals'.

From these two rooms the two men set forth to inspect the ruins, guided by the French Consul, Louis-François-Sébastien Fauvel, a dealer in ancient relics, and Lord Elgin's agent, Giovanni Battista Lusieri. The conscientious Hobhouse, as befitted the future author of *A Journey through Albania, and other Provinces of Turkey in Europe and Asia . . . during the years 1809 and 1810*, paid far closer attention to what he was told than Byron, who was more concerned with impressions than with unadorned facts and became irritated by his friend, whose 'dogged perseverance' as he pottered about with map and compass 'to ascertain the site of some ancient temple' was certainly to be envied but was one of the reasons why they wrangled every day.

'I have no hobby and no perseverance,' Byron admitted. 'I gazed at the stars

142 The Grand Vizier giving audience to the English Ambassador.

and ruminated; took no notes, asked no questions.' He visited all the sites that the guide-books required him to visit, but he was happier riding off to Piraeus, swimming in the Bay of Phaleron, diving for tortoises and making love to women and boys; and he was much more at his ease when, having been to Smyrna, the Dardanelles and Constantinople, and having enjoyed the proud satisfaction of swimming across the Hellespont in an hour and ten minutes, he went back to Athens without Hobhouse, who had gone home after their tour of Turkey.

On his return to Athens, Byron took rooms at the Capuchin which were more commodious than any he had yet occupied in Greece. He was 'by no means solitary there', since, for companions, he had not only 'il Padre Abbate' but 'his "scuola" consisting of six "Ragazzi"', 'sylphs' with whom there was 'nothing but riot from noon to night'. Setting out from the Convent, Byron made two trips to the Peloponnese, fell seriously ill with a fever at Patras and sailed home aboard the *Hydra* in April 1811, taking with him 'four ancient Athenian skulls, dug out of sarcophagi – a phial of Attic hemlock – four live tortoises – a greyhound (died on the passage) – two live Greek servants . . . and myself'.

Byron had originally intended to travel far further east than Constantinople, as

Fynes Moryson had done in the sixteenth century, as Thomas Coryate and William Lithgow had done in the seventeenth, and as those no less celebrated travellers Lady Jane Digby, Lady Hester Stanhope and A.W. Kinglake all did in the nineteenth.

Lady Jane Digby seems to have found happiness there. Born in 1807, the daughter of rich parents, she was married when young and, ignored by her husband, followed a lover to Paris on the way to the Orient. Having married two other husbands, taken several lovers and given birth to six children, Lady Jane settled down in Damascus and in the desert with Sheikh Mezrab, remaining in the Middle East for thirty-five years, admired alike for her beauty, her good nature, her superb horsemanship and her easy command of nine languages.

Lady Hester Stanhope's story is equally romantic but less happy in its ending. Tall, passionate, extravagant, outspoken and overbearing, she was the eldest daughter of the third Earl Stanhope and a niece of William Pitt, for whom she kept house and to whom she was devoted. After Pitt's death, she sailed for the Levant with a companion, Miss Williams, a personal physician, Dr Meryon, and a retinue of servants which increased in size as she progressed. Sailing from Portsmouth in February 1810, she landed at Gibraltar where she met a man, Michael Bruce, ten years her junior, who became her lover and accompanied her to Malta. From Malta she sailed in a frigate to Zante, then to Patras, where she and Bruce were joined by Lord Sligo and on, in a Greek felucca, through the Gulf of Corinth. She then rode across the isthmus of Corinth, the villagers and fishermen gazing at the tall, pale woman in a high plumed hat, riding haughtily by with a handsome young man on either side of her, a guide and interpreter leading the way, a train of servants following in her wake. After staying in a cottage on Mount Olympus, where she enjoyed meals of pilaff and meat balls wrapped in vine leaves and, having changed into men's dress, visited harems and Turkish baths, she set off for Alexandria. On the way the boat was wrecked in a storm; crew and passengers clambered to safety on a rock where, when help came, all the sailors were found to be drunk and Lady Hester had lost all her clothes, together with her jewels and her dog. 'Starving thirty hours on a bare rock, even without fresh water, being half naked and drenched with wet, having traversed an almost trackless country, over dreadful rocks and mountains, partly on foot and partly on a mule for eight hours, laid me up at a village for a few days,' she told a friend. 'But I have since crossed the island [Rhodes] on an ass, going for six hours a day, which proves I am pretty well now at least.'

From Egypt, Lady Hester went to Jerusalem and then to Damascus, shocking Christians by visiting the Holy Sepulchre in men's clothes and on the arm of her lover, and Muslims by entering Damascus unveiled. From Damascus she rode to Palmyra at the head of forty camels and seventy Arabs, and amidst the ruins of

Palmyra she presided over a vast Bedouin encampment before moving on to the foothills of Mount Lebanon. Abandoned by her lover and struck by the plague, which affected both her brain and her lungs, she became increasingly autocratic and eccentric. Regarded by the local people as a prophetess, she had over thirty personal attendants, mostly Syrians who, though dirty and dishonest, were gratifyingly obsequious and prepared to be on call at all hours of the day and night. She dressed like an Arab chieftain, with a turban covering her shaved head, smoking a long pipe. To her visitors she talked at inordinate length in what Dr Meryon called 'unbroken discourse', so exhausting one of them that, after hours of listening to her, he fainted away from fatigue. Dr Meryon left; Miss Williams died; but Lady Hester lived on, impoverished, attended by unpaid servants, in debt and ill, without teeth, with failing eyesight, suffering from consumption, compelled by vanity to receive no visitors in daylight, yet still impressive in her splendid self-regard.

One evening in the 1830s she received A.W. Kinglake, the author of *Eothen*, who was immediately struck by the 'large commanding features of the gaunt woman' and by 'the most astonishing whiteness' of her skin. She was wearing a very large turban, and a voluminous dress of white linen. Two black slave girls brought in pipes and coffee, and then, 'for hours and hours, this wondrous white woman poured forth her speech'. She related anecdotes of her Arab life; she talked 'long and earnestly' of religion, of race and of the occult and the magic arts; and she indulged her talent for mimicry by describing her encounter with Byron. 'She had seen him, it appeared, soon after his arrival in the East, and was vastly amused at his little affectations.' Kinglake could not tell 'whether Lady Hester's mimicry of the bard was at all close, but it was amusing: she attributed to him a curiously comical lisp'.

Kinglake had embarked upon his tour as a young lawyer, 'not flying from his country because of ennui' but to strengthen his will and temper, 'the metal of his nature'. He and his friend, Lord Pollington, had made their way to Belgrade and then to Constantinople, crossing the Golden Horn in a caique, landing 'dripping and sloshing and looking very like men who had been turned back by the Royal Humane Society for being incurably drowned', then going south towards Smyrna with a large retinue which he explained was not as pompous as it might appear:

For an Englishman journeying in the East must necessarily have with him Dragomen capable of interpreting the Oriental languages. The absence of wheeled-carriages obliges him to use several beasts of burthen for his baggage, as well as for himself and his attendants; the owners of the horses and camels, with *their* slaves or servants, fall in as part of his train, and altogether the cavalcade becomes rather numerous.

It also became rather slow, covering no more than five miles an hour, and in difficult country less than this.

143   An English traveller in the Turkish Empire, riding a camel with a native soldier as escort.

The English traveller in the East, Kinglake said, had also to grow accustomed to meagre rations and to the custom of his dragomen obtaining what provisions might be available not by payment but by intimidation. It was common for the natives to declare 'that their hens were mere old maids, and all their cows unmarried'. But then the traveller's attendants swore and shouted and fingered their daggers until eggs and milk were produced. Payment might subsequently be made,

but so to order the matter that the poor fellows who have been forced to contribute should be the persons to receive the value of their supplies is not possible; a traveller to attempt anything so grossly just as that would be too outrageous. The truth is that the usage of the East in old times required the people of the village at their own cost to supply the wants of travellers; and the ancient custom is now adhered to – not in favour of travellers generally – but in favour of those who are deemed sufficiently powerful to enforce its observance.

As for accommodation, it was advisable to seek shelter in a monastery where lodgings could be found, or to be content with a camp life. In Tiberias, Kinglake took up his quarters in a church where his servant soon made him a home on the southern side with 'portmanteaux, carpet bags, books and maps', but the congregation of fleas which also attended the church 'must have been something enormous'. After passing a night in a place like this, assaulted by swarms of insects, 'you are glad to gather up the remains of your body long before morning dawns. Your skin is scorched – your temples throb – your lips feel withered and dried – your burning eye-balls are screwed up inwards against the brain. You have no hope but only in the saddle.'

On their way to Smyrna, Lord Pollington fell ill, and the travellers consulted 'a solemn Armenian, half soothsayer, half doctor', who 'while counting his beads, fixed his eyes steadily upon the patient, and then suddenly dealt him a violent blow on the chest'. This affecting no cure, the patient had to be carried along in a rough and bumpy cart without springs. From Smyrna, Kinglake sailed down the Aegean towards the Mediterranean in a Greek brigantine, calling at Cyprus on the way to Beirut. He then toured the Holy Land, visiting Jerusalem, Nazareth, Bethlehem and the shores of the Sea of Galilee where he was shown 'some massive fragments, the relics', so he was earnestly informed by a Christian guide, 'of that wondrous banquet' of loaves and fishes, now turned into stone. 'The petrefaction was most complete.' He bathed in the Dead Sea and, before he began to dress, found that the sun had already evaporated the water, leaving him 'thickly encrusted with salts'. He crossed the Jordan in a raft propelled by naked men swimming in the water with inflated skins tied to their loins, and he crossed the desert to Cairo with four camels – two for his servants, one for his baggage and one for himself – and with four Arabs, the owners of the camels, on foot. His stores were 'a small soldier's tent, two bags of dried bread, a couple of bottles of wine, two goatskins filled with water, tea, sugar, a cold tongue, and (of all things in the world) a jar of Irish butter purchased from some merchant. There was also a small sack of charcoal, for the greater part of the desert is void of fuel.'

In Cairo he found the plague was raging, the deaths being reckoned at twelve hundred a day. But, having recovered from a lesser illness himself, he rode about the streets on a donkey, whose footfalls could scarcely be heard as its hooves fell on the sandy soil strewed on the surface by way of pavement; he visited the pyramids and wondered at the 'lonely Sphynx' whose 'comeliness is not of this world'. He went on to Suez, entered the desert again to take the unfrequented route to Gaza, moved north to Nablus and Damascus, and, before sailing home, explored the ruins of Baalbec.

The Ruins of Baalbec was the title of a book published in 1757 by Robert Wood who, some years earlier, had written *The Ruins of Palmyra*. These books, together with *The Antiquities of Athens* by Stuart and Revett and Robert Adam's *The Ruins of the Palace of the Emperor Diocletian at Spolatro* (1764), were to have a decisive influence on a new neo-Classical style in England, a taste which the later stages of the Grand Tour did so much to develop and which was to find expression in such houses as Grange Park in Hampshire, remodelled by William Wilkins in 1810 and enlarged by C.R. Cockerell in 1823–5, and Bilsay Castle in Northumberland, designed for himself by Sir Charles Monck who, prevented by the Napoleonic Wars from making the usual Grand Tour, had gone to Greece for a long honeymoon in 1804 and, with his wife, had made a detailed study of its temples.

144 The Hippodrome at Constantinople in 1813, with the minarets of the Hagia Sophia in the distance.

Throughout the age of the Grand Tour the English hotly debated its worth. Adam Smith, who resigned his professorship of Moral Philosophy at Glasgow in 1764 to accompany the third Duke of Buccleuch on his travels, expressed a widespread opinion when he said that, although his own pupil had profited by his experiences, most did not:

A young man who goes abroad at seventeen or eighteen and returns home at one and twenty . . . commonly returns more conceited, more unprincipled, more dissipated and more incapable of any serious application either to study or to business, than he could well have become in so short a time had he stayed at home. . . . Nothing but the discredit into which the universities are allowing themselves to fall could ever have brought into repute so very absurd a practice as that of travelling at this early period of life.

A chorus of parents, of former tourists, of tutors, pedagogues and preachers agreed with him. Lord Chesterfield ridiculed those young men who returned from their travels as ill-informed as they had been on their departure: 'They go abroad, as they call it; but, in truth, they stay at home all that while; for being very awkward . . . and not speaking the languages, they go into no foreign company, at least none good; but dine and sup with one another only at the tavern.' John Moore agreed:

To go to France and Italy and there converse with none but English people, and merely that you have it to say that you have been in these countries is certainly absurd. Nothing can be more so, except to adopt with enthusiasm the fashions, fopperies, taste and manners of these countries and transplant them to England where they never will thrive. . . . There are instances of Englishmen who, while on their travels, shock foreigners by an ostentatious preference of England to all the rest of the world, and ridicule the manners, customs and opinions of every other nation; yet on their return to their own country, immediately assume foreign manners and continue during the remainder of their lives to express their highest contempt for everything that is English.

Similar sentiments were expressed by John Locke, Vicesimus Knox, Samuel Johnson and Lord Macaulay – all of whom considered that the Grand Tour was undertaken at the wrong time in a man's life – and by scores of other critics of the institution. Steele, for example, considered the 'most irksome conversation of all others' was that conducted with travellers who had 'passed through France and Italy with the same observations that the Carriers and Stage Coachmen do through Great Britain, that is their Stops and Stages have been regulated according to the Liquor they have met with in their Passages'. Lord Cowper ordered on his

145 (Opposite) Charles Towneley and friends, depicted by Zoffany, in the gallery of his house in Park Street in which were housed the Towneley collection of marbles, reliefs and coins. They were purchased from his executors by the British Museum in 1805.

deathbed that his son should never go on the Tour, since he had discovered himself that 'there was little to be hoped, and much to be feared from travelling'. A writer in the *World* contended that the 'majority of young travellers return home, entirely divested of the religion of their country without having acquired any new one in its place'.

Laurence Sterne thought that there was 'nothing in which we are so much deceived, as in the advantages proposed from our connections and discourse with the literati, etc., in foreign parts; especially if the experiment is made before we are matured by years of study'. Smollett had 'seen in different parts of Italy a number of raw boys, whom Britain seemed to have poured forth on purpose to bring her national character into contempt; ignorant, petulant, rash, and profligate, without any knowledge or experience of their own, without any director to improve their understanding, or superintend their conduct'. Count Berchtold proposed that 'those who are naturally destitute of judgement and prudence become still greater fools by their travelling than they were before, it being impossible for him, who is a fool in his own country, to become wise by running up and down' in others. Dr Sharp had not seen one young Englishman on his travels who was not eager to return to his friends and country and would have done so had they not all considered 'the Grand Tour a kind of apprenticeship for qualifying a gentleman'. Baretti had never heard of an English tourist who 'ever went a step out of those roads which from the foot of the Alps lead straight to our most famed cities; none of them ever [would] deign to visit those places whose names [were] not in everybody's mouth'. Lady Mary Wortley Montagu characterised young English tourists as

the greatest blockheads in nature . . . the worst company in the world . . . their whole business abroad (as far as I can perceive) being to buy new cloaths, in which they shine in some obscure coffee-house, where they are sure of meeting only one another; and after the important conquest of some waiting gentlewoman of an opera Queen . . . return to England excellent judges of men and manners . . . and no more instructed than they might have been at home by the help of a map.

Charles de Brosses wrote,

The money that the English spend at Rome and the practice of making a journey there, which forms a part of their education, do not profit much the majority of them. There are some of them who are persons of intelligence and endeavour to instruct themselves, but they form no great number. The majority have a hired carriage harnessed in the Piazza di Spagna that is at their service throughout the day until they go together to play billiards, or to some other similar amusement. I see some of them who will leave Rome without having seen any but English people and without knowing where the Coliseum is.

According to a report from Rome printed in the *Newcastle Courant* in 1751 the

English then in the city were 'so numerous as to be able to form among themselves a society as considerable as that of the Roman Noblesse', and went so far in their disdain of the diversions that Rome had to offer that they hired a palace where they met every evening for gambling, for 'a concert of musick and a supper'.

Many tourists, moreover, were said to be more or less permanently drunk. According to Walpole, Sir Francis Dashwood and Lord Middlesex, later second Duke of Dorset, were seldom sober the 'whole time they were in Italy'.

English periodicals, novels and plays of the time are full of satirical comments on, and absurd characterisations of, fussy, lazy servants, pompous, ignorant, prejudiced tutors, and spoilt and profligate young gentlemen who have returned from their travels either as little refined as the character in Congreve's *Way of the World*, who comes home as much improved as 'a Dutch skipper from a whale-fishing', or, as a dandified Macaroni, a 'kind of animal, neither male nor female', in the words of the *Oxford Magazine*, a creature in a painfully tight suit and with elaborately curled hair which 'talks without meaning, smiles without pleasantry, rides without exercise, wenches without passion' and often speaks in a kind of broken Italian in place of the English it pretends to have forgotten.

In the pages of the *World* in the 1750s there appeared several typical satires on the Grand Tour, in one of which a correspondent describes how, conscious of his own ignorance of continental lands and foreign manners, he sends his son abroad in the care of a Swiss tutor and is 'cruelly disappointed':

During his stay in Paris he only frequented the worst English company, with whom he was unhappily engaged in two or three scrapes, which the credit and good nature of the English ambassador helped him out of. He hired a low Irish wench, whom he drove about in a hired chaise. . . . He did not learn one word of French and never spoke to Frenchmen or Frenchwomen, excepting some vulgar and injurious epithets, which he bestowed upon them in very plain English. His governor very honestly informed me of this conduct . . . and advised their removal to Italy which accordingly I immediately ordered. His behaviour there will appear in the truest light to you by his own letter which I here give:

Sir – In the six weeks that I passed at Florence, and the week I spent at Genoa, I never had time to write to you, being wholly taken up with seeing things of which the most remarkable is the steeple of Pisa: it is the oddest thing I ever saw in my life; it stands all awry; I wonder it does not tumble down. I met with a great many of my countrymen, and we live together very sociably. I have been here now a month, and will give you an account of my way of life. Here are a great many agreeable English gentlemen; we are about nine or ten as smart bucks as any in England. We constantly breakfast together, and then either go and see sights, or drive about the outlets of Rome in Chaises; but the horses are very bad, and the chaises do not follow well. We meet before dinner at the English coffee-house; where there is a very good billiard-table and very good company.

From thence we go and dine together by turns at each other's lodgings. Then after a cheerful glass of claret, for we have made a shift to get some here, we go to the coffee-house again; from thence to supper, and so to bed. I do not believe these Romans are a bit like the old Romans; they are a parcel of thin-gutted, snivelling, cringing dogs; and I verily believe that our set could thrash forty of them. We never go among them; it would not be worth while; besides, we none of us speak Italian and none of those signors speak English; which shows what sort of fellows they are. We saw the Pope go by 'tother day in a procession, but we resolved to assert the honor of Old England; so we neither bowed nor pulled off our hats to the old rogue. Provisions and liquor are but bad here; and, to say the truth, I have not had one thorough good meal's meat since I left England. No longer ago than last Sunday we wanted to have a good plum-pudding; but we found the materials difficult to procure, and were obliged to get an English footman to make it. Pray, Sir, let me come home; for I cannot find that one is a jot the better for seeing all these outlandish places and people. But if you will not let me come back, for God's sake, Sir, take away the impertinent mounseer you sent with me. He is a considerable expense to you, and of no manner of service to me. All the English here laugh at him, he is such a prig. He thinks himself a fine gentleman, and is always plaguing me to go into foreign companies, to learn foreign languages, and to get foreign manners; as if I were not to live and die in Old England, and as if good English acquaintance would not be more useful to me than outlandish ones. Dear Sir, grant me this request, and you shall ever find me

Your most dutiful son,

G.D.

ROME, May the 3d, 1753.

A similar letter from a son in Paris to his father, baronet of Simpleton Hall, Norfolk was printed in the *Gentleman's Magazine* in 1736:

Honour'd and Worshipful Sir,
This is to let you know that I am well in Health, hoping that you and my Mother and Brother Bob are the same. I got safe to Harwich, and went aboard soon after; But as we came over the Salt Sea it rag'd like any mad, and made me sick to Death: When I was a little recover'd, I had Recourse to the Neat's Tongue which my loving Mother put into my Pocket the last Thing she did at parting, and it kept the Wind out of my Stomach, as she said it would.

We arriv'd at Holland on Thursday, and as soon as my Things were ashore I made our John put on his Livery: he looks very well in it. . . . I makes Remarks on the Countries as you and Mr Martext, our Curate, advis'd me. Tho' I have seen several Counties in England, yet I never saw so many Rivers in any one of them as there are in Holland; however this I could not but observe, that we have larger Plains and a greater Number of Oaks and Timber growing than they have, and our John says the same. . . .

146 (Opposite above) The south side of West Wycombe Park, which was modelled on the Palazzo Chiericati at Vicenza by Palladio.

147 (Below) A capriccio by Pannini, 1741, showing many of the most famous classical buildings of Rome, including the Pantheon and Trajan's Column. The picture was brought back by Henry Blundell, who built a rotunda based on the Pantheon at Ince Blundell House to house his collection of Grand Tour trophies.

When we came into the Popish Countries, we met then with Cathedrals, many's the one, of which I was very glad and so was John: But when I went into one of them I would not cross myself with their Holy Water, as they call it, which was put up against a Pillar, nor would I pull off my Hat, because it belong's to the Papishes; and the Place, as I have heard our Curate often say, was a Place of Idolatry. At last a great fat Parson, (a Parson I believe he was, tho' nothing like our Parsons in Norfolk, for he was without a Shirt or a Pair of Shoes, and had a great Rope about his Middle) be he what he will, this greazy Fellow came up to me as much as to say, pull off your Hat; I was plaguily afraid being in a Strange Place, so made no Words but pull'd it off. I was uneasy in my Conscience about this Affair, 'till I went to John, who entirely clear'd all Scruples, by remembering me of a Maxim he had often heard my grandfather use, that when you are at Rome you must do as they do at Rome. You can't imagine how learned the People are in these Popish Countries, or which seem so at least, for they all of them have their Common-Prayer Book in Latin.

I observ'd in my travelling to Paris that the common People wear a wooden Kind of Shoes, and was told by an English Gentleman that it was owing to passive Obedience. . . . Tho' I heard so much of the French cookery, their Kickshaws and Fricasees, and their Ragous, yet I don't find they live near so well as we do in Norfolk. We exel 'em much in our Beef, which is fatter than theirs by at least an Inch in the Rib; and what very much 'maz'd me they never make any Dumpling: But 'stead of Beef and Dumpling or Pudding, they eat Frogs like mad, and devour the Devil and all of Garlick and Onions: Our John is quite Heart-sick of their Diet, and wants to be at Simpleton-Hall again.

As for this Town of Paris it is very large, and has a power of People. . . . I make a pretty Figure in my Silver Button'd Cloaths, which I have kept very fresh, as our John can vouch: I wore it two Days ago at a Ball among People of the best Fashion: They dance here extremely well, yet I was confounded when I call'd for Moll Placket and Roger o'Coverly, neither the Company or the Fidlers knew any Thing of the Matter.

This, Sir, with kind Love and Service to you, my Mother and Brother Bob, I desire you would accept, an so no more at present from
Your dutiful Son, 'till Death,

The writer of this letter, who signs himself Tim Shallow, was drawn from life, as was William Cowper's youthful tourist in *The Progress of Error:*

> From school to Cam or Isis, and thence home;
> And thence with all convenient speed to Rome,
> With reverent tutor clad in habit lay,
> To tease for cash, and quarrel with all day;
> With memorandum book for every town,
> And every post, and where the chaise broke down;
> His stock a few French phrases got by heart,
> With much to learn but nothing to impart;
> The youth, obedient to his sire's commands,
> Sets off a wanderer into foreign lands,
> Surprised at all they meet, the gosling pair,

With awkward gait, stretch'd neck and silly stare,
Discover huge cathedrals built in stone,
And steeples towering high much like our own;
But show peculiar light by many a grin
At popish practices observed within . . .
Returning he proclaims by many a grace,
By shrugs and strange contortions of his face,
How much a dunce that has been sent to roam,
Excels a dunce, that has been kept at home.

Cowper's young tourist is much like Pope's in *The Dunciad:*

Led by my hand, he saunter'd Europe round
And gather'd ev'ry Vice on Christian ground;
Saw ev'ry Court, heard ev'ry King declare
His royal sense of Op'ras or the Fair;
The Stews and Palace equally explor'd
Intrigu'd with glory and with spirit whor'd;
Try'd all *hors d'oeuvres*, all liqueurs defin'd,
Judicious drank, and greatly daring din'd;
Dropt the dull lumber of the Latin score,
Spoil'd his own language and acquir'd no more;
All Classic learning lost on Classic ground,
And last turn'd Air, the Echo of a Sound!
See now, half-cur'd and perfectly well-bred,
With nothing but a Solo in his head.

Samuel Foote took particular pleasure in lampooning young English travellers on the stage. His *Englishman in Paris, Englishman Returned from Paris,* and *The Capuchin* - a revised version of *The Trip to Calais* which the Lord Chamberlain banned at the instigation of the Duchess of Kingston – all show Englishmen abroad as ill-mannered as they are ignorant, as pretentious as they are extravagant. In *The Capuchin*, Sir Harry Hamper is making the Grand Tour with a tutor and is determined to cut a fine figure:

Hamper: Come, come! Come along, Doctor! Give the positilions 30 sous apiece.
Tutor: 'Tis put down they are to have but five in the book.
Hamper: No matter; it will let them know we are somebody.
Tutor: What significations that? Ten to one we shall never see them again.
Hamper: Do as you are bid.
Tutor: Then! See how they grin. I dare be sworn you hadn't seen such a sum this many a day.
1st Postilion: Serviteur! Bonne voyage! Monsieur, my Lor!
Hamper: There, there! '*My Lord*'! I have purchased a title for tenpence. That is dog cheap, or the Devil's in it!

There undoubtedly were numerous tourists like Sir Harry Hamper who returned to England either with all their prejudices against foreign life and art confirmed or with an undiscriminating preference for all things continental to everything at home. Shelley's father, for example – who once advised his younger son, 'Never read a book, Johnnie, and you will be a rich man' – was said to have come from his travels with nothing more than a bad painting of Vesuvius and a few ill-pronounced words of French. Yet there were many others who came back richer in mind if not in pocket, who brought to English life and culture a cosmopolitan influence, an intellectual curiosity and refinement of manner of inestimable value to the society in which they lived. They kept in touch with each other at Almack's in Pall Mall, eventually forming a club of their own which became known as Brooks's; they joined the Dilettanti Society; later they joined the Travellers' Club, founded after the Grand Tour had been disrupted by the Napoleonic Wars. Their educated taste eventually brought about a lasting transformation in English art and manners, a deep appreciation of music as well as art and architecture.

The reputation of many of the painters most admired in the eighteenth century has since fallen, while the genius of others, Botticelli and Tintoretto among them, was not then fully recognised, and contemporary French artists, such as Watteau and Fragonard, were almost completely disregarded. Yet the treasures which found their way into England, either as purchases made on the Grand Tour, or in consequence of tastes formed on continental travels, were of an extraordinary range. To take as an example one county alone, Norfolk provides an indication of the effect the Grand Tour had upon the collections in country houses.

Felbrigg Hall, Houghton Hall, Wolterton and Holkham were all built or reconstructed in the first half of the eighteenth century and filled with works of art purchased on the Grand Tour or in the style of works admired on the Continent. So was Narford, whose owner, Sir Andrew Fountaine, was described as 'one of the keenest virtuosi in Europe' and as one who 'out-Italianised the Italians themselves'. Narford contained the finest collection of majolica in the country, thousands of prints, a Canaletto, sculptures by Peter Scheemakers and Camillo Rusconi, and splendid examples of the work of Giovanni Antonio Pellegrini, the Venetian artist who, together with Marco Picci, had been brought to England by the fourth Earl of Manchester in 1708. At Houghton, Sir Robert Walpole's house, the influences of the Grand Tour were no less apparent: the collections here, which included sculptures by Rysbrack, pictures by Canaletto and Salvator Rosa, bronzes attributed to Le Sueur, vases of Volterra alabaster and Scagliola tables, were augmented by all three of Sir Robert's surviving sons. The youngest, Horace, also formed his own collection by buying bronzes and medals, busts and pictures (including two views of Florence by Thomas Patch), a bust of Vespasian which he was told in Rome was second only to that of Caracalla in the Farnese

148 A group portrait by Sir Joshua Reynolds of the Members of the Society of Dilettanti at a meeting in 1771 on the occasion of the introduction of Sir William Hamilton, seated with his arm on the table.

Collection, and a medal of Severus Alexander found by a peasant in Rome, sold for sixpence to an antiquarian and purchased by Walpole for seven and a half guineas, though 'to virtuosi [it was] worth any sum'.

At Holkham, which like Houghton Hall was decorated by William Kent, there were splendid works by Benedetto Luti and Giuseppe Chiari, Gaspar van Wittel, Canaletto, Salvator Rosa, Nicolas Poussin and Claude Lorraine, books and manuscripts, drawings and prints bought in France and Germany, Switzerland and Italy, as well as statues and bronzes and numerous other works purchased by Matthew Brettingham, who spent nearly seven years in Italy on Thomas Coke's behalf. At Felbrigg Hall, a special cabinet was designed for pictures bought on the Grand Tour by William Windham whose architect, James Paine, with his patron's help, drew careful plans to indicate where each of the forty-odd paintings should be placed. There are Grand Tour cabinets similar to this one, which can still be seen at Felbrigg, at Corsham Court, Chippenham and Saltram House, Plymouth.

As it was with painting and sculpture so it was with architecture in England

 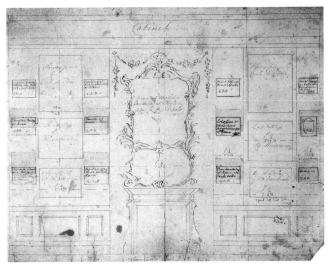

149 (Left) The Cabinet at Felbrigg Hall, Norfolk, which was designed by James Paine for William Windham to house works of art purchased on the Grand Tour.

150 (Right) Paine's and Windham's plan for the Cabinet at Felbrigg, indicating where the pictures were to be placed, and where most of them still remain.

where, it has been calculated, in the thirty years between 1710 and 1740 alone, 148 country houses were built or rebuilt, mostly by owners who had been on the Grand Tour. Sir Roger Pratt, one of the most successful architects of the seventeenth century, expressed the belief that foreign travel was as essential for those who hoped to live in a well-designed modern building as it was for those who intended to design one. He himself, having travelled throughout Europe, had returned to design Kingston Lacy near Wimborne for Sir Ralph Bankes, Lord Allington's house at Horseheath, and Sir George Pratt's at Coleshill. He had also designed Ryston Hall, Norfolk for himself and Clarendon House, Piccadilly, which, completed in 1667 for the first Earl of Clarendon, served as a model for several smaller London houses built during the Restoration.

Inigo Jones, whose work Pratt much admired, was also deeply influenced by his extensive continental travels. He had been in Florence and Venice in his twenties, had later returned to Italy in the suite of the Earl of Arundel, one of the greatest patrons and art collectors of his time, and had travelled, too, in France. He had studied Vitruvius, the great Roman architect whose treatise *De Architectura Libri Decem* was to have so profound an influence on the originators of the Classic revival; he had read and re-read Palladio's *Quattro libri dell' architettura* and had visited the buildings illustrated in it; he had also studied the works of Alberti, Serlio, Labacco and the French theorist, Philibert de L'Orme; in Venice he had

151   Mount Vernon, home and burial place of George Washington, one of many houses in the United States built in the eighteenth century to a neo-Classical design.

met Scamozzi, whose *Idea dell' architettura universale* influenced him as much as did Palladio. On Jones's return to England, where he became the country's principal architect, the effects of his studies and travels were unmistakable. The Banqueting House in Whitehall contains strong echoes of the Palazzo Thiene in Vicenza; the piazza and church of St Paul at Covent Garden, as John Evelyn noticed, were at least partially inspired by vistas in Leghorn; while the Queen's House at Greenwich, which was completed in 1640 for Queen Henrietta Maria, is, in Sir John Summerson's words, 'a *quattrocento* idea of a Roman patrician villa, brought to the Thames, subjected to the full rigour of Palladio and Scamozzi, and resolved into such a serene and simple statement that it might as easily belong to 1816 as 1616'.

Once the idea of neo-Classicism had taken root, it was to dominate English architecture for more than two centuries, and every leading architect from Wren and Vanbrugh (who added to it strong elements of baroque), to Kent, Chambers and James Gibbs, was to demonstrate in his work the strong influence of either the classical buildings he had seen on his travels or the recognised Italian authorities he had consulted. Several of their patrons required specifically a house in the style of Palladio, as Lord Burlington had done; while the ninth Earl of Pembroke himself designed a Palladian bridge at Wilton which, in James Lees-Milnes's opinion, is 'not excelled by any building of Palladio in Venezia' and is 'one of the most beautiful buildings in all England'. Mereworth Castle in Kent was built for the Hon. John Fane, afterwards seventh Earl of Westmorland, by Colen Campbell, the Scottish architect of Wanstead House (prototype of many neo-Palladian houses in England) who based his designs on illustrations in the *Quattro libri dell' architettura*. Houghton Hall by Campbell and Thomas Ripley, with interiors by William Kent, is another splendid example of Palladian architecture. Holkham was designed after Thomas Coke's architectural tutor had been paid to draw plans of the Palazzo Farnese in Rome and after long discussions between Coke and Burlington, William Kent and Matthew Brettingham the elder. For those who could not afford the fees of a leading architect, or quailed at the thought of realising some of the grander designs described by William Chambers in his *Treatise on Civil Architecture*, the first edition of which appeared in 1759, there were such pattern books as *A Complete Body of Architecture* by Isaac Ware, a protégé of Lord Burlington who seems to have travelled in Italy at his patron's expense; and *A Book of Architecture* (1728) by James Gibbs, Carlo Fontana's former pupil who, in presenting his designs for fairly modest houses, as well as for windows, doors and garden pavilions, expressed the hope that his work would 'be of use to such Gentlemen as might be concerned in Building, especially in the remote parts of the Country, where little or no assistance for Designs can be procurred'.

Several houses based on Gibbs's designs were also built in America, where neo-Classical buildings soon began to appear in profusion. The plantation owners of the South, some of whom had been on the Grand Tour, built themselves mansions in the Palladian style. President Jefferson, who had been appointed United States Minister to the French government in 1784 and had later travelled in Italy, had the University of Virginia designed on the lines of one of Palladio's villas and wanted the President's house in Washington to be built as a replica of another. Charles Bulfinch, who was largely responsible for introducing the Adam style into America and who provided New England with several of its most imposing buildings – including the Massachusetts State House, Boston – received his architectural training and inspiration during a long continental tour in 1785–7.

The gardens that surrounded the new Palladian houses were also influenced by continental models. The formal, regular and artificial gardens of the past gave way, as Alexander Pope recommended in an influential essay, to more natural landscapes in the romantic manner of Nicolas Poussin and his adopted son, Gaspard; while, inside the houses, the decorations of the rooms were strongly affected by continental styles and often executed by continental artists. The whole character of the interior of West Wycombe Park, for example, was transformed by Joseph Borgnis whom Sir Francis Dashwood had met on the Grand Tour and had persuaded to come to England in 1736.

In the second half of the eighteenth century no architect had a greater influence on interior decoration than Robert Adam. When he returned from Italy in 1759

152 (Left) The neo-Classical hall at Heveningham, Suffolk, which was built for Sir Gerard Vanneck by Sir Robert Taylor in 1778–80 and completed by Sir James Wyatt in 1780–4.

153 (Right) Robert Adam's design for the staircase at Home House, Portman Square, built in 1773–7 for Elizabeth Countess of Home.

many of his fellow-architects' patrons were growing tired of the rather heavily pretentious forms into which neo-Palladianism had fallen since the death of its earlier advocates, and Adam and his brothers and successors, notably James Wyatt, who had trained as an architect in Venice and Rome, set out to provide them with something more delicate, extravagant and ornate. For twenty years this new style dominated architectural taste, although it had many disapproving critics, among them George III who voiced a common opinion when he said there was too much sweetness in their work, too much that looked like confectionery. Then, with George Dance, James Wyatt, John Soane and John Nash, all born between 1740 and 1755, there came a new wave of neo-Classicism, incorporating certain aspects of the picturesque which few tourists of an earlier generation, with the notable exceptions of Horace Walpole and William Beckford, would have appreciated.

When Beckford died in 1844, his fortune much depleted by the creation of Fonthill, that huge Gothic folly, that 'glittering waste of laborious idleness', as Hazlitt called it, the age of the Grand Tour was over and Gothicism was no longer so decried as disorderly, tasteless, unscholarly, lacking in cohesion and rhythm. The Tour had never recovered its former importance after having been brought almost to a halt by the Napoleonic Wars. Within a year of the Emperor's defeat at Waterloo, the English Channel was being crossed by steamers; within six years there was a regular steamer service; and within twenty years railway tracks were being built all over Europe and hotels at every terminus. By then the aristocratic institution known as the Grand Tour had been replaced by 'A Great Circular Tour of the Continent' advertised by that pioneer of travel agents, Thomas Cook.

Cook's 'Great Circular Tour' promised to take the vexation and exasperation out of travelling. No longer did tourists have need to contend with those 'disagreeable things' of which Edward Gibbon complained, 'bad roads, and indifferent inns, taking very often a good deal of trouble to see things which do not deserve it, and especially the continental converse one is obliged to have with the vilest part of mankind – innkeepers, post-masters, and custom-house officers'. But how amply, as Gibbon added, was the eighteenth-century traveller rewarded in his slow and leisurely peregrinations by the excitement and the variety of the journey, 'the pleasure and knowledge he finds in almost every place'.

154 The end of the Tour.

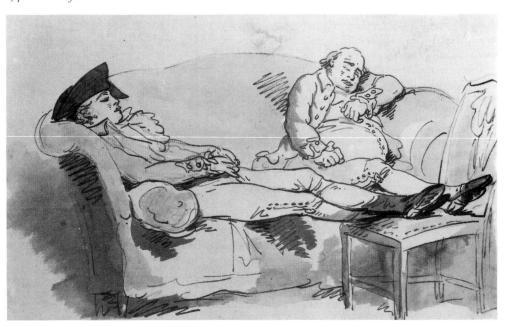

MANUSCRIPT

Lyttelton Papers (Hagley Hall); Elton Papers (Clevedon Court); Bell Papers (Thirsk Hall); Pococke MSS (BL Add 22978); Francis MSS (BL Add 40759); Newcastle Papers (BL Add 32753/27734); Fox Letters (BL Add 47576); North Papers (BL Add 61980); Duke of Marlborough MSS (BL Add 61667); St Vincent MSS (BL Add 31192); Mitchell MSS (BL Add 58314); Edward Southwell, 'Journal of a Journey', September 1723 (BL Add 34753); Hardwych Papers (BL Add 35538/35541); 'Journal of Travel to Luneville', 1721 (BL Add 60522); Essex MSS (BL Add 60387/22626); Grey Journal (BL Add 5957).

PRINTED

Ackerman, James S., *Palladio* (1966)
Addison, Joseph, *Remarks on Several Parts of Italy, 1701–1703* (1705)
Anderson, Patrick, *Over the Alps* (1969)
Archenholz, Baron J.W. von, *A Picture of Italy* (Trans. Joseph Trapp, 2 vols., 1791)
Babeau, Albert *Les Voyageurs en France, etc.* (1885)
Baretti, Giuseppe Marc' Antonio, *An Account of the Manners and Customs of Italy* (2 vols., 1769)
    A Journey from London to Genoa, etc. (2 vols., 1770)
Barthélemy, M.l'Abbé, *Travels in Italy* (1802)
Bates, E.C., *Touring in 1600* (1911)
Berchtold, Count Leopold, *An Essay to Direct and Extend the Inquiries of Patriotic Travellers* (1787)
Birbeck, Morris, *Notes of a Journey through France, etc.* (1815)
Bisoni, Bernado, *Aventures d'un Grand Seigneur Italien à travers l'Europe* (1899)
Black, Jeremy, *The British and the Grand Tour* (1985)
Blake, Robert, *Disraeli's Grand Tour* (1982)
Blanch, Lesley, *The Wilder Shores of Love* (1954)
Bonnaffé, Edmond, *Voyages et Voyageurs de la Renaissance* (1895)
Bonnard, Georges A., (ed.) *Edward Gibbon: Memoirs of My Life* (1966)
    Gibbon's Journey from Geneva to Rome: His Journal from 20 April to 2 October 1764 (1961)
Boorde, Andrew, *Fyrst Boke of the Introduction of Knowledge* (?1541)
Bourrit, Marc Theodore, *A Relation of a Journey to the Glaciers in the Dutchy of Savoy* (1775)
Breval, John Durant, *Remarks on Several Parts of Europe, etc.* (2 vols., 1738)
Bromley, William, *Several Years' Travels, etc.* (1702)
Brosses, Charles de, *Lettres historiques et critiques sur l'Italie* (3 vols., 1799)
Canaletto: Paintings and Drawings (The Queen's Gallery, 1980)
Carnarvon, Earl of, (Ed.) *Lord Chesterfield's Letters to his Godson* (1890)
Carr, John, *The Stranger in France, etc.* (1803)
Caylus, Comte de, *Voyage d'Italie, 1714–1715* (1914)
Chambers, James, *The English House* (1985)
Chandler, Richard, *Travels* (1775–76)
Chapman, Guy, (ed.) *The Travel Diaries of William Beckford of Fonthill* (1928)
Clark, Anthony M., *Pompeo Batoni* (1985)
Clay, Edith, (ed.) *Ramage in South Italy* (1965)
Clenche, John *A Tour in France and Italy, etc.* (1676)
Coe, Richard N., (ed. and trs.) *Rome, Naples and Florence by Stendhal* (1959)
Cogan, Thomas, *The Rhine, etc.* (1793)

Coghlan, Francis, *Hand-book for Italy* (1847)

Connell, Brian, *Portrait of a Whig Peer* (1957)

Cork and Orrery, Earl of, *Letters from Italy in 1754 and 1755* (1774)

Coryat's Crudities. Hastily gobled up in five Moneths travells in France, Savoy, Italie (2 vols., 1905)

Coxe, William, *Travels in Switzerland* (1789)

de Beer, E.S., (ed.) *The Diary of John Evelyn* (6 vols., 1955)

de Beer, G.R., (ed.) *A Journey to Florence in 1817* (1951)

du Chesne, André, *Les Antiquités et Recherches des villes, Chasteaux, et Places plus Remarquables de toute la France* (1647)

Duclos, Charles Pineau, *Voyage en Italie* (1766)

Dupaty, l'Abbé, *Travels through Italy in a series of Letters, 1785* (1789)

Ebel, Johann Gottfried, *The Traveller's Guide through Switzerland* (1818)

Eliot-Drake, Lady, (ed.) *Lady Knight's Letters from France and Italy 1776–1795* (1905)

Essex, James, *Journal of a Tour Through Parts of Flanders and France, etc. in 1773* (1888)

Este, Charles, *A Journey in the year 1793 through Flanders, Brabant and Germany to Switzerland* (1795)

Eustace, Rev. J.C., *A Classical Tour through Italy, etc.* (1819)

Evelyn, *see* de Beer

Fleming, John, 'Lord Brudenell and his Bear-Leaders' in *English Miscellany* (1958)
    Robert Adam and His Circle in Edinburgh and Rome (1962)

Gentleman's Guide in His Tour through France, etc., The (1770)

Gentleman's Pocket Companion for Travelling into Foreign Parts, The (1722)

Foote, Samuel, *Dramatic Works* (4 vols., 1788)

Ford, Brinsley, 'The Grand Tour' in *Apollo* (December 1981)

Fothergill, Brian, *Sir William Hamilton: Envoy Extraordinary* (1969)

Fremantle, Anne, (ed.) *The Wynne Diaries 1789–1820* (3 vols., 1935–1940)

Glover, Cedric Howard, *Dr Charles Burney's Continental Travels* (1927)

Goethe, Johann Wolfgang, *Italian Journey 1786–1788* (Trans. W.H. Auden and Elizabeth Mayer, 1962)

Graf, Arturo, *L'Anglomania e l'influsso inglese in Italia nel secolo XVIII* (1911)

Grosley, P.J., *Observations on Italy and the Italians made in 1764* (1770)

Gunn, Peter, *Naples: A Palimpsest* (1961)

Guys, Pierre Augustin, *Voyage, Litéraire de la Grèce* (1771)

Halsband, Robert, (ed.) *The Complete Letters of Lady Mary Wortley Montagu* (1965, etc.)

Hawkins, E., (ed.) *Brereton's Travels in Holland, 1634–1635* (1844)

Hazlitt, William, *Notes of a Journey through France and Italy* (collected works, vol. 9, 1904)

Heylyn, Peter, *A full Relation of Two Journeys, etc.* (1656)

Hilen, Andrew, (ed.) *The Diary of Clara Crowninshield* (1956)

Holcroft, Thomas, *Travels from Hamburg through Westphalia, Holland and the Netherlands* (1804)

Howard, Clare, *English Travellers of the Renaissance* (1914)

Howell, James, *Instructions for Forreine Travell* (1642, ed. 1867)

Hunt, James Henry Leigh, *Autobiography* (ed. J.E. Morpurgo, 1949)

Hurd, Bishop Richard, *Dialogue on the Uses of Foreign Travel* (1764)

Images of the Grand Tour: Louis Ducros, 1748–1810 (1985)

Ireland, Samuel, *A Picturesque Tour through Holland, Brabant and Parts of France* (1789)

Jesse, J.H., *George Selwyn and His Contemporaries* (1843)

Jones, Rev. William, *Observations on a Journey to Paris by way of Flanders* (2 vols. 1777)

Keysler, John George, *Travels through Germany, etc.* (1760)

Kinglake, *Eōthen* (1844)

Klima, Slava, (ed.) *Joseph Spence: Letters from the Grand Tour* (1975)

Knox, Vicesimus, *Liberal Education, etc.* (1789)

Lalande, Jérôme Lefrançais de, *Voyage d'un Français en Italie fait dans les anneés 1765 et 1766* (1768)

Lambert, R.S. (ed.) *The Grand Tour: A Journey in the Tracks of the Age of Aristocracy* (1935)

Lassells, Richard, *The Voyage of Italy, etc.* (1670)

Lee, Vernon, *Studies of the Eighteenth Century in Italy* (1880)

Lees-Milne, James, *The Earls of Creation* (1962)

Lewis, W.S., (ed.) *The Correspondence of Horace Walpole* (1937, etc.)

Links, J.G., *Travellers in Europe* (1980)

Lithgow, William, *Travels and Voyages through Europe* (1771)

Locke, John, *Some Thoughts Concerning Education* (1693)

Logan, Henry, *Directions for such as shall Travel to Rome* (1654)

Low, D.M., *Edward Gibbon* (1937)

Mahon, Lord, (ed.) *Lord Chesterfield's Letters to His Son* (1845–1853)

Marchand, L.A., *Byron: a Biography* (3 vols., 1957)

Martyn, Thomas, *Sketch of a Tour through Swisserland* (1787)
    A Tour through Italy, etc. (1791)
    A Gentleman's Guide in his Tour through France (1787)

Mason, Haydn, *Voltaire* (1981)

Massingham, Hugh and Pauline, *The Englishman Abroad* (1962)

Maugham, H. Neville, *The Book of Italian Travel, 1580–1900* (1903)

Mead, William Edward, *The Grand Tour in the Eighteenth Century* (1914)

Mikhailovich, Nikolai, (ed.) *Letters of a Russian Traveller* [N.M. Karamzin] (Trans. Florence Jonas, 1957)

Miller, Lady Anne, *Letters from Italy* (1776)

Misson, François Maximilien, *A New Voyage of Italy, with Curious Observations on Germany, Switzerland, Savoy, France, Flanders and Holland* (1724)

Montagu, *see* Halsband

Montesquieu, Charles Louis de Secondat, *Voyages* (1894–6)

Moore, Andrew W., *Norfolk and the Grand Tour* (1985)

Moore, John, *A View of Society and Manners in Italy* (1792)
    A View of Society and Manners in France, Switzerland and Germany (1792)

Morris, James, *Venice* (1960)

Morritt, J.B.S., *A Grand Tour: Letters and Journeys 1794–96* (ed. G.E. Marindin, introduction, Peter J. Hogarth (1985)

Moryson, Fynes, *An Itinerary Containing His Ten Yeeres Travell, etc.* (1617, reprinted 1907)

Northall, Captain John, *Travels through Italy* (1766)

Nugent, Mr [Sir Thomas], *The Grand Tour containing an exact description of most of the Cities, Towns and Remarkable Places of Europe* (4 vols., 1749)

Ortolani, Giuseppe, *Voci e visioni del settecento veneziano* (1926)

Parks, George Bruner, *The English Travellers to Italy* (1954)

Piozzi, Mrs Hester Lynch, *Observations and Reflections made in the Journey through France, Italy, and Germany* (1789)

Pottle, Frederick A., (ed.) *Boswell on the Grand Tour: Germany and Switzerland, 1764* (1953)
    (with Frank Brady) *Boswell on the Grand Tour: Italy, Corsica and France, 1765–1766* (1955)
    James Boswell, The Earlier Years (1966)

Pratt, Samuel Jackson, *Gleanings through Holland and Westphalia* (1795)

Quennell, Peter, *Byron in Italy* (1941)

Radcliffe, Ann, *A Journey made in the summer of 1794 through Holland, etc.* (1796)

Ray, John, *Travels through the Low Countries, etc.* (1738)

Raymond, John, *An itinerary contayning a voyage made through Italy in the yeares 1646 and 1647* (1648)

Remarks on the Grand Tour lately performed by a Person of Quality (1692)

Richardson, Jonathan, *An Account of The Statues, etc., in Italy, France, etc.* (1722)

Riesbeck, Baron, [Johann Caspar Risbeck] *Voyages en Allemagne* (1792)

Rigby, Dr Edward, *Letters from France, etc., in 1789* (1880)

Robinson, Henry Crabb, *Diary, etc.* (1872)

Roget, S.R., (ed.) *Travels in the Last Two Centuries of Three Generations* (1921)

Rowdon, Maurice, *The Silver Age of Venice* (1970)

Russell, John, *A Tour in Germany, etc.* (1828)

Sadleir, Thomas, *An Irish Peer on the Continent (1801–1803). As Related by Catherine Wilmot* (1924)

Sherlock, Martin, *Letters from an English Traveller* (1780)

   New Letters from an English Traveller (1781)

   Short Account of a Late Journey to Tuscany, Rome, etc. (1741)

Smith, James Edward, *Sketch of a Tour on the Continent* (1807)

Smith, Logan Pearsall, *Life and Letters of Sir Henry Wotton* (1907)

Smollett, Tobias, *Travels through France and Italy* (1766)

Southey, Robert, *Journal of a Tour in the Netherlands* (ed. 1849)

Starke, Mariana, *Letters from Italy, 1792–1798* (1800)

Steegman, John, *The Rule of Taste from George I to George IV* (1936)

Stephen, Leslie, *The Playground of Europe* (1871)

Sterne, Laurence, *A Sentimental Journey through France and Italy* (1768)

St John, James, *Letters from France, etc., in 1787* (1788)

Stoneman, Richard, *A Literary Companion to Travel in Greece* (1984)

Stoye, John Walter, *English Travellers Abroad 1604–1667* (1952)

Summerson, John, *Inigo Jones* (1966)

Swinburne, Henry, *Travels in the Two Sicilies, 1777–1780* (1790)

Taylor, Thomas, *The Gentleman's Pocket Companion for Travelling into Foreign Parts* (1722)

Temple, R.C., (ed.) *The Travels of Peter Mundy, etc., 1608–1667* (1907–1924)

Thicknesse, Philip, *Observations on the Customs and Manners of the French Nation, etc.* (1766)

   A Year's Journey through France (1777)

   Useful Hints to Those who Make the Tour of France (1768)

Thierry, Luc Vincent, *Almanach de Voyageur à Paris, etc.* (1785)

   Tour through Germany, containing Full Directions, etc. (1793)

Tovey, D.C., *Gray and his Friends* (1890)

Travels of Edward Brown, Esq., formerly a Merchant of London, The (1753)

Trease, Geoffrey, *The Grand Tour* (1967)

   (ed.) *Matthew Todd's Journal: A Gentleman's Gentleman in Europe, 1814–1820* (1968)

Trechmann, E.J. (ed. and trans.) *The Diary of Montaigne's Journey in 1580–1581* (1929)

Tregaskis, Hugh, *Beyond the Grand Tour* (1979)

Trevelyan, George Otto, *The Life and Letters of Lord Macaulay* (1876)

Trevelyan, Raleigh, *The Shadow of Vesuvius* (1976)

Vaussard, Maurice, *Daily Life in Eighteenth Century Italy* (trans. Michael Heron) (1962)

Views of Paris and Places Adjoining. Written by a Gentleman lately residing at the English Ambassador's (1701)

Warcup, Edmund, *Italy in its Original Glory, Ruine and Revival* (1660)

Windham, William, *A Letter from an English Gentleman giving an Account of . . . the Ice Alps in Savoy* (1744)

Wordsworth, William, *Letters* (ed. Ernest de Selincourt, 1935, etc.)

Wraxall, Nathaniel, *Tour through the Western, Southern and Interior Provinces of France* (1777)

Wright, Edward, *Some Observations made in Travelling through France, Italy etc.* (1764)

Young, Arthur, *Travels in France in 1787–1789* (1889)

INDEX